Date Due

VISUAL PERCEPTION

VISUAL PERCEPTION
The Influence of H. W. Leibowitz

Edited by

JEFFREY ANDRE

D. ALFRED OWENS

LEWIS O. HARVEY, JR.

DECADE
of BEHAVIOR
2000-2010

AMERICAN PSYCHOLOGICAL ASSOCIATION

WASHINGTON, DC

Published by
American Psychological Association
750 First Street, NE
Washington, DC 20002
www.apa.org

To order   Tel: (800) 374-2721, Direct: (202) 336-5510
APA Order Department   Fax: (202) 336-5502, TDD/TTY: (202) 336-6123
P.O. Box 92984   Online: www.apa.org/books/
Washington, DC 20090-2984   Email: order@apa.org

In the U.K., Europe, Africa, and the Middle East, copies may be ordered from
American Psychological Association
3 Henrietta Street
Covent Garden, London
WC2E 8LU England

Typeset in Century Schoolbook by NOVA Graphic Services, Ft. Washington, PA

Printer: Phoenix Color Corporation, Hagerstown, MD
Cover Designer: Anne Masters, Washington, DC
Project Manager: NOVA Graphic Services, Ft. Washington, PA

The opinions and statements published are the responsibility of the authors, and such opinions and statements do not necessarily represent the policies of the American Psychological Association.

Library of Congress Cataloging-in-Publication Data
Visual perception : the influence of H. W. Leibowitz / edited by Jeffrey Andre, D. Alfred Owens, Lewis O. Harvey, Jr.—1st ed.
     p. cm.—(Decade of behavior)
   Includes bibliographical references and indexes.
   ISBN 1-55798-945-1 (alk. paper)
     1. Visual perception.   2. Leibowitz, Herschel W.   I. Andre, Jeffrey.   II. Owens, D. Alfred.   III. Harvey, Lewis O.   IV. Series.

   BF241 .V568 2003
   152.14—dc21   2002033218

British Library Cataloguing-in-Publication Data
A CIP record is available from the British Library.

Printed in the United States of America
First Edition

APA Science Volumes

Attribution and Social Interaction: The Legacy of Edward E. Jones

Best Methods for the Analysis of Change: Recent Advances, Unanswered Questions, Future Directions

Cardiovascular Reactivity to Psychological Stress and Disease

The Challenge in Mathematics and Science Education: Psychology's Response

Changing Employment Relations: Behavioral and Social Perspectives

Children Exposed to Marital Violence: Theory, Research, and Applied Issues

Cognition: Conceptual and Methodological Issues

Cognitive Bases of Musical Communication

Cognitive Dissonance: Progress on a Pivotal Theory in Social Psychology

Conceptualization and Measurement of Organism–Environment Interaction

Converging Operations in the Study of Visual Selective Attention

Creative Thought: An Investigation of Conceptual Structures and Processes

Developmental Psychoacoustics

Diversity in Work Teams: Research Paradigms for a Changing Workplace

Emotion and Culture: Empirical Studies of Mutual Influence

Emotion, Disclosure, and Health

Evolving Explanations of Development: Ecological Approaches to Organism–Environment Systems

Examining Lives in Context: Perspectives on the Ecology of Human Development

Global Prospects for Education: Development, Culture, and Schooling

Hostility, Coping, and Health

Measuring Patient Changes in Mood, Anxiety, and Personality Disorders: Toward a Core Battery

Occasion Setting: Associative Learning and Cognition in Animals

Organ Donation and Transplantation: Psychological and Behavioral Factors

Origins and Development of Schizophrenia: Advances in Experimental Psychopathology

APA Decade of Behavior Volumes

Contents

Contributors

Jeffrey Andre, School of Psychology, James Madison University, Harrisonburg, VA

Christopher J. Best, School of Psychology, Deakin University, Malvern, Australia

Bruce Bridgeman, Departments of Psychology and Psychobiology, University of California, Santa Cruz

Peter R. Cavanagh, Lerner Research Institute, The Cleveland Clinic Foundation, Cleveland, OH

Malcolm M. Cohen, NASA/Ames Research Center, Moffett Field, CA

Boris Crassini, School of Psychology, Deakin University, Malvern, Australia

Ross H. Day, School of Psychological Science, La Trobe University, Melbourne, Australia

Sheldon M. Ebenholtz, (emeritus) College of Optometry, State University of New York, New York

Jay M. Enoch, School of Optometry, University of California, Berkeley

Kenneth Grice, New England College of Optometry, Boston, MA

Lawrence T. Guzy, Department of Psychology, State University of New York, Oneonta

Jane Gwiazda, New England College of Optometry, Boston, MA

Lewis O. Harvey, Jr., Department of Psychology, University of Colorado, Boulder

Richard Held, New England College of Optometry, Boston, MA

Jill S. Higginson, Center for Locomotion Studies, Pennsylvania State University, University Park

Chris A. Johnson, Discoveries in Sight Research Laboratories, Devers Eye Institute, Portland, OR

Herschel W. Leibowitz, (emeritus) Department of Psychology, Pennsylvania State University, University Park

James McLellan, New England College of Optometry, Boston, MA

D. Alfred Owens, Department of Psychology, Franklin & Marshall College, Lancaster, PA

Chad W. Patton, Department of Psychology, Clemson University, Clemson, SC

Robert B. Post, Department of Psychology, University of California, Davis

Sharon Toffey Shepela, Department of Psychology, Hartford College for Women, Hartford, CT

Robert M. Stern, Department of Psychology, Pennsylvania State University, University Park

Frank Thorn, New England College of Optometry, Boston, MA

Richard A. Tyrrell, Department of Psychology, Clemson University, Clemson, SC

Robert B. Welch, NASA/Ames Research Center, Moffett Field, CA

Foreword

In early 1988, the American Psychological Association (APA) Science Directorate began its sponsorship of what would become an exceptionally successful activity in support of psychological science—the APA Scientific Conferences program. This program has showcased some of the most important topics in psychological science and has provided a forum for collaboration among many leading figures in the field.

The program has inspired a series of books that have presented cutting-edge work in all areas of psychology. At the turn of the millennium, the series was renamed the Decade of Behavior Series to help advance the goals of this important initiative. The Decade of Behavior is a major interdisciplinary campaign designed to promote the contributions of the behavioral and social sciences to our most important societal challenges in the decade leading up to 2010. Although a key goal has been to inform the public about these scientific contributions, other activities have been designed to encourage and further collaboration among scientists. Hence, the "APA Science Series" has continued as the "Decade of Behavior Series." This represents one element in APA's efforts to promote the Decade of Behavior initiative as one of its endorsing organizations. For additional information about the this initiative, please visit http://www.decadeofbehavior.org.

Over the years, the Science Conference and Decade of Behavior Series has allowed psychological scientists to share and explore cutting-edge findings in psychology. The APA Science Directorate looks forward to continuing this successful program and to sponsoring other conferences and books in the years ahead. This series has been so successful that we have chosen to extend it to include books that, although they do not arise from conferences, report with the same high quality of scholarship on the latest research.

We are pleased that this important contribution to the literature was supported in part by the Decade of Behavior program. Congratulations to the editors and contributors of this volume on their sterling effort.

Kurt Salzinger, PhD
Executive Director for Science

Virginia E. Holt
Assistant Executive Director for Science

Introduction

This volume was assembled by students and colleagues of Herschel W. Leibowitz as a tribute to his wide-ranging contributions to psychological science and his unique approach to teaching and investigating problems of visual perception and human performance. In contrast with current trends toward increasing specialization in science, Leibowitz's interests and contributions crossed many of the familiar boundaries within and beyond psychological science. Identified as one of the most influential researchers in perception,[1] Leibowitz's investigations ranged also to clinical psychology, cross-cultural psychology, the history of psychology, and hypnotic age regression as well as numerous perceptual topics such as visual illusions, the eye's focusing mechanism (accommodation), the two visual system hypothesis, and spatial vision. Throughout this work, Leibowitz showed a remarkable talent for seamlessly integrating basic research and applied problems.

The following chapters present a sample of Leibowitz's intellectual agility and exemplify his penchant for blending scientific inquiry with teaching and public service. While focusing on some facet of Leibowitz's broad scientific interests, most chapters also share stories about his disarming modesty, infectious humor, and unselfish outlook on life and science. His personal style and positive regard for both students and colleagues inspired many toward broader conceptual integration and cross-disciplinary collaboration while building productive bridges between different areas of psychology and outward to other disciplines.

The volume begins with a brief account of Leibowitz's collaborative approach to research, followed by a prologue that focuses on his strong commitment to integrating basic and applied research. During his 50-year career, Leibowitz contributed important research on a wide variety of topics in visual perception and beyond; the remaining chapters present a partial legacy of Leibowitz's diverse interests from the latter half of his career. Chapters are divided into seven topical sections, including applications in clinical vision, investigations of ocular accommodation, interactions with visual information, implications for traffic safety, and visual perception applied to other disciplines.

Part I: A Symbiosis of Science, Service, and Mentorship

Leibowitz always challenged his students to think independently and to frame their empirical questions in the broader contexts of practical consequence and historical precedent. In part I, the editors' tribute to Hersh, "Herschel W. Leibowitz's Approach to Psychological Science," takes a somewhat biographical approach to highlight some of his scientific contributions as well as his unique style of mentorship and pedagogy. Leibowitz's students enjoy remembering his engaging personality and try to emulate it wherever possible. Hersh and

---

[1]White, M. J. (1987). Big bangs in perception: The most often cited authors and publications. *Bulletin of the Psychonomic Society, 25*, 458–461.

Eileen Leibowitz's affection and dedication to students and colleagues have resulted in an academic family for whom they express pride and love that would be a blessing in any natural family. This is where the volume starts. The first two chapters attempt to describe the mystique of Hersh Leibowitz. "Mystique" is not an overstatement; Hersh's approach to research and scholarship seems so simple in concept yet is so rarely attained in practice.

In the following chapter, "Why Is That Important? Herschel W. Leibowitz As a Model for Mentors," Sharon Toffey Shepela offers an anecdotal account of Hersh's personal style. This chapter was created from discussions and correspondence about why students and colleagues found Hersh so special. Interwoven throughout both chapters is our understanding of how Hersh thought science should be done and how individuals should be treated. The title of the chapter was Hersh's favorite probing question to students and colleagues alike. We think that these chapters provide useful groundwork for appreciating the voices that speak through rest of the volume.

Part II: Integrating Basic and Applied Research

The hallmark of Leibowitz's research is his rare talent for blending basic and applied research. To Hersh, there is no useful distinction between the two. In accord with William James's pragmatic philosophy, the primary value of basic research is the discovery of fundamental insights whose importance is grounded in their implications for solving practical problems. Conversely, persistent practical problems hold great potential value in directing basic inquiry, as they often reflect gaps in our knowledge. The first chapter of Part II is this argument in Leibowitz's own words, "The Symbiosis Between Basic and Applied Research," reprinted from his 1996 *American Psychologist* article. Here, Hersh argues for such a symbosis through past experiments that exemplify his pragmatic approach. In the following chapter, Hersh's first doctoral student, Lewis O. Harvey, Jr., discusses how psychology seeks to describe quantitative relationships between the physical world and human physiology. Harvey's chapter, "Living With Uncertainty in an Uncertain World: Signal Detection Theory in the Real World" shows how the basic precepts of signal detection theory can be used to describe complex human cognitive processes, such as the decision of whether a convict should be given parole.

Part III: Clinical Applications

Can basic visual phenomena be used to help develop techniques for detecting eye disease? Chris A. Johnson answers that question in "The Use of a Visual Illusion to Detect Glaucoma: Frequency Doubling Technology Perimetry." His report on how the frequency doubling illusion that is seen when sinusoidal gratings are rapidly reversed in contrast is proving to be a powerful tool for detecting early stages of glaucoma, a leading cause of blindness. This "application" of the illusion is now providing new insight into early physiological stages of the visual system. Keeping with the theme of clinical applications and reflecting Hersh's great appreciation for the history of science (for many years, he taught a course in the history of psychology at Penn State, and many of his lessons for graduate students focused on the ways new research fits into historical context), Jay M. Enoch, Dean Emeritus from the School of Optometry at University of California at Berkeley, describes in "On the Earliest Known Lenses" the earliest ophthalmic lenses and how those lenses were used in art as well as health care.

Part IV: Accommodations

Some of Leibowitz's most cited research grew from his interest in optometry and, more generally, optimization of performance under challenging visual conditions. In the next chapter, "Controversies Concerning the Resting State of Accommodation: Focusing on Leibowitz," Jeffrey Andre recounts early research and theories of the eye's focusing system, in which we find antecedents of the discovery by Hersh and his students that the resting state corresponds to an intermediate focus (i.e., *dark focus* of accommodation), which exhibits wide individual differences. Andre also presents a recent experiment that clarifies the basis of contradictory findings that have generated some controversy concerning the eye's resting state. The following chapter, "Early Astigmatism Contributes to the Oblique Effect and Creates Its Chinese–Caucasian Difference" by Richard Held, Frank Thorn, James McLellan, Kenneth Grice, and Jane Gwiazda, provides yet another good example of the symbiosis of clinical and basic research. Their investigations of the oblique effect, a phenomenon that Leibowitz studied nearly 50 years ago, are revealing a fascinating link between parallel development of the eye's optical system and its retinocortical neural pathways, both of which are strongly, although not completely, determined by genetic factors.

Part V: Interactions With Visual Information

The chapters in this section drew inspiration from Leibowitz's long-standing interests in visual illusions and multiple modes of visual processing. Leibowitz enjoyed numerous opportunities to collaborate with colleagues, often from neighboring disciplines and far-off geographical locations. Two of the three chapters were written by authors who spent time with Hersh at Penn State as visiting researchers. In "Misperceiving Extents in the Medial Plane: The Paradox of Shepard's Tables Illusion," our voice from "down under," Australian author Boris Crassini, along with his colleagues Christopher J. Best and Ross H. Day, lead off with an intriguing account of Shepard's Table Illusion and its presence in our daily environment. Following this is a chapter contributed by three of Leibowitz's collaborators from New York and California. In "Field Dependence With Pitched, Rolled, and Yawed Visual Frame Effects," Lawrence T. Guzy, Malcolm M. Cohen, and Sheldon M. Ebenholtz discuss their recent research, which has revealed a surprising relationship: the visual control of posture, perception of height, and the personality variable called "field dependence." This work links with Leibowitz's studies of the inter-actions of visual perception, postural stability, and eye movements—complex systems that must be coordinated with fine precision to enable virtually all "higher level" aspects of perception and behavior. In the last chapter of this section, "Perception and Action: Two Modes of Processing Visual Information," Leibowitz's former student Robert B. Post and his colleagues Robert B. Welch and Bruce Bridgeman discuss two modes of processing visual information. Their research contributes to a fuller understanding of the functional differentiation between parallel neural processes that serve perception of objects and the control of action, a conceptualization that has been heuristic in studies of transportation safety.

Part VI: Traffic Safety

Along with his research and teaching at Penn State, Leibowitz devoted a great deal of energy to service as a consultant to numerous government agencies and as an expert witness in matters of litigation, particularly those concerning various types of transportation accidents. Transportation human factors is an area in which there are plenty of applied problems that reflect substantial gaps in our fundamental knowledge. This section on traffic safety issues begins with "Twilight Vision and Road Safety: Seeing More Than We Notice but Less Than We Think," D. Alfred Owens's account of problems of perception in nighttime road safety. A central concept here is the *selective degradation hypothesis*, which extends insights from behavioral science and neuroscience on multiple modes of vision to the fact that many drivers are unaware of their visual limitations at night. "Educating Pedestrians About Their Own Nighttime Visibility: An Application of Leibowitzian Principles," by Richard A. Tyrrell and Chad W. Patton, follows. This chapter discusses Tyrrell's recent studies of pedestrians' misperception of their own visibility at night and his development and evaluation of techniques to encourage pedestrians to dress more safely. This ingenious work illustrates how "Leibowitz-ian" principles can literally be put to use saving lives.

Part VII: Perceptual Applications to Other Disciplines

The last section of the volume presents contributions from two of Leibowitz's Penn State collaborators. Hersh delighted in opportunities to collaborate with colleagues in other specialty areas. Robert M. Stern, a close friend and colleague in the Department of Psychology, presents his unique psychophysiological research on nausea in "Basic and Applied Nausea Research Using an Optokinetic Drum." His work connected with Leibowitz's interest in the role of visual–vestibular interactions in the symptoms of space sickness that are experienced by most astronauts and thus represents another fruitful blend of basic and applied issues. The last chapter, "What Is the Role of Vision During Stair Descent," by Peter R. Cavanagh, Distinguished Professor of Kinesiology, and his graduate student, Jill S. Higginson, describes their recent studies of the role of vision in guiding locomotion on stairs, the leading site of disabling injuries among the older population.

We hope that you enjoy reading this volume and that it raises your interest about the diversity of psychological research, about how psychology research is done, and about how to treat both students and colleagues. For the authors and editors, this volume was a labor of love dedicated to a man who taught us so much, even when we did not think we were in a classroom.

Jeffrey Andre
D. Alfred Owens
Lewis O. Harvey, Jr.

Part I

A Symbiosis of Science, Service, and Mentorship

1

Herschel W. Leibowitz's Approach to Psychological Science

D. Alfred Owens, Jeffrey Andre, and Lewis O. Harvey, Jr.

Herschel Leibowitz's scholarly contributions were extraordinary. He taught and published in four languages, including more than 250 scientific papers in journals ranging from the *Annual Review of Psychology* to *Reader's Digest*. He served on the editorial boards of numerous journals including *Journal of Experimental Psychology, Human Factors, Perception and Psychophysics,* and *Journal of Experimental Psychology: Applied.* Hersh's research stands among the most frequently cited contributions to the literature on perception, earning him the formal designation of one of the "Big Bangs in Perception" (White, 1987). He has taught at multiple American universities as well as research centers in Germany, the Netherlands, and Japan, and he has received an honorary doctor of science degree from SUNY College of Optometry.

Hersh has received awards and fellowships from the Guggenheim Foundation, the Alexander von Humboldt Foundation, and the Center for Advanced Study in the Behavioral Sciences at Palo Alto. On several occasions, Hersh offered testimony before the United States Congress on behalf of the Federation of Behavioral Sciences, the National Safety Foundation, the Federal Railroad Administration, and the Defense Department. He served on the National Research Council Committees on Vision and Human Factors, and worked frequently on review panels of the National Institutes of Health and the National Science Foundation's programs in Psychobiology and Sensory Physiology and Perception. He served as the President of Division III of the American Psychological Association, and in 1993, he received the American Psychological Association's Distinguished Scientific Award for the Applications of Psychology.

As impressive as these awards and achievements are, somehow they fail to reflect the real character of Herschel Leibowitz. They miss the best reasons that Hersh deserves the accolades he has received and why he stands as an extraordinary model for academic scientists. His approach to psychological science is unusual for its breadth of inquiry, its commitment to public service, and its high regard for the creative talents of colleagues and students alike.

One of the striking characteristics of Leibowtiz's approach is an unusual breadth of interests and research. A dominant theme in Hersh's career has been the credo that "research and teaching and public service are all thoroughly interdependent and mutually reinforcing." He demonstrated that basic research need not be narrowly specialized or esoteric or disconnected from the problems of everyday life. Indeed, his accomplishments prove the contrary. Among academic psychologists, Hersh is probably best known for his work in perception, and that certainly represents a substantial part of his scientific contributions—from his early studies of visual psychophysics under the direction of Clarence Graham at Columbia, to later work on illusions, perceptual development, oculomotor processes, size perception, night vision, visual control of posture and locomotion, and, finally, dynamic contrast sensitivity. In addition to his well-known research on perception, Hersh contributed important studies of hypnosis, cross-cultural psychology, clinical neurology, and a wide variety of problems in human factors.

The citation for Leibowitz's Distinguished Scientific Award for the Applications of Psychology applauded his "approach to the interaction between psychological science and its applications." This perspective disposed Hersh to explore the links of psychological science to disciplines ranging from anthropology to zoology. Hersh never spent a sabbatical leave at another psychology department. Rather, he chose to forge new collaborations with colleagues in other disciplines. Hersh would observe that in each of these collaborations, he learned new lessons and gained new insights about psychological processes. We also suspect he was just irrepressibly curious.

A central motive of Hersh's approach was his deep appreciation of real-world problems. He always stressed the intellectual value of simple facts and practical implications (Leibowitz, 1996). Early on, his graduate students learned about Leibowitz's first law: "You can't see a damn thing in the dark." The law is simple and it is practical. And, of course, it seems laughably obvious. But we came to understand that Leibowitz's law embodies a more subtle lesson: It is useful to think in practical terms and to appreciate the complementary nature of basic insight and applied problems. Never an intellectual snob, Leibowitz always championed the view that so-called applied problems are interesting and challenging because they often reflect gaps in our basic knowledge. Thus, they can serve as useful guides for finding better questions, for devising more incisive experiments, and for improving and expanding our theoretical understanding. From this perspective, no idea or observation, no experiment or model, no matter how clever, is self-justified. They all have to address Hersh's favorite question: "Why is that important?" The question may sound simple, but the apparent simplicity is deceptive.

A satisfactory answer to Leibowitz's favorite question requires a broader view than most modern theories command. It requires that the finding or concept hold implications beyond the laboratory and model. Hersh's perspective pays serious attention to matters outside the conventional boundaries of psychology. It rejects claims of privilege through erudition. It demands respect for the simple facts of everyday life and the practical consequences of abstract ideas.

No account of Hersh Leibowitz would be complete without a reflection of his faith in the creative ingenuity of his colleagues and of his students, who he always treated as colleagues. Throughout his career, Hersh had the reputation of never giving a student a straight answer, which, though largely true, is not quite fair. Hersh never presumed that he had the right answers. And he was loathe to tell anyone—even his students—what to do. He even appeared reluctant to impose his research agenda on the students' creative efforts. In any event, he seemed to believe that good students left to their own devices, would come up with something new—something Hersh hadn't thought of yet.

Of course, we students found such an attitude incredible and sometimes frustrating until we actually came up with some sort of worthwhile novelty. Now, it should be understood that "something new" need not be a theoretical breakthrough: It could be a new twist on a standard methodology (like using signal detection theory to evaluate hypnotically induced tunnel vision), a new stimulus (like the laser speckle pattern or a sinusoidal grating), a new lab tool (like a glue gun or duct tape), or a new conceptual connection (like the one from hamster brains to highway safety). It would be interesting to collect a list of all the minor novelties and serendipitous discoveries that Hersh applauded much to the student's exhilaration. The list would be remarkable for its variety and for the appearance of some items that seem mundane or maybe even bizarre. But we would wager that the critical feature for every item on the list would be that it passed the test of Hersh's favorite question: It had some general importance.

Given his respect for the events of everyday life, it should not be surprising to hear that Hersh has always been devoted to "family values" in the best sense of the term. Indeed, those who know Hersh cannot think of him without thinking of his family. He and his wife, Eileen, seemed to view the concept of "family" as broadly as Hersh views the field of psychology: Scores of undergraduate and graduate students, postdoctoral students, collaborators, and visiting colleagues were welcomed to the Leibowitz family. Patience, support, and love were never lacking for Hersh's academic family

Finally, it should be noted that we almost lost Hersh years before his time. One Saturday evening in early March of 1994, Hersh was running in Rec Hall at Penn State. Almost no one was in the gym except for a recent journalism graduate named Tim Greb, who was playing basketball with a young boy. Investigating a strange noise, Tim found that Hersh had fallen and was clearly in serious trouble. Hersh's heart had stopped beating. Fortunately, Tim had been trained in CPR, and although he had never had occasion to use it, when the time came, he knew what to do. He saved Hersh's life. It took 11 minutes for the emergency medical team to arrive. It took Hersh another 3 days to awaken from a coma. But, by the beginning of June, Hersh was able to participate in Jeff Andre's comprehensive oral exam.

In sum, we his students admire Hersh for his energy, his kindness and support, his sense of humor, his synthetic view of basic and applied research, and his tireless dedication to psychological science and to public service. And we marvel at the way he made it all look simple—and exciting for its simplicity.

References

Leibowitz, H. W. (1996). The symbiosis between basic and applied research. *American Psychologist, 51*, 366–370.

White, M. J. (1987). Big bangs in perception: The most often cited authors and publications. *Bulletin of the Psychonomic Society, 25*(6), 458–461.

2

Why Is That Important?

Hersh Leibowitz As a Model for Mentors

Sharon Toffey Shepela

Hersh's legacy as a mentor is not limited to those students of his who have continued in the study of perception and vision but includes students whose careers went in different directions and colleagues from many fields with whom he works and continues to mentor with his own inimitable style. And the model of mentorship he offers cannot be understood without his wife, Eileen, who is an integral part of the team that taught and formed us as professionals who were more than the sum of our academic courses and classes. None of the common definitions of mentoring do justice to the way this gentle giant of a man poked and prodded, encouraged, allowed, and guided his colleagues. His students were his colleagues—no rigid hierarchy there, though I recall calling him Dr. Leibowitz to his face and Big Daddy among my fellow students until I was several years out of the nest. It had to do with awe.

I asked several other former students for comments on Hersh's mentoring, and ubiquitous learning leaped to the top of the list. Bob Hennessy wrote,

> Mentoring by Hersh does not stand in contrast to non-mentoring by Hersh. There never was a time or condition when this distinction could have any meaning. Hersh just was and is. I finally realized the reason was that Hersh's mentoring was what we would now call an immersion experience. There were no disconnected activities—now we are learning and now we are not. All interactions with Hersh were part of a continuous mentoring process that went on all the time. When I first met Hersh he casually took me in, in the best sense of the word, bought me a sticky bun and began a gentle, magnificent dialog that went on for years in school and continues to this day.

Jeff Andre, the latest of Hersh's students, said that learning was a constant activity.

Conversations about Hersh with other former students always involve hoots of laughter as we recount his awful jokes (most of which we can all repeat to this day), and the distinction between goofing off in the lab (bad) and goofing around (good). "Why," he would ask, "does a Frenchman only eat one

---

The thoughts presented here come from my distillation of conversations with a number of Hersh's former students and colleagues who attended the Festschrift. Several of them wrote notes to me, and I have quoted them extensively here. They are, in a way, coauthors and I want to thank them for the time and thought they put in to their comments: Charles Abernethy, Jeff Andre, Jay Enoch, Lew Harvey, Bob Hennessy, Chris Johnson, Bob Miller, and Charlotte Shupert.

egg?" After a pause, he would respond to his own joke. "Because one egg is an œuf!" A silly grin would follow.

I want to focus on Hersh's mentoring influence in three areas that transcend the specific field of vision—teaching, scholarship and professionalism, and personal life.

Teaching

Respect your students and their ideas. Bob Hennessy said,

> Hersh never told anyone to do anything, or tried to persuade anyone to think otherwise about some idea. He taught analytical skills, research design, and good writing by example and engaging his students in his activities. He would frequently hand you a paper he was reviewing and ask you for your opinion, implying he did not understand something and would value your input. . . . Discussing such papers you never thought you were being taught or tested, rather you were simply doing the business of science with a more experienced colleague.

This model of mentoring can be unnerving to students who are hoping for hand holding, and remarkably empowering when they find out they have something to contribute. And we all did. Hersh primed the pump with good questions and let us go. And then he got genuinely excited when we came up with a good question, an interesting methodology, a useful application. "Why?" he would ask. "What is important about that?" "What did you learn?"

Push and stretch your students and support them so that they can meet your standards. Hersh's students always gave presentations at scientific meetings, from the very beginning of their careers. Hersh paid our way, coached us at home, and came to every presentation. If we were nervous about difficult or hostile questions, he told us to say, "Dr. Leibowitz and I were just discussing that point, and I think he would like to respond." I don't know if anyone ever had to use that, but it was perfect protection against the "werewolves" in the audience, and it gave us confidence. I've used it with my students.

Share opportunities. Hersh took us not only to professional meetings but also on consulting site visits and to conferences. As a first-year graduate student I remember going with Hersh and Steve Pollard, now a physician, to the Pentagon for a meeting on training animals to serve as messengers in Vietnam. There was a long discussion about using pigs as couriers, because they are so smart, and the disadvantage of using them because they are so tasty.

Hersh always introduced his students to important colleagues in the field, and because he treated us with such respect, he engendered some of that same respect for us in professionals often more used to ignoring graduate students. Chris Johnson said

> When I was midway through my graduate training, Hersh arranged for all of his graduate students to be invited to attend a two-day meeting of the

National Academy of Sciences/National Research Council Committee on Vision in Washington, DC. The members of that committee were a Who's Who of vision science. For two days, I had the benefit of hearing the greatest minds in vision science deliberate over many issues, as well as an opportunity to interact with them during coffee breaks and meals. I was privileged to have one-on-one discussion with my academic vision science "heroes." It was the first time I met Jay Enoch, with whom I eventually did a postdoctoral fellowship. . . . The whole experience was remarkable. It was instrumental in shaping my future career aspirations and has had a lasting impact on me.

Collaboration. In Hersh's labs, the collaboration among students and with Hersh was both the norm and virtue. In a general climate in which stories circulated of faculty members appropriating student ideas and research, or of competition between students leading to hoarding of ideas, Hersh's students learned that good ideas benefited everyone and that anyone who could help out should do so. We all learned from one another, and Hersh was a part of the team, taking delight in anyone's innovation and creative problem solving. He taught us, by his example, to give credit where credit is due. Teamwork has been recently discovered as a creative device in the corporate world. We learned it from the start. From this teamwork we also came to realize that faculty can learn from students, to everyone's advantage. I have had occasion to be instructed or corrected by undergraduates in a classroom, and I think of Hersh when I praise them for their ideas and clarifications, for their courage in offering those ideas, and when I tell them that we can all learn from each other as long as we keep an open mind. Hersh learns from everyone he meets. It is a powerful lesson for all of us.

Take risks in choosing students. Hersh often picked up students with unlikely credentials and from unlikely places, seeing in each one a capacity for intellectual and scientific achievement. I think he believes that almost everyone can be grown into a scientist if his or her natural curiosity is fostered in a nurturing environment. He would have been an adventurous gardener, growing flourishing plants from both healthy and problematic seedlings.

Wacky works. Hersh's students cannot talk about Hersh as a teacher without talking about jokes and witticisms and wacky memorable examples. His humor was present in large classrooms as well as the lab, and we learned that it is an effective teaching tool. To this day my husband cringes when he hears what antics I've used in class, but I learned well that letting my sense of humor out works better than would some distancing stiff decorum, and vivid examples stick.

Scholarship and Professionalism

This section may be best be presented as a simple listing of "Hersh pearls" known by every one of his students and colleagues. They constitute a philosophy of empiricism and social responsibility, of the intellectual life well lived.

Study what bugs you. Lew Harvey said that after he finished his master's thesis, Hersh took him out to lunch and they talked about possible dissertation topics. (The setting and the rapid focusing are typical.) When Lew said he was uncertain about what to work on, Hersh said, "What question really bugs you? What do you often think about and wonder about? That's what you should work on." This advice guarantees interest and commitment to your research and is a far cry from advocating following the current trends or politically correct or funding-driven topics. The fundamental question must always be answered—"Why is that important?"

Ask why it developed. Bob Miller said that Hersh initiated us into the functionalist tradition, and that whenever he, Bob, is lost in a research problem and doesn't know how to understand it, he asks himself, "Why would such a system or tendency evolve in the first place?" or "Why would people have such characteristics; what purpose do they serve?" The answers help him find his way out of the confusion.

Applied research is valuable. This maxim grows out of the perspective that a synergy exists between applied problems and basic theoretical understanding, and it runs counter to the prevailing idea that applied research is the lesser cousin to "pure" research. Hersh also taught and modeled the responsibility inherent in the privileged position we had been given as educated people. We owed it to society to work on real-life problems. Charles Abernethy wrote that Hersh's influence launched his career in human factors and kept him focused on good products designed through both fundamental and applied research, and introduced through effective political skills. This acceptance of applied research led me to public policy research when I switched my field to social psychology.

Simplicity of language, breadth of measurement. Bob Hennessy wrote that simplicity in research ideas, design, and preparation and delivery of results is a Leibowitz theme. Simplicity, he went on, is not trivial, but rather fundamental and obvious. Size constancy works in everyday perception, so study the perception of the size of people at different distances outdoors, from near to far. Investigating over as wide a range of values of a parameter as possible is something Hersh learned from his own mentor at Columbia University, Clarence Graham: "important, real world yet simple and elegant." We learned that research should be communicated in such a way that our grandmothers could understand it. Hersh told us that no one would ever criticize us for making a presentation too simple. "Never try to make more than three points in a presentation" is a standard I pass on to my students to this day.

Avoid the three-cone effect. Statistical results so small that they affect only three cones, even if they are statistically significant, are likely to be irrelevant. Hersh preferred the "interocular test of significance"; that is, if the results hit you between the eyes, *then* they are significant.

Research should both add and subtract from the literature. That good research adds new knowledge seems obvious. By subtracting from the literature, Hersh meant that good data and good analysis can consolidate previously disconnected findings into a new whole. In this way what was once 12 independent studies might be understood as representing 1 interesting new concept or model. Higher order thinking was always encouraged in Hersh's lab.

Do it right. We learned that sound methodology must be the hallmark of all our research, whether it is done in a lab with elaborate equipment or on a darkened road in Centre County. That is a given. It is a hallmark of Leibowitz students. Having learned that has been important in getting my public policy research accepted by skeptical legislators or judges and in gaining acceptance and funding for the findings of other former students now working in applied areas.

Personal Lives

Hersh Leibowitz's influence on his students and colleagues goes far beyond his philosophy of science or his pedagogical techniques and into the fiber of our being. His is the power of decency to bring out decency in others. Again, Bob Hennessy writes,

> When I think of the character of Hersh's influence on my life, personal and professional, the first thing that always pops up is his kind, tolerant, and gentle attitude toward people and ideas. He is constitutionally unable to approach people or research from a negative position. He can never speak ill of anyone and his criticism of research is always stated positively. He will say, "this paper could have gone a bit further" rather than "this is trivial nonsense." He always gives it the positive spin. If he asks someone a question about their work it is because he wants to know, not because he wants to make them look stupid. He can't even be metaphorically mean. We often have heard him say he could never eat eggs sunny-side up because it is too much like poking an eye.

And yet this does not preclude righteous anger and action. I recall that when one of our colleagues reported to Hersh that a corporate recruiter from a firm with which Hersh consulted had propositioned her in an interview, he returned to us in a few days and said that the man was not doing college recruiting any more. The head of the undergraduate psychology honors program at Penn State wrote a letter supposedly in support of my graduate school applications that said, to paraphrase, "She is a superb student with a high GPA and several publications; however, she is attractive and personable and I seriously doubt she will complete her degree." These things happened in the mid-1960s. It was enough to result in my being rejected from every graduate school to which I had applied. When I told Hersh, he convened an emergency meeting of the graduate admissions committee of the department the next morning, and by 10 a.m. I was admitted as his student with a research assistantship. He saved my career.

He taught us to keep our priorities straight. "What will be more important in 5 years?" he would ask. Jay Enoch wrote of a National Academy of Sciences committee meeting in which members argued for hours about the addition of serifs to standard visual acuity charts. Hersh called a break and whispered to Jay, "What the hell is a serif?" Jay continues, "I told him that these were not the seraphs of the Bible, but rather the little tails at the end of letters in certain font styles. He [Hersh] looked me in the eye and said, 'If that is what we have been arguing about for four hours, they must all be mad!'" He ended the discussion promptly when the committee reconvened.

We watched him learn from everyone. We watched him laugh at himself. We watched him give talks to the local PTA. We watched him patiently and kindly answer a parent's question on bedwetting when the parent thought a psychologist might be able to help. We watched his kindness and we thrived in its light and we wanted to emulate him. I was Hersh Leibowitz's student for 1 year more years ago than I can count, and I am still trying to grow my heart to be as big as his—as are we all.

Part II

Integrating Basic and Applied Research

3

The Symbiosis Between Basic and Applied Research

Herschel W. Leibowitz

In thinking about basic science and its applications, I cannot recall a time when I considered them as separate. The war years in particular provided countless examples of their close relationship. This issue was not a topic of conversation or instruction in my undergraduate years, although the presence of the Psychological Clinic at the University of Pennsylvania seemed both natural and appropriate. Some of the staff at Columbia had contributed to the war effort and had experienced these problems, but I do not recall any discussion of the issues.

I have always felt that reaching out to learn from other disciplines was an essential aspect and privilege of an academic career. There is no question in my mind that the opportunity to work with colleagues in other fields has broadened my outlook and, I hope, has made our research more meaningful. Collaboration with colleagues in neurophysiology, zoology, neurology, optometry, biomechanics, law, industry, human factors, and various governmental agencies in both basic research and its applications has significantly enriched the scope of research from our laboratory.

I believe that an approach that views the search for fundamentals and the solution of societal problems to be interdependent is worthy of serious consideration. Examples of this are notable in the history of science. Some of my favorites are the contributions of Selig Hecht, Karl von Frisch, Erich von Holst, and Paul Fitts. However, I will confine my remarks in this document to two examples which, from our work at the Pennsylvania State University, illustrate the symbiotic and mutually supportive relationship between basic and applied research.

Note. Reprinted from *American Psychologist*, 1996, *51*, pp. 366–370. A version of this chapter was originally presented as part of a Distinguished Scientific Award for the Applications of Psychology address at the 103rd Annual Convention of the American Psychological Association, New York, NY, August 1995.

I wish to express my gratitude and appreciation to D. Alfred Owens and Eileen Leibowitz for advice and assistance, and to gratefully acknowledge support from the National Science Foundation, the National Institutes of Health, the Guggenheim Foundation, the Wisconsin Alumni Research Foundation, the Alexander von Humboldt Foundation, the Center for Advanced Study in the Behavioral Sciences, the American Automobile Association Foundation for Traffic Safety, and the Evan Pugh Professorial Fund of the Pennsylvania State University. The contributions of Clarence H. Graham, Jay Enoch, Hans Lukas Teuber, Clinton Woolsey, Gerald B. Stein, Conrad Kraft, Johannes Dichgans, Yun Hsia, Conrad Mueller, Richard M. Held, David A. Grant, Alfred Lit, Peter Cavanagh, and David Rosenhan are noteworthy and deeply appreciated. Sincere thanks go to my students, from whom I have learned so much.

Night Myopia

Night myopia, or night nearsightedness, illustrates how concentration on applications in the absence of an understanding of basic mechanisms can be insufficient. In 1789, Lord Maskelyne, the director of the Royal Observatory in Greenwich, England, reported that although he could see normally during daylight without optical correction, he became nearsighted at night (Levene, 1965). This phenomenon, referred to as *night myopia*, can present a serious handicap in tasks for which the appreciation of distant objects under low illumination is critical. Although it was not an issue for astronomers, inasmuch as they can adjust the focus of their telescopes to compensate for (spherical) refractive errors, it was later recognized as a serious problem for military personnel attempting to detect targets at night with unaided vision. Following Maskelyne's observations, a number of researchers attempted to understand the cause of night myopia and to find a method for correction. During World War II, various laboratories in Germany, Japan, Spain, and the United States supported active research programs on this problem.

In addition to its implications for human performance, night myopia posed a challenge for visual scientists because it represented an example in which the focusing mechanism of the eyes—accommodation—appears to malfunction. Ordinarily, accommodation automatically focuses the eyes for objects at different distances. One is not usually aware of this process until it begins to fail in middle age with the appearance of *presbyopia,* the loss of elasticity of the lens, which creates the need for reading glasses or bifocals. The paradoxical aspect of night myopia is that it represents a case in which this ordinarily efficient mechanism responds in a manner that is biologically maladaptive.

Despite many efforts throughout the international vision research community, the problem remained unsolved. In 1954—165 years after Maskelyne's observations—Herbert Schober suggested that the basis for night myopia was not essentially an aberrant response (Schober, 1954). Rather, he proposed that the classical assumption—attributed to Helmholtz—that the eyes relax to focus on distant objects when there is no stimulus to accommodation required modification. In terms of this assumption, the resting posture of the eyes corresponds to distant stimuli so that any accommodation whatsoever for a distant object would represent an inappropriate response. However, Schober's hypothesis that the resting posture of the eye is at an *intermediate* position provided an alternative interpretation. Specifically, night myopia would be the result of a *passive* return of the eyes under the degraded conditions of nighttime viewing toward their intermediate resting posture. In this view, night myopia would be considered the natural consequence of a basic oculomotor mechanism—the intermediate resting tonus of the ciliary muscle.

In the mid-1970s, with the availability of lasers and the development of the laser optometer, we tested Schober's hypothesis empirically (Leibowitz & Owens, 1975). The data, in confirmation of Schober, indicated that with few exceptions the eye does in fact rest at an intermediate position and, furthermore, this resting posture exhibits high intersubject variability (see Figure 3.1). The data vary from the classical infinity position to 10 in., with a mean of about 2 ft. Subsequent data on night myopia, as well as other examples of the anomalous myopias, demonstrated that the anomalous response could be

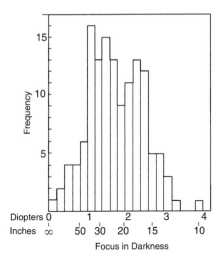

Figure 3.1. Scatterplot of the resting position of accommodation in total darkness. $N = 124$; $M = 1.71$ diopters; $SD = 0.72$.

reliably predicted from the resting posture of the individual observer. In Figure 3.2, the magnitude of the anomalous myopias is plotted as a function of the observer's dark focus. The straight line indicates the prediction that the dark focus determines the magnitude of the anomalous myopias.

The general rule is that whenever the stimulus is degraded by low illumination—or when vision is blurred by a cloudy medium, uncorrected refractive error, fog, or rain—the eyes tend to focus toward or at the individual's characteristic resting position. Confirmation of Schober's (1954) hypothesis of the intermediate resting position and the identification of its high intersubject variability not only has provided an understanding of the basis for night and the other anomalous myopias but also has suggested a means for ameliorating them. Basically, at night or when viewing in an empty field such as the sky, or under any condition when the image is degraded or blurred, one should wear an additional negative lens correction approximating the optical distance between the observer's individual resting position and optical infinity. Details of these developments have been presented in other research (e.g., Leibowitz & Owens, 1975, 1978; Leibowitz, Sheehy, & Gish, 1985; Owens, 1979, 1984; Owens & Leibowitz, 1976; Post, Owens, Owens, & Leibowitz, 1979).

The relevance of this research in the present context is that progress in solving the applied problem was possible only after basic research had provided insights into the nature of the mechanism subserving accommodation. Viewed simply as an aberrant response, night myopia resisted solution for almost 2 centuries. In contrast, when viewed as a manifestation of a basic mechanism, both the understanding of the phenomenon and its amelioration were readily amenable to solution. The appreciation of both basic and applied aspects of accommodation—each of which complemented the other—proved to be the key to understanding. Specifically, the fundamental nature of accommodation and night, as well as empty field and instrument myopia, visual fatigue, and any condition that degrades the stimulus such as unclear optical media or refrac-

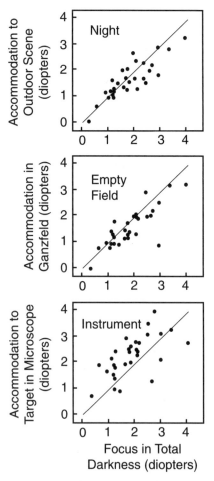

Figure 3.2. Magnitude of night, empty field, and instrument myopia as a function of the observer's resting position of accommodation. The straight line designates the prediction that the individual observer's dark-focus determines the magnitude of the anomalous myopia.

tive errors, share a common mechanism (Owens, 1984). It is clear that both the societal problem and our basic understanding have, in this case, been incremented by consideration of both aspects. I believe that many problems involving lack of basic understanding are more apparent in nonlaboratory situations. Consideration of practical problems can help to reveal the limitations of theory that sometimes tend to become self-perpetuating.

Nighttime Traffic Accidents

An illustrative example of the many values of fundamental knowledge follows from research carried out by Gerald Schneider in his doctoral dissertation at the Massachusetts Institute of Technology (Schneider, 1967). Schneider was interested in the neural mechanisms subserving vision and conducted a series of experiments in which he systematically removed various parts of the brain of the golden hamster. His basic finding was that, as expected, ablation of the cortex interferes with the ability to recognize objects. However, removal of the superior colliculi, which are part of the midbrain, interferes with the ability to orient spatially. Animals with cortical lesions could orient but not recognize, whereas animals with midbrain lesions could, if properly oriented, recognize normally. These findings, taken together with results of studies by Held, Ingle, and Trevarthen, led to the development of the concept of *two visual systems* (Held, 1968; Ingle,1967; Trevarthen, 1968). The more familiar recognition system, referred to as *focal vision*, subserves object recognition. The spatial orientation or visual guidance system, referred to as *ambient vision*, underlies spatial orientation or visual guidance. In the hamster, these systems are subserved by different parts of the brain and can be independently dissociated surgically. In humans, although the two functions can be dissociated functionally, the neurology is not as clear, and it is preferable to refer to two "modes" of visual processing (Held, 1970).

Not only do these two modes subserve different functions but they also respond differentially to changes in the visual environment. As is well known, reduction of illumination interferes with the ability to recognize objects and other tasks involving appreciation of fine detail such as reading. However, the same procedure has very little effect on visual guidance of locomotion. A familiar example is provided by the tasks of reading and walking, both of which can be carried out quite routinely under high illumination levels. However, under low illumination—when it is no longer possible to read or recognize objects efficiently—it is still possible to orient even in an unfamiliar environment. In research from our laboratory, we refer to the differential response to lowered illumination of the recognition and guidance modes as the *selective degradation* of vision (Leibowitz & Owens, 1977).

Selective degradation is helpful for understanding a major problem associated with nighttime traffic accidents. In terms of miles driven, the frequency of high fatalities is approximately 3.5 times higher at night than during the day (National Safety Council, 1993). In spite of this, drivers typically do not slow down at night, nor are they required to by government regulations. Of course, accidents have many causes; however, a possible explanation for a significant number of them may follow from the concept of two modes of processing and selective degradation. Specifically, as illumination is lowered, the ability to steer the car—assuming there is some light available—is still possible, by utilizing the ambient system that is relatively insensitive to illumination level. In contrast, the ability to recognize hazards in the road such as pedestrians, animals, potholes, disabled vehicles, or other low-contrast objects is severely degraded. Because the occurrence of such hazards on the highway is an infrequent event (itself a factor in reducing detection and recognition) and steering a continuous process, drivers remain unjustifiably self-confident about their driving ability on the basis of frequent feedback from steering. As a consequence, drivers are not aware of their degraded recognition ability, resulting in nighttime driving speeds that are too fast for the illumination levels provided by automobile headlights. Because of selective degradation of the two modes, motorists are not prepared for the infrequent demands on their degraded recognition system (Leibowitz & Owens, 1986). A striking example is provided by nighttime driving accidents involving pedestrians in which drivers report that either they did not see the pedestrian in time or, in approximately 25% of cases, they did not see the pedestrian at all (Allen, 1970)!

The degraded ability to see at night is noteworthy for pedestrians as well as drivers. In many cases, a pedestrian can actually see much better than a driver can in the night road environment because the pedestrian's eyes are adapted to a lower level of ambient illumination. Their superior visual sensitivity may be one reason that pedestrians overestimate drivers' ability to see them at night (Allen, Hazlett, Tacker, & Graham, 1969; Shinar, 1984). Ironically, the pedestrian's better night vision may lead to unnecessary risk taking. Improved conspicuity of pedestrians, through the use of well-designed reflective markings, would enhance nighttime road safety (Owens, Antonoff, & Francis, 1994).

Possible ameliorative solutions are to increase public awareness of the implications of selective visual degradation through the media, the educational system, and transportation literature; to promote the use of devices to increase the visibility of nighttime hazards; and to introduce differential, day-or-night speed limits that would not only reduce nighttime driving speeds but also serve to communicate the generally unappreciated hazards of the nighttime driving environment.

For the purposes of this article, a noteworthy aspect of this research is the fact that the original studies by Schneider (1967) were designed to investigate the function of neural pathways without any thought of implications for nighttime driving accidents. As frequently happens, increased appreciation of fundamental mechanisms suggested a possible means for understanding the basis of a serious societal problem that was conceptually remote from the objectives of the original studies. The present examples demonstrate how increasing our comprehension of basic functions can lead to totally unanticipated applications, in these cases in relation to both a classical human factors problem and one of the most serious public health problems faced by contemporary technological societies. In the United States, driving accidents are the leading cause of death from ages 1 through 38 and are responsible for more deaths than all other causes combined between the ages of 15 and 24 (National Safety Council, 1993)!

A Historical Strength of Psychological Science

The preceding examples were chosen to illustrate the mutually beneficial relationship between the search for fundamentals and the solution of societal applications as advocated by the functionalist school of psychology. The research on anomalous myopias and accommodation demonstrates how an understanding of fundamentals can provide an effective means of solving a persistent applied problem. It also illustrates how interest in both fundamentals and applications can serve to suggest directions for basic research and augment our ability to solve societal problems. In the case of the two modes of visual processing, research designed to elucidate basic neurological mechanisms suggested a possible means for understanding the basis of a serious societal problem that was conceptually remote from the objectives of the original studies.

The presence of these examples should not suggest that interest in societal problems should in any way diminish the traditional goal of research to identify fundamental mechanisms. On the contrary, awareness of the usefulness of research can stimulate innovative directions and strategies for basic studies as well as facilitate applications (Leibowitz, 1992). I believe it is this message, inherent in the Functionalist philosophy, that has played a major role in stimulating the growth of psychology in so many fruitful directions, has fueled the vigorous expansion of psychology during this century and, it is hoped, will play a positive role in psychology's future.

References

Allen, M. J. (1970). *Vision and highway safety*. Philadelphia: Chilton.

Allen, M. J., Hazlett, R. D., Tacker, H. L., & Graham, B. V. (1969). *Actual pedestrian visibility and the pedestrian's estimate of his own visibility*. Paper presented at the 13th Annual Conference of The American Association for Automotive Medicine, Minneapolis, MN.

Held, R. M. (1968). Dissociation of visual functions by deprivation and rearrangement. *Psychologische Forschung, 31*, 338–348.

Held, R. M. (1970). Two modes of processing spatially distributed visual stimulation. In F. O. Schmitt (Ed.), *The neurosciences: Second study program* (pp. 317–324). New York: Rockefeller University Press.

Ingle, D. (1967). Two visual mechanisms underlying the behavior of fish. *Psychologische Forschung, 31*, 44–51.

Leibowitz, H. W. (1992). Functional psychology and its societal contributions. In D. A. Owens & M. Wagner (Eds.), *Progress in contemporary psychology: The legacy of American Functionalism* (pp. 17–29). Westport, CT: Praeger.

Leibowitz, H. W., & Owens, D. A. (1975). Night myopia and the intermediate dark-focus of accommodation. *Science, 189*, 646–648.

Leibowitz, H. W., & Owens, D. A. (1977). Nighttime accidents and selective visual degradation. *Science, 197*, 422–423.

Leibowitz, H. W., & Owens, D. A. (1978). New evidence for the intermediate position of relaxed accommodation. *Documenta Ophthalmologica, 46*(1), 133–147.

Leibowitz, H. W., & Owens, D. A. (1986, January). We drive by night. *Psychology Today*, 77–80.

Leibowitz, H. W., Sheehy, J. B., & Gish, K. W. (1985). Correction of night myopia: The role of vergence accommodation. *Proceedings of the 1983 NASAINRC Conference on Night Vision*. Washington, DC: National Research Council.

Levene, J. R. (1965). Nevil Maskelyne, F. R. S. and the discovery of night myopia. *Royal Society of London Notes and Reports, 20*, 100–108.

National Safety Council. (1993). *Accident facts, 1993 edition*. Itasca, IL: Author

Owens, D. A. (1979). The Mandelbaum Effect: An accommodative bias toward intermediate distances. *Journal of the Optical Society of America, 69*, 646–652.

Owens, D. A. (1984). The resting state of the eyes. *American Scientist, 72*, 378–387.

Owens, D. A., Antonoff, R. J., & Francis, E. L. (1994). Biological motion and nighttime pedestrian conspicuity. *Human Factors, 36*, 718–732.

Owens, D. A., & Leibowitz, H. W. (1976). Night myopia: Cause and a possible basis for amelioration. *American Journal of Optometry and Physiological Optics, 53*, 709–717.

Post, R. B., Owens, R. L., Owens, D. A., & Leibowitz, H. W. (1979). Correction of empty field myopia on the basis of the dark-focus of accommodation. *Journal of the Optical Society of America, 69*, 89–92.

Schneider, G. E. (1967). Contrasting visuomotor functions of tectum and cortex in the golden hamster. *Psychologische Forschung, 31*, 52–62.

Schober, H. A. W. (1954). Üeber die Akkommodationsruhelage [The resting position of accommodation]. *Optik, 11*, 282–290.

Shinar, D. (1984). Actual versus estimated night-time pedestrian visibility. *Ergonomics, 27*, 863–871.

Trevarthen, C. (1968). Two mechanisms of vision in primates. *Psychologische Forschung, 31*, 229–337.

4

Living With Uncertainty in an Uncertain World

Signal Detection Theory in the Real World

Lewis O. Harvey, Jr.

When I arrived at Penn State for graduate study in the fall of 1964, I was told that Professor Herschel W. Leibowitz would be my advisor and that I should arrange an appointment with him. What a stroke of good fortune for me. Hersh was unlike any teacher I ever knew in college. His wry sense of humor as well as keen sense of curiosity was a deep source of inspiration. Silly jokes and stupid stories flowed from him in an endless stream, but in retrospect these jokes and stories were used with the skill of a wise Zen master: Each one was crafted to illustrate a scientific point. One such story was about a person's arduous search for the meaning of life. After years of studying, learning, and searching, he finds a Tibetan monk high in the Himalayas who gives him the answer: "Life is like a fountain." After he expresses anger, dismay, frustration, and disbelief that his lifelong quest should end in such an ambiguous statement, the monk looks him directly in the eyes and says, "Well, maybe it's not."

I dedicate this chapter to Hersh. I owe him much for what he taught me. I also dedicate this chapter to his wife, Eileen. The two of them together have over the years been mentor and friend, father and mother, brother and sister to me. They have been an inspirational source of unconditional love and support. I treasure them. Thank you.

Representing Uncertainty

Uncertainty is a fundamental property of our physical world. Figure 4.1 illustrates the distribution of water drops falling from a vertical stream of water at the center of a fountain. The drops cluster near the center, but some fall quite far away. Although it is not possible to predict where each individual drop will fall, it is possible to describe the pattern of the drops by means of a probability distribution having an appropriate central tendency and spread. Thus uncertainty can be quantified.

Uncertainty has played a central role in psychophysics from its beginning (Fechner, 1860), but only recently has it received more widespread attention in mainstream psychological theory. Fechner assumed that internal sensory thresholds were not constant but fluctuated from moment to moment. Urban (1908), who coined the term "psychometric function," asserted that the characteristic S shape of this function was a consequence of stimuli having noisy,

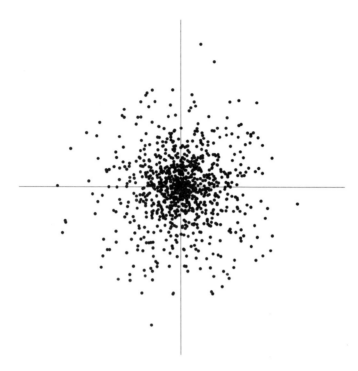

Figure 4.1. Pattern of water droplets from a fountain. The stream flows up from the center of the graph.

fluctuating internal representations, a concept that became the cornerstone of Thurstone's ideas of how stimuli are represented in the mind (Thurstone, 1927a, 1927b). The psychometric function is the integral of the underlying probability density function representing the stimulus. Early writers assumed this distribution to be Gaussian, based on Fechner's ideas (see, for example, p. 104 in Fechner, 1889; or p. 86 in Fechner, 1966) and consistent with Galton's use of this distribution when he introduced the concept of percentiles to describe distributions of measured properties (Galton, 1885).

The Need for a Psychological Model

Some of the uncertainty arises from the physical nature of stimuli, and some of it comes from the biological and psychological processes that create internal representations. To achieve quantitative precision and predictive power, an explicit conceptual framework is needed (Garner, Hake, & Eriksen, 1956). At minimum there are two psychological processes in this framework: a *sensory process* and a *decision process* (Krantz, 1969; Swets, 1961; Swets, Tanner, & Birdsall, 1961). The sensory process transforms physical stimulation into an internal representation; the decision process decides what actions to take based on the properties of the internal representation. Current theoretical frameworks contain numerous additional processes, as is illustrated in Figure

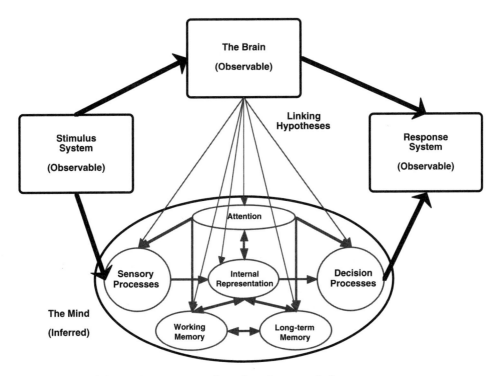

Figure 4.2.   Schematic representation of modern psychology.

4.2, but for the purposes of this chapter we need consider only the sensory and decision processes.

Two Components: Internal Representation and Decision Maker

The idea of a sensory process that transforms physical stimuli into a fluctuating internal representation and the idea of a decision process that makes decisions about what to say or do based on that internal representation were both made explicit by Louis Thurstone (1927a; 1927b), although their essence had been already expressed by Fechner in *Elements of Psychophysics* (Fechner, 1860). These ideas reached full maturity with the development of signal detection theory (Green & Swets, 1966/1974; Swets, 1961; Swets et al., 1961; Tanner & Swets, 1954): The fluctuating output of the sensory process is modeled by a probability density function (usually Gaussian), and the decision process uses rules from statistical decision theory to make decisions consistent with achieving certain goals. Another key element of signal detection theory is the assumption that in the absence of a stimulus an internal representation is still created by the sensory process, the so-called noise distribution. Finally, the theory proposes that there is no sensory threshold. Fechner had already explicitly stated this last assumption and thus could have developed signal detection theory a century earlier:

> Im Gebiete der intensiven Lichtempfindung kann der directe Nachweis, dass es erst einer gewissen Stärke des Lichtreizes bedürfe, um Empfindung

zu erwecken, also eine Schwelle für die Lichtempfindung bei einem endlichen Werthe des Lichtreizes bestehe, nicht geführt werden, weil das Auge, wie mehrfach besprochen, *durch eine innere Erregung stets über der Schwelle ist, wozu jeder äussere Lichtreiz nur einen Zuschuss giebt.* (Fechner, 1889, p. 240; italics added)

For intensive light sensations we cannot prove directly that there is need for a certain stimulus intensity in order to arouse our sensations, or in other words, that a threshold for visual sensation exists for any finite value of a light stimulus. As we have noted several times, the eye is always above threshold *because of its internal excitation, so that each external light stimulus can only add to the excitation already present.* (Fechner, 1966, p. 200; italics added)

For more about the relationship between Fechner's ideas and modern signal detection theory the reader is directed to the excellent paper by Link (1994).

The probability density function used to model the noisy internal representation is most commonly the familiar Gaussian distribution. Other probability density functions have been proposed to replace it (for example, see DeCarlo, 1998), but the fit of the Gaussian distribution to most data is better than the fit of other distributions; even when it is slightly worse, the Gaussian model usually cannot be rejected on statistical grounds. Among these alternate distributions are the logistic distribution, the Weibull distribution, and the extreme minimum value and extreme maximum value distributions (for complete descriptions of numerous probability distributions, see Johnson & Kotz, 1970a, 1970b).

The decision process operates by establishing one or more decision criteria and by comparing the output of the sensory process with the criteria to decide what response to make. The simplest situation is illustrated in the upper panel of Figure 4.3, in which the observer must discriminate between two conditions in a detection experiment: stimulus absent and stimulus present. The internal representations of these conditions are modeled in the figure by Gaussian probability density functions: The left one, labeled noise, represents the output of the sensory process when the signal is absent, and the one labeled signal represents the output when the signal and noise are present. The decision process establishes a decision criterion (the vertical line) for generating a response. If the output of the sensory process on an experimental trial exceeds this decision criterion, the observer says "yes" and if not, says "no." Although a different model of the decision process has recently been proposed for recognition memory (Van Zandt, 2000), the classic model just described is sufficient for a wide variety of tasks involving human judgment.

The magnitude of the internal representation is a continuous variable, and observers can therefore give more than two responses ("yes" and "no") by establishing more than one decision criterion. This model of the decision process is illustrated in the middle panel of Figure 4.3. The response ratings illustrated in Figure 4.3 range from 1 = *sure that the stimulus was not present* to 5 = *sure that the stimulus was present*. Observers can hold as many as 15 decision criteria and use them reliably and consistently (Macmillan & Creelman, 1991). The lower panel of Figure 4.3 illustrates the most general model, with several different stimulus representations and several decision criteria. Let us look more closely at this general model of noisy internal representation.

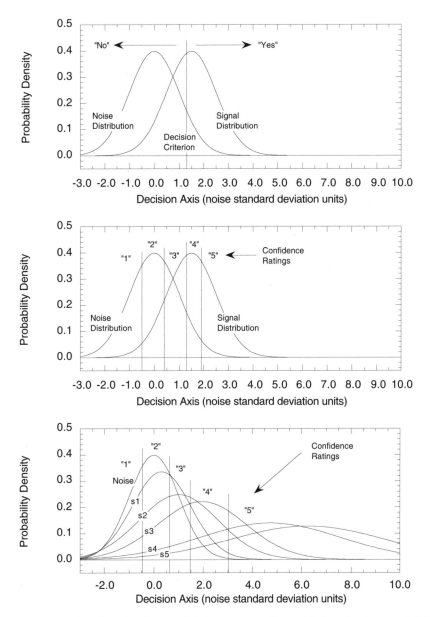

Figure 4.3. Single criterion model (upper panel), multiple criterion model (middle panel), and multiple signal, multiple criterion model (lower panel).

Visual Detection

40-year-old male observer, using his left eye, was asked to detect a series of faint visual targets, 30 min of arc in diameter, projected onto the white hemisphere of a Tübinger Perimeter (Aulhorn & Harms, 1972). The target was presented at a retinal locus of 5 deg on the horizontal meridian of the left visual field. On each trial, indicated by an auditory click, one of six possible events occurred: No stimulus was presented, or one of five targets, ranging from −2.5 to −2.1 log relative luminance units, was presented. The observer indicated his confidence that a stimulus had been presented by responding on a scale from 1 to 5, as illustrated previously. There were 40 blank trials and from 23 to 34 trials of each stimulus intensity, presented in a random order.

The raw data are the number of times each rating category was used under each of the six target conditions. From these data we want to figure out the means and standard deviations of the Gaussian internal representations of the target conditions as well as the position of the decision criteria that would best predict them. A maximum-likelihood fitting technique, originally developed by Dorfman (Dorfman & Alf, 1969; Dorfman, Beavers, & Saslow, 1973), was used to compute these parameters of the best fitting model.[1]

The success of a model is assessed by comparing the rating frequencies given by the observer with those predicted by the model. As one can see in Figure 4.4, the fit between the predictions of the model and data is very good. The goodness of this fit is measured by the chi-square statistic: The smaller the chi-square, the better the fit (Chapter 15 in Press, Teukolsky, Vetterling, & Flannery, 1992). Chi-square, with 10 deg of freedom, was 6.8. Because the probability of obtaining this value or higher by chance alone, assuming that the model is correct, is .75, we conclude that the small discrepancies between the observed data and those predicted by the model are due to chance alone. The Gaussian distributions of each target condition and the position of the four decision criteria are plotted in the lower panel of Figure 4.3.

From the means M and standard deviations SD of the Gaussian internal representations of the six stimulus conditions, we compute measures of the ability of the observer's sensory process to discriminate each target from the blank condition. The distance between the noise distribution and a target distribution is taken as a measure of sensitivity. The classic measure of sensitivity when the distributions have the same standard deviation is d prime (Green & Swets, 1966/1974):

$$d' = \frac{\mu_t - \mu_n}{\sigma_n}$$

where the subscript t stands for target and the subscript n stands for noise. When the standard deviations of the two distributions are not equal, the best measure of this distance is d_a, a metric using both standard deviations (Simpson & Fitter, 1973):

$$d_a = \frac{\mu_s - \mu_n}{\sqrt{\dfrac{\sigma_s^2 + \sigma_n^2}{2}}}$$

---

[1] The computer program to carry out signal detection analyses (Rscore+) is available from the author at his Web site: http://psych.colorado.edu/~lharvey/. Address correspondence to Department of Psychology, University of Colorado, 345 UCB, Boulder, Colorado 80309-0345 or to lharvey@psych.colorado.edu.

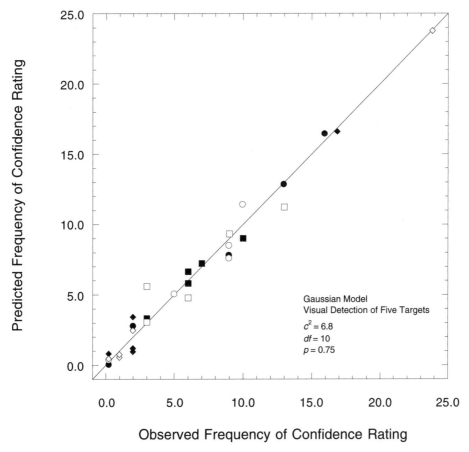

Figure 4.4. Frequency of ratings predicted by the best-fitting multiple Gaussian, variable criteria signal detection model as a function of the observed frequencies.

The psychometric function based on d_a is linear (Laming, 1986), as can be seen in the upper panel of Figure 4.5.

For a given level of sensitivity, the performance of an observer is nicely illustrated by the receiver operating characteristic (ROC), the relationship between the hit rate and the false alarm rate for various decision criteria. The ROCs for the five targets are plotted in Figure 4.6. The symbols represent the observed data; the solid lines are the predicted values of the best fitting model. The diagonal line represents zero detectability. As the signal strength increases, the ROC becomes more bowed.

The sensitivity of the sensory process may also be measured by the area under the ROC. This measure is called A_z and is easily computed from d_a (Harvey, 1992; Simpson & Fitter, 1973):

$$A_z = z^{-1}\left(\frac{d_a}{\sqrt{2}}\right)$$

where $z^{-1}()$ is the inverse z-score transformation based on the unit normal Gaussian probability distribution. A_z is equal to the percentage correct you

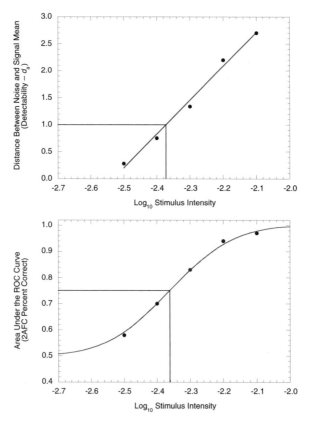

Figure 4.5. Two psychometric functions for detecting faint visual targets. In the upper panel, detection sensitivity, d_a, is plotted as a function of stimulus intensity. The vertical line marks the intensity required to achieve a sensitivity of 1.0. The straight line is the linear regression. In the lower panel, area under the ROC (equivalent to percentage correct in a 2AFC task) is plotted as a function of stimulus intensity. The vertical line marks the intensity required to achieve a detection probability of .75. The smooth curve is a Gaussian integral fit to the data with a maximum-likelihood technique.

would get with the same targets in a two-alternative, forced-choice (2AFC) detection paradigm. Even though they are equivalent to each other, the term *accuracy* will be used to mean A_z and the term *sensitivity* will be used to mean d_a. When A_z is plotted as a function of the target luminance, the familiar S-shaped psychometric function results, as may be seen in the lower panel of Figure 4.5.

The main point here is that signal detection theory provides a means for distinguishing the characteristics of the sensory process from those of the decision process. When the performances of two observers differ, it could be that the observers have different sensitivity in their sensory processes or that they are using different decision rules in their decision processes or both. The upper panel of Figure 4.7 presents traditional psychometric functions of three observers. The dependent measure of performance is the probability of saying "yes" on the detection task: a classic frequency-of-seeing curve. The three observers clearly differ

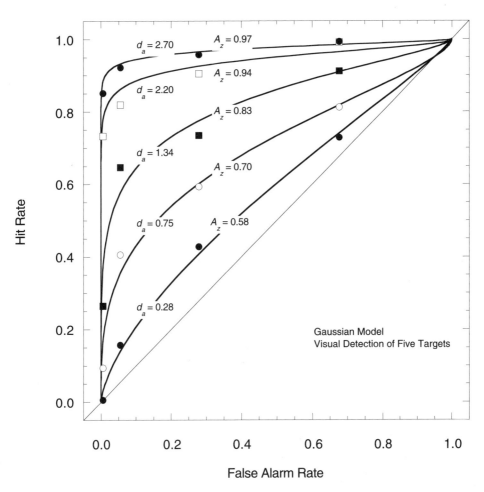

Figure 4.6. Receiver operating characteristic (ROC) of five visual targets differing in intensity. The sensitivity (d_a) and the accuracy (A_z) of the ROC for each target are marked on it.

in their detection performance: Observer 1 requires the least amount of stimulus intensity to reach .5, and Observer 3 requires the most.

What is the basis of this different performance? To answer this question we must use a model of the detection process. We can compute the sensitivity of the sensory process within the signal detection framework by taking the probability of saying "yes" when the signal is present (hit rate) together with the probability of saying "yes" when the signal is absent (false alarm rate) and computing d_a and A_z. The lower panel of Figure 4.7 shows the psychometric functions of the same observers based on the accuracy of the sensory process (A_z). Now the three psychometric functions are much more similar to one another. Some slight differences still exist among the three observers, but most of the variability seen in the upper panel has disappeared and was therefore due to differences in decision criteria.

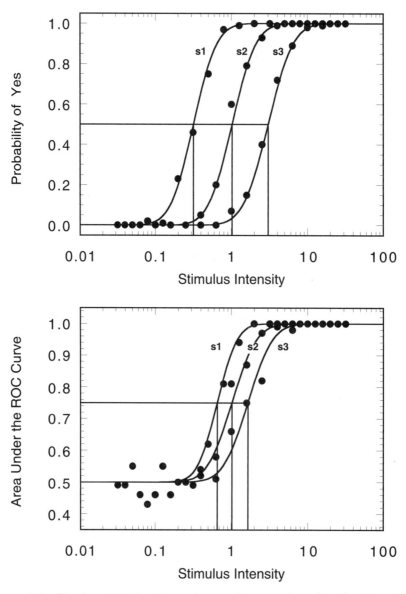

Figure 4.7. Psychometric functions of three observers based on the biased measure of sensitivity, probability of saying "yes" (upper panel), and the unbiased measure, area under the ROC curve (lower panel).

The signal detection model, as outlined previously, has received widespread acceptance among researchers in psychophysics. But it has not gained much acceptance in psychology and related fields as a model of decision-making in the face of uncertainty, in spite of compelling evidence that supports it (Hammond, Harvey, & Hastie, 1992b; Harvey, 1992; Harvey, Hammond, Lusk, & Mross, 1992; Swets, 1986; Swets, Dawes, & Monahan, 2000; Swets & Picket, 1982). I will illustrate the generality of the noisy representation model and show that with the application of signal detection theory we can decompose human judgment performance into a sensory or, more generally, an information-processing component (sensitivity and accuracy) and a decision-making component. These are the two major psychological processes that connect stimuli in the environment to action, as illustrated in Figure 4.2.

Detection of Severe Weather by Research Forecasters

Severe weather can be life threatening, and weather forecasters continuously seek new ways to improve forecasting accuracy. Mueller, Wilson, and Heckman (1987) studied the ability of forecasters to predict severe weather at runway approaches to Stapleton International Airport in Denver. At 1-hr intervals the forecasters estimated the probability that a severe downdraft would occur within the next 15 min, the next 30 min, the next 45 min and the next hour. Approximately 520 forecasts were made. The forecasters used 15 different probability values, ranging from 0.0 to 1.0, to express their judgment that a severe downdraft would occur. Fifty severe downdraft events occurred during the experiment. The signal detection model can be applied to these data by treating the probability estimates as confidence ratings. We (Harvey et al., 1992) computed the means and standard deviations of the four Gaussian distributions representing the four forecasting intervals and the value of the 14 decision criteria that generate the 15 response categories by finding the maximum-likelihood fit of the model to the actual data. The results of this analysis are summarized in Figure 4.8. The upper panel shows the four Gaussian distributions representing severe weather at the four forecasting intervals and the distribution representing the no severe weather condition. The 14 decision criteria are shown as vertical lines. All four downdraft distributions are shifted well to the right of the no downdraft distribution, indicating that rather high forecasting accuracy is possible. The mean of the 15-min forecast is the farthest to the right followed by the 30-min forecast.

In the lower left panel of Figure 4.8 the data predicted by the bestfitting model are plotted as a function of the observed data. The fit of the model to the data is extremely good, as is seen in the figure. Chi-square for 40 deg of freedom was 32.1. The probability that the deviations of the data from the predicted values are due to chance alone is .87 so we conclude that the model is a good representation of the forecasting process. The ROCs of the four forecasting intervals are shown in the lower right panel of Figure 4.8. One can see that these forecasters achieved a high degree of accuracy, as measured by the area under each of the ROC curves. Accuracy is highest for the 15-min forecast (.97) and diminishes slightly to .92 for the 60-min forecast. Comparing Figure 4.8 with the ROCs in Figure 4.6, one can see that the weather forecasters achieve the same accuracy as and have performance similar to an observer trying to detect a simple visual target.

Detection of Precipitation by Weather Forecasters

Forecasting for the next 24 hr is not as accurate as for the next 15 min. Murphy and Winkler (1987) reported the results of 2,820 probability of precipitation (PoP) forecasts made by National Weather Service forecasters at Chicago, Illinois, from July 1972 to June 1976. The forecasts were for the 12-hr period

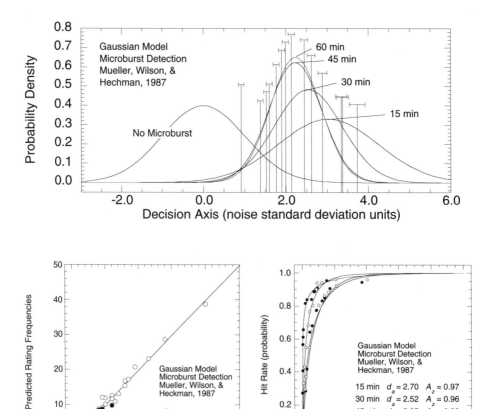

Figure 4.8. Forecasting of severe weather at 15, 30, 45, and 60 min into the future (data are from Harvey et al., 1992). Shown are the complete Gaussian signal detection model with decision criteria (upper panel); the fit between the observed data and those predicted by the model (lower left panel); and the receiver operating characteristics of the four forecasts (lower right panel).

from 12 to 24 hr following the forecast. We treat the probability forecasts as confidence ratings and calculate the best fitting signal detection model. In this case logistic distributions (Johnson & Kotz, 1970b) fit the data even better than Gaussian distributions, and so the logistic model is presented in Figure 4.9.

How well the model depicted in the upper panel of Figure 4.9 fits is shown in the lower left panel of the same figure. The chi-square of the fit is 12.9, and for 10 deg of freedom the probability of getting that value or higher by chance alone is .227, so we conclude that the model cannot be rejected. The ROC of the forecasters is plotted in the lower right panel of Figure 4.9. The impressive agreement between the hit rate–false alarm rate pairs (open circles) generated by the decision criteria separating the response categories and the hit rates and false alarm rates predicted by the model (smooth line) is obvious in the figure. Overall sensitivity to predicting rain is not as high as for predicting

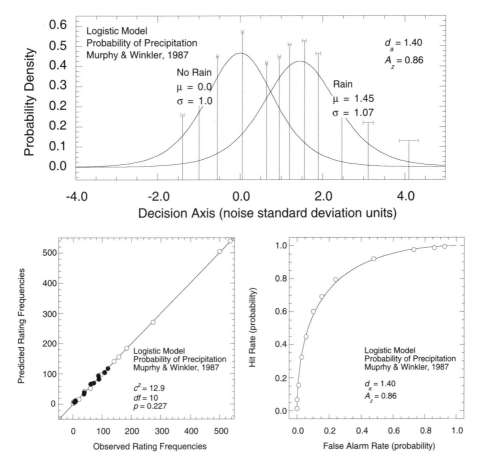

Figure 4.9. Forecasting the probability of precipitation (PoP). The complete logistic signal detection model with decision criteria (upper panel); the fit between the observed data and those predicted by the model (lower left panel); and the ROC of the PoP forecasts (lower right panel).

severe weather. The area under the ROC curve is only .86 for the PoP forecasts compared with .97 to .92 for the prediction of severe weather. One factor causing this loss of accuracy is the longer time period of the PoP forecast.

Detection of Liars by Polygraph Operators

How do weather forecasters compare with the ability of polygraph operators to detect liars? We can apply the same psychological model of noisy internal representation and multiple decision criteria to judgments made by professional polygraph operators and compare their accuracy with those of weather forecasters. Kleinmuntz and Szucko (Kleinmuntz & Szucko, 1984; Szucko & Kleinmuntz, 1981) asked six professional polygraph operators to examine 100 individuals, 50 of whom were actually guilty of theft. Using a confidence scale

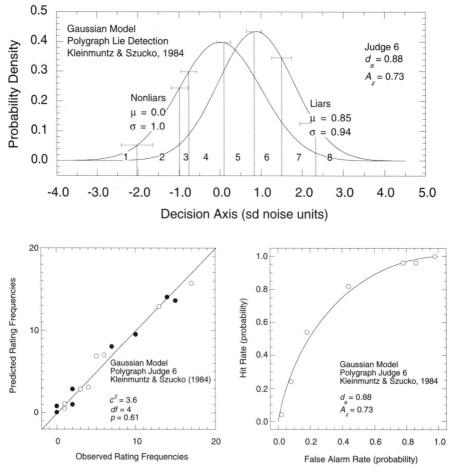

Figure 4.10. Detection of liars by professional polygraph judges. Shown are the complete Gaussian signal detection model with decision criteria for Judge 6 (upper panel); the fit between the observed data and those predicted by the model (lower left panel); the ROC of the judge (lower right panel).

from 1 to 8, in which 1 meant confident *no* and 8 meant confident *yes*, they judged whether or not each person was lying about stealing. In the original paper (Kleinmuntz & Szucko, 1984), the authors collapsed ratings 1–4 to mean *no* and ratings 5-8 to mean *yes*. In the reanalysis of their data presented here, the frequency of each confidence rating form the data set used to compute the noisy representation model for each of the six judges.

The results for Judge 6, who is representative of the other judges, are shown in Figure 4.10. The upper panel shows the two Gaussian distributions, one for the nonliars and one for the liars. The vertical lines indicate the seven decision criteria that partition the internal representation space into the eight different response categories. In the lower left panel the response frequencies predicted by the best fitting model are plotted as a function of the observed response frequencies. Chi-square is 3.6. With 4 deg of freedom, the probability that the differences between the model and the data are due to random error is

.61. We therefore conclude that the Gaussian signal detection model cannot be rejected. In the lower right panel of Figure 4.10 the hit rate generated by each decision criterion is plotted as a function of the corresponding false alarm rate. Again one sees that the dual Gaussian variable criterion model is a very good description of the judgment behavior of the polygraph operator. The area under Judge 6's ROC is .73, which is lower accuracy than either of the weather fore-casting situations described previously. The accuracies of the other five judges were .73, .67, .78, .81, and .72. This low overall accuracy is the main reason that polygraph testing is not admissible in most courts of law (Office of Technology Assessment, 1983). Again we see that the behavior of experts making complex judgments is well modeled by an information-processing process having noisy internal representations and a decision process holding a series of decision criteria that are used to determine which of the possible responses will be made.

Detection of Successful Parolees

Finally, we apply the signal detection model to the process of deciding whether or not to release a prisoner on parole. A parole board is in fact performing a detection task: They try to detect which prisoners are safe to release back into society and which prisoners should not be released. Several tools are available to assist a parole board in making this decision. One such tool, the Salient Factor Score (SFS) of the United States Parole Commission, has been widely used since the 1970s as an aid in making parole decisions. Hoffman (1983) reported the performance of the SFS in assessing the risk of granting parole to 6,294 parolees. The SFS score ranges from 0 (a poor risk for parole) to 10 (a good risk). The parolees were classified into two groups: those who had no problems during the 2 years following their release from prison (the success-ful outcome group); and those who got into trouble with the law (failure outcome group). As part of a larger project on parole board decision making (a manuscript is in preparation), my colleague Tim Brennan and I calculated the number of parolees having each of the 11 possible SFS scores, for each of the two groups, using the data presented in Hoffman's published Table 1 and then fit the Gaussian signal detection model to these data.

The best fitting model is shown in the upper panel of Figure 4.11. The model is a very good description of the observed frequencies, as can be seen in the lower left panel of Figure 4.11. The chi-square for 8 deg of freedom is 12.7, which has an associated probability of .12. We therefore have no reason to reject this model as a valid description of the detection performance. The ROC of the SFS is plotted in the lower right panel of Figure 4.11. The accuracy of the score is above chance (.5), but at .67, it is well below the accuracy of the polygraph judges and the weather forecasters.

Discussion

The simple idea of noisy internal representations that can be modeled by prob-ability distributions combined with the simple idea of responses based on one or more decision criteria leads to a powerful model with great predictive power

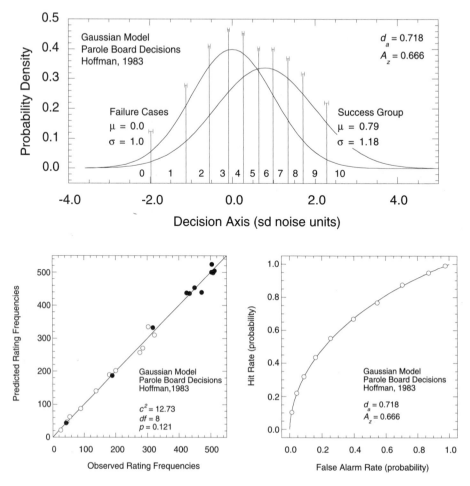

Figure 4.11. The Salient Factor Score (SFS) as a tool for releasing prisoners on parole. Shown here are the complete Gaussian signal detection model with decision criteria (upper panel); the fit between the observed data and those predicted by the model (lower left panel); and the ROC of the SFS (lower right panel).

and widespread applicability beyond the narrow psychophysical domain from which it sprang. I have shown how this model can describe the sensitivity and accuracy of the sensory process in the detection of visual targets in a way that is not contaminated by the rules of the decision process. I have then demonstrated that the model is an excellent description of how humans make judgments about severe weather, about the probability of rain, about lying, and about releasing prisoners on parole. Other examples of signal detection theory's extensibility can be found in several sources (e.g., Harvey, 1992; Swets, 1986; Swets et al., 2000; Swets & Picket, 1982). This approach to understanding human performance offers a reconciliation between two rival points of view in science—correspondence and coherence (Hammond, 1996)—because it contains elements of both.

The ROCs of the five examples discussed previously show that mistakes are unavoidable in situations in which one must discriminate between two or more overlapping internal representations. The decision maker faces a dilemma: He or she can lower the false alarm rate by adopting a more conservative decision criterion but at the price of a lower hit rate. The decision maker can increase the hit rate by adopting a more liberal decision criterion but at the cost of having a higher false alarm rate. For a fixed level of sensitivity, there is no way out of this dilemma.

The sensitivity and accuracy of a judge or diagnostic system may be compared unambiguously to that of any other. We have seen in this paper that research meteorologists can predict severe weather with an accuracy of .97, whereas National Weather Service forecasters can predict rain with an accuracy of .86. Both of these forecasters in turn have a higher accuracy than polygraph judges who detected liars with an accuracy of only .73. Finally, we see that a widely used instrument for aiding parole boards in making parole decisions achieves an accuracy of only .67.

For a situation with a fixed level of accuracy, which decision criterion to use is often not a scientific question but a public policy question. For example, a parole board could release all prisoners with a SFS score higher than 5 or release only those prisoners with scores of 8 or higher. The consequences of using different decision criteria may be calculated in a straightforward manner, and public policy decisions can be made in as rational a way as possible. More detailed discussions of these important issues may be found in several papers (e.g., Hammond, Harvey, & Hastie, 1992a; Hammond et al., 1992b; Harvey, 1992; Swets, 1992).

Life, like water drops from fountains, is indeed filled with uncertainty. But this fact should not be a source of despair because uncertainty may be quantified through the use of probability distributions whose properties *are* completely specified. Using probability distributions to describe noisy internal representations combined with appropriate decision processes provides a simple yet powerful model of human judgment and decision making in a wide variety of domains.

References

Aulhorn, E., & Harms, H. (1972). Visual perimetry. In D. Jameson & L. M. Hurvich (Eds.), *Handbook of sensory physiology: Vol. 7. Part 4. Visual psychophysics* (pp. 102–145). New York: Springer.

DeCarlo, L. T. (1998). Signal detection theory and generalized linear models. *Psychological Methods, 3*(2), 186–205.

Dorfman, D. D., & Alf, E., Jr. (1969). Maximum-likelihood estimation of parameters of signal-detection theory and determination of confidence intervals—Rating method data. *Journal of Mathematical Psychology, 6*(3), 487–496.

Dorfman, D. D., Beavers, L. L., & Saslow, C. (1973). Estimation of signal detection theory parameters from rating-method data: A comparison of the method of scoring and direct search. *Bulletin of the Psychonomic Society, 1*(3), 207–208.

Fechner, G. T. (1860). *Elemente der Psychophysik.* Leipzig, Germany: Breitkopf and Härtel.

Fechner, G. T. (1889). *Elemente der Psychophysik* (2nd unaltered ed., Vol. 1). Leipzig, Germany: Breitkopf and Härtel.

Fechner, G. T. (1966). *Elements of Psychophysics* (H. E. Adler, Trans.) (Vol. 1). New York: Holt, Rinehart and Winston.

Galton, F. (1885). Some results of the Anthropometric Laboratory. *Journal of the Anthropological Institute of Great Britain and Ireland, 14,* 275–287.

Garner, W. R., Hake, H. W., & Eriksen, C. W. (1956). Operationism and the concept of perception. *Psychological Review, 63*(3), 149–159.

Green, D. M., & Swets, J. A. (1974). *Signal detection theory and psychophysics*. Huntington, NY: Robert E. Krieger.

Hammond, K. R. (1996). *Human judgment and social policy*. New York: Oxford University Press.

Hammond, K. R., Harvey, L. O., Jr., & Hastie, R. H. (1992a). Comment on application of decision science: Reply. *Psychological Science, 3*(6), 383–384.

Hammond, K. R., Harvey, L. O., Jr., & Hastie, R. H. (1992b). Making better use of scientific knowledge: Separating truth from justice. *Psychological Science, 3,* 80–87.

Harvey, L. O., Jr. (1992). The critical operating characteristic and the evaluation of expert judgment. *Organizational Behavior and Human Decision Processes, 53*(2), 229–251.

Harvey, L. O., Jr., Hammond, K. R., Lusk, C. M., & Mross, E. F. (1992). Application of signal detection theory to weather forecasting behavior. *Monthly Weather Review, 120*(5), 863–883.

Hoffman, P. B. (1983). Screening for risk: A revised salient factor score (SFS 81). *Journal of Criminal Justice, 11,* 539–547.

Johnson, N. L., & Kotz, S. (1970a). *Continuous univariate distributions-1*. New York: John Wiley & Sons.

Johnson, N. L., & Kotz, S. (1970b). *Continuous univariate distributions-2*. New York: John Wiley & Sons.

Kleinmuntz, B., & Szucko, J. J. (1984, March 29). A field study of the fallibility of polygraphic lie detection. *Nature, 308,* 449–450.

Krantz, D. H. (1969). Threshold theories of signal detection. *Psychological Review, 76*(3), 308–324.

Laming, D. (1986). *Sensory analysis*. New York: Academic Press.

Link, S. W. (1994). Rediscovering the past: Gustav Fechner and signal detection theory. *Psychological Science, 5*(6), 335–340.

Macmillan, N. A., & Creelman, C. D. (1991). *Detection theory: A user's guide*. Cambridge, England: Cambridge University Press.

Mueller, C. K., Wilson, J. W., & Heckman, B. (1987). *Evaluation of the TDWR aviation nowcasting experiment*. Paper presented at the Third International Conference on the Aviation Weather System, Boston, MA.

Murphy, A. H., & Winkler, R. L. (1987). A general framework for forecast verification. *Monthly Weather Review, 115*(7), 1330–1338.

Office of Technology Assessment. (1983). *Scientific validity of polygraph testing: A research review and evaluation—a technical memorandum* (OTA-TM-H-15). Washington, DC: Office of Technology Assessment, Congress of The United States.

Press, W. H., Teukolsky, S. A., Vetterling, W. T., & Flannery, B. P. (1992). *Numerical recipes in C: The art of scientific computing* (2nd ed.). New York: Cambridge University Press.

Simpson, A. J., & Fitter, M. J. (1973). What is the best index of detectability? *Psychological Bulletin, 80*(6), 481–488.

Swets, J. A. (1961). Is there a sensory threshold? *Science, 134,* 168–177.

Swets, J. A. (1986). Form of empirical ROC's in discrimination and diagnostic tasks: Implications for theory and measurement of performance. *Psychological Bulletin, 99*(2), 181–198.

Swets, J. A. (1992). The science of choosing the right decision threshold in high-stakes diagnostics. *American Psychologist, 47*(4), 522–532.

Swets, J. A., Dawes, R. M., & Monahan, J. (2000). Psychological science can improve diagnostic decisions. *Psychological Science in the Public Interest, 1*(1), 1–26.

Swets, J. A., & Picket, R. M. (1982). *Evaluation of diagnostic systems: Methods from signal detection theory*. New York: Academic Press.

Swets, J. A., Tanner, W. P., Jr., & Birdsall, T. G. (1961). Decision processes in perception. *Psychological Review, 68*(5), 301–340.

Szucko, J. J., & Kleinmuntz, B. (1981). Statistical versus clinical lie detection. *American Psychologist, 36*(5), 488–496.

Tanner, W. P., Jr., & Swets, J. A. (1954). A decision-making theory of visual detection. *Psychological Review, 61*(6), 401–409.

Thurstone, L. L. (1927a). A law of comparative judgment. *Psychological Review*, 34, 273–286.

Thurstone, L. L. (1927b). Psychophysical analysis. *American Journal of Psychology, 38,* 368–389.

Urban, F. M. (1908). *The application of statistical methods to problems of psychophysics.* Philadelphia: The Psychological Clinic Press.

Van Zandt, T. (2000). ROC curves and confidence judgments in recognition memory. *Journal of Experimental Psychology: Learning, Memory, and Cognition, 26*(3), 582–600.

Part III

Clinical Applications

5

The Use of a Visual Illusion to Detect Glaucoma

Frequency Doubling Technology Perimetry

Chris A. Johnson

I could not imagine a better mentor than Herschel W. Leibowitz. It has now been 25 years since I completed my graduate training with Hersh, and I have come to realize how especially unique and invaluable this experience has been to my career and my life. It would be impossible within the confines of this manuscript to express my gratitude fully for this experience, nor would it be possible to recount all the things that I learned under his tutelage. Pearls of wisdom such as "A good study should both add to and subtract from the literature," and "How important will this be 5 years from now?" and numerous others have served me well throughout my career.

Many qualities also make Herschel Leibowitz a truly unique scholar and mentor. Among the many notable characteristics, several stand out for me. First, Herschel Leibowitz has an uncanny ability to view old research problems within a new context and to recognize potential relationships among problems that had previously been thought to be unrelated. He was able to convey this to his students, who were thereby able to view research problems with fewer pre-existing biases, leading them to seek innovative and novel approaches to these problems. Another of Hersh's attributes was to study problems that had practical as well as theoretical importance. In this view, Herschel Leibowitz exposed his students to many different real-world applications of visual perception; he brought those students along on consulting and advisory visits related to the design of heads-up displays for pilots, to visual problems associated with traffic accidents, and to a myriad of other topics. This practice instilled in his students the enduring question "Why is this problem important?" Research questions that have practical, real-world significance as well as theoretical merit are ones that have the greatest importance. For these experiences and others too numerous to mention, I offer a most heartfelt "Thank you!"

Most appropriately, this chapter describes a novel application of a perceptual effect to a real-world problem, the use of a visual illusion to detect glaucoma and other eye diseases.

Supported in part by National Eye Institute Research Grant #EY-03424. The author is a paid consultant for Welch Allyn, the manufacturer of the commercial version of the Frequency Doubling Technology (FDT) perimeter.

The Frequency Doubling Illusion

The study of visual illusions has played a longstanding role in the history of experimental psychology and visual perception (Gregory, 1997; Hochberg, 1971; Leibowitz, 1965; Tolansky, 1964). Visual illusions have served both as a challenge to explain their underlying basis and as a tool to evaluate the properties of mechanisms involved in normal visual processing. There are also many practical real-world situations in which visual illusions play an important role, including night visual approaches by airline pilots (Mertens & Lewis, 1981, 1982, 1983), spatial orientation under weightless conditions in space (Lackner, 1992a, 1992b; Lackner & DiZio, 1993), accidents and falls in the elderly (Cohn & Lasley, 1985, 1990), and the interpretation of radiologic images (Daffner, 1989; Jaffe, 1984). In this chapter, I would like to describe another real-world application of a visual illusion, the use of the frequency doubling illusion for detection of glaucoma and other eye diseases.

Kelly (1966) was the first to describe the frequency doubling illusion. It occurs when viewing a low spatial frequency (less than one cycle per degree) sinusoidal grating undergoing high temporal counterphase flicker frequency (greater than 15 Hz). Under these conditions, one perceives twice as many light and dark bars than are physically present on the display; that is, the spatial frequency appears to be doubled. Kelly (1966, 1981) concluded that the frequency doubling illusion was produced by a nonlinearity present in the visual system and developed a model to account for this effect. Tyler (1974) established that the type of nonlinearity was most likely a rectification, as illustrated schematically in Figure 5.1.

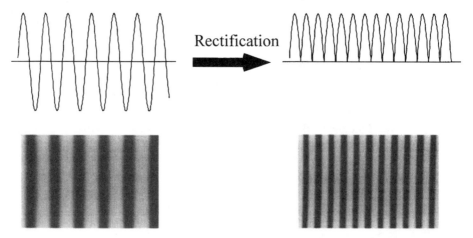

Figure 5.1. Schematic representation of rectification of a sinusoidal grating to produce a doubling of the spatial frequency. As illustrated here, the rectifier inverts the sine wave each time it becomes negative (goes below the horizontal line). In the case of a retinal ganglion cell, rectification would consist of the same burst of activity whether a portion of the sine wave goes from light to dark or from dark to light. (Note that this figure is intended to illustrate that the spatial frequency of the grating appears to be doubled and is not meant to present an accurate depiction of a rectified sinusoidal waveform.)

According to Maddess and Henry (1992), the frequency doubling illusion is believed to be mediated by a subset of retinal ganglion cells that project to the magnocellular layers of the lateral geniculate nucleus. The magnocellular retinal ganglion cells (M-cells) tend to have large-diameter axons and fast conduction velocities, and they are most sensitive to low spatial frequencies and high temporal frequencies. Because of this, M-cells are believed to be primarily involved in the processing of visual motion, rapid flicker, and other visual functions involving quick temporal changes (Livingston & Hubel, 1987, 1988). Maddess and Henry further attribute the frequency doubling illusion to a subset of M-cell fibers (My-cells) that have nonlinear response properties. In particular, the My cells appear to function like a rectifier, in accordance with Tyler's (1974) explanation of the frequency doubling illusion.

Because evidence exists that retinal ganglion cells with large-diameter axons (Quigley, Dunkelberger, & Green, 1988, 1989; Quigley, Sanchez, & Dunkelberger, 1987) and retinal ganglion cells that project to the magnocellular layers of the lateral geniculate nucleus (Chaturvedi, Hedley-Whyte, & Dreyer, 1993; Dandona, Hendrickson, & Quigley, 1991) may be preferentially damaged early in glaucoma, Maddess and Henry (1992) suggested that the frequency doubling illusion might be useful as a screening procedure for detecting glaucoma. Their preliminary findings indicated that contrast thresholds for detecting a frequency doubling stimulus were elevated in patients with glaucomatous visual field loss in comparison with normal observers. We have extended these initial findings to optimize the performance of this test procedure and define its clinical characteristics (Adams, Bullimore, Wall, Fingeret, & Johnson, 1999; Chauhan & Johnson, 1999; Johnson, 1995; Johnson, Cioffi, & Van Buskirk, 1999b; Johnson & Demirel, 1997; Johnson & Samuels, 1997; Johnson, Wall, Fingeret, & Lalle, 1998). However, before any further discussion of the frequency doubling illusion, I will present a brief overview of glaucoma.

Glaucoma

Glaucoma is one of the leading causes of blindness in the United States and other industrialized countries. It is estimated that in the United States approximately 2 million people have glaucoma, and 80,000 people are legally blind from it (USDHEW, 1973). Glaucoma is the leading cause of blindness in African Americans and the third leading cause of blindness in Whites. The prevalence of glaucoma in African Americans is about 5 times higher than in Whites, with rates of 1.23% in those between the ages of 40 and 49 and 11.26% in those older than 80 (Tielsch et al., 1991). By comparison, the prevalence of glaucoma in Whites is 0.92% in those between the ages of 40 and 49 and 2.16% in those older than 80. Accurate prevalence rates are not yet available for other ethnic groups.

It has been estimated that an additional 3 to 6 million people in the United States (3%–8% of the population older than 40 years of age) are at increased risk of developing glaucoma because of elevated pressure in the eye, a family history of glaucoma, or other factors known to be associated with the development of glaucoma (Kass, 1994).

Glaucoma is a disease process that causes damage to retinal ganglion cells at the optic nerve head, the point at which the ganglion cell nerve fibers exit the eye and travel to the lateral geniculate body. In its most common form (primary open-angle glaucoma), glaucomatous damage is caused either by mechanical insult to ganglion cells at the optic nerve head resulting from elevated pressure in the eye or by a lack of adequate blood flow to portions of the optic nerve or by a combination of both factors. The damage typically occurs to small bundles of nerve fibers in localized portions of the optic nerve, and therefore peripheral visual field sensitivity losses mimic the anatomic arrangement of retinal ganglion cells as they exit the eye at the optic nerve head. Figure 5.2 illustrates the arrangement of retinal ganglion cell nerve fiber bundles entering the optic nerve head (top) and a typical form of peripheral visual field loss associated with damage to a nerve fiber bundle (bottom).

From a clinical ophthalmic standpoint, there are three main characteristics of importance in the detection and evaluation of glaucoma: (a) the intraocular pressure (IOP) of the eye, (b) the appearance of the optic nerve head, and (c) the differential light sensitivity (increment threshold) of the peripheral visual field, usually referred to as perimetry. Currently, the primary means of treating glaucoma is to lower the IOP of either by applying medicine topically to the eye or by surgery.

One of the major problems associated with glaucoma is detecting the earliest signs of damage. Glaucoma patients do not usually notice symptoms until the disease has significantly progressed and a large proportion of the retinal ganglion cells have been lost. Screening for glaucoma, particularly in populations at increased risk of developing glaucoma, is therefore extremely important (Harper & Reeves, 1999). The easiest method of screening is to measure the IOP. Unfortunately, it is not very effective. In patients with glaucoma, a single measurement of IOP will be within normal limits approximately 50% of the time (Tielsch et al., 1991). In addition, there is a subgroup of glaucoma patients who have IOP measurements that are within normal limits but who still develop glaucomatous damage to retinal ganglion cells (low-tension glaucoma). Thus, more than half of all patients with glaucoma will not be detected by a single IOP measurement. A much larger group of individuals (those with ocular hypertension) have elevated IOP that is beyond normal limits but do not have glaucomatous damage. Although patients with ocular hypertension are at greater risk of developing glaucoma, they may never sustain any damage or require treatment. Those with ocular hypertension greatly outnumber glaucoma patients. Thus, screening for glaucoma on the basis of IOP measurements will result in low sensitivity (correct determination of glaucoma) and low specificity (incorrect determination of glaucoma in persons without damage).

Evaluating the appearance of the optic nerve head for evidence of glaucomatous damage is an effective method of screening for glaucoma. However, it requires highly experienced and skilled examiners who are able to detect evidence of glaucomatous injury to the optic nerve head, particularly the earliest subtle signs of damage. This method is complicated by the fact that there are wide variations in the appearance of normal optic nerve heads, and even glaucoma specialists do not always agree upon features that represent

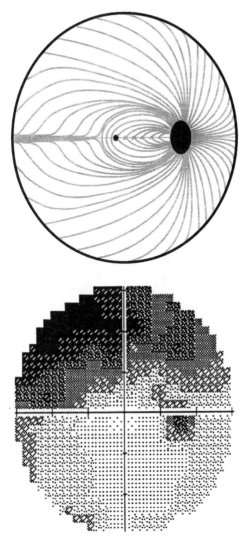

Figure 5.2. (Top) The arrangement of retinal ganglion cell nerve fiber bundles as they enter the optic nerve head. (Bottom) A typical example of glaucomatous visual field loss corresponding to damage to nerve fiber bundles in a localized portion of the optic nerve head. Sensitivity is represented by a grayscale plot, with high sensitivity represented by lighter areas and low sensitivity represented by dark areas. The darker arcuate region in the superior visual field indicates damage to the corresponding nerve fiber bundle.

normal variations and those that represent damage from glaucoma. For these reasons, it is not practical to screen for glaucoma in large populations using this method.

Another effective method of screening for glaucoma is to test the peripheral visual field for evidence of localized areas of sensitivity loss resulting from glaucomatous damage. Although this method has been shown to have high sensitivity and specificity for detection of glaucoma (Harper & Reeves, 1999;

Katz, Sommer, Gaasterland, & Anderson 1991), the equipment needed to perform this testing is quite expensive and is not very portable. In addition, the time required to test both eyes is too long to make the method a practical means of screening large populations. Clearly, there is an important need for a fast, simple, and portable method of accurately screening for glaucoma.

The Frequency Doubling Illusion for Detecting Glaucoma

We have refined the original test procedure described by Maddess and Henry (1992) to form the basis of a commercially available clinical test procedure that utilizes the frequency doubling illusion. The Frequency Doubling Technology (FDT) perimeter, produced jointly by Welch Allyn (Skaneateles, NY) and Humphrey Systems (Dublin, CA), is shown in Figure 5.3. It has a number of advantages for glaucoma screening, including portability, ease of use, rapid test procedures, high sensitivity and specificity, good reproducibility of test results, and resistance to the effects of blur, pupil size changes, and related factors. The FDT perimeter consists of a custom video monitor and control circuitry, an internal microprocessor, a display panel for selecting test procedures and monitoring the progress of testing, a printer for providing hard copies of test results, and a patient response button.

The FDT perimeter uses two stimulus presentation patterns to evaluate the central visual field. The first stimulus pattern consists of 16 targets (4 per quadrant) whose dimensions are 10 deg by 10 deg, plus a central circular target of 5 deg diameter. Because our initial investigations revealed that a few early glaucomatous visual field defects were missed because they were located beyond the limits of the display in the nasal visual field (Johnson & Samuels, 1997), two additional test locations were added along the nasal horizontal meridian. Both stimulus presentation patterns are shown in Figure 5.4.

The stimulus consists of a 0.25 cycle/deg sinusoidal grating undergoing 25-Hz counterphase flicker. During the test procedure, one of the target locations is selected on a random basis. Each stimulus is presented for a maximum of 720 ms. The person being tested is instructed to press a response button each time a stimulus is detected. In the first 160 ms, the stimulus contrast is increased from zero to the contrast selected for that trial. If the stimulus is not seen, it remains at this contrast for 400 ms and then is gradually decreased to zero during the final 160 ms. This ramping up and down of contrast is done to avoid temporal transients in the stimulus presentation that might produce spurious responses. If the target is seen, the stimulus is prematurely truncated at the time of the response. Between stimulus presentations, there is a variable random interstimulus interval to reduce anticipation and rhythmic responses by the person being examined.

To determine contrast thresholds for all visual field locations, a modified binary search (MOBS) procedure is employed (Tyrrell & Owens, 1988). MOBS is a variant of the standard staircase threshold estimation procedure that is more robust to false-positive and false-negative response errors and is therefore well suited for a clinical test procedure. This procedures takes between 4 and 5 min per eye. Results are presented in terms of contrast sensitivity in

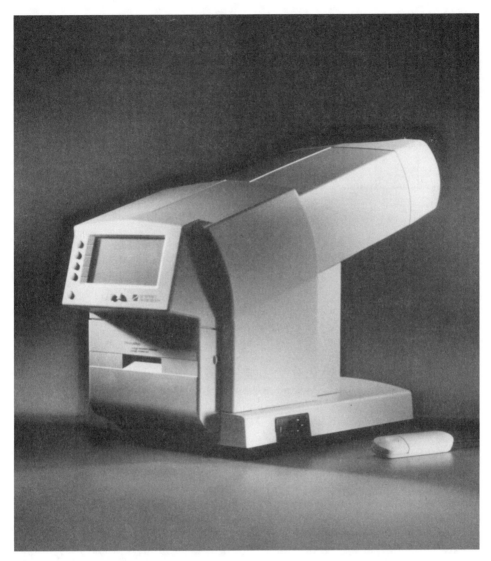

Figure 5.3. The commercial version of the Frequency Doubling Technology (FDT) perimeter.

decibels (dB), which is the inverse of the contrast threshold. A contrast sensitivity of 0 dB corresponds to a stimulus with 100% contrast. The dB scale is logarithmic, and therefore a 10-dB contrast sensitivity corresponds to a stimulus with 10% contrast, a 20-dB contrast sensitivity corresponds to a stimulus with 1% contrast, and so forth. This test procedure has a sensitivity of better than 92% and a specificity of better than 96% (Cello, Nelson-Quigg, & Johnson, 2000; Johnson & Samuels, 1997). False-positive (response when no stimulus is presented), false-negative (failure to respond to a stimulus of maximum contrast), and fixation loss (response to a stimulus presented to the normal blind spot region) "catch" trials are also presented during the test procedure, every 6 to 10 presentations. A minimum of 6 of each of the catch trials

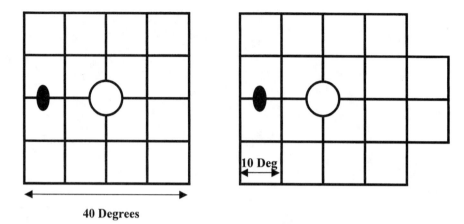

40 Degrees

Figure 5.4. The two stimulus presentation patterns currently used by FDT perimetry. The display is presented for a left eye. The position of the blind spot is indicated by the small dark oval.

are presented during the test, and if any of them equals or exceeds an error rate of 33%, the test is labeled potentially unreliable.

Test results are immediately compared with a database of test results from more than 700 normal eyes to determine whether an individual's sensitivity at each visual field location is within or outside normal limits. Because previous studies have shown that normal age-related changes in vision affect the sensitivity for detecting the frequency doubling stimulus (Adams, Bullimore, Wall, Fingeret, & Johnson, 1999), the normative database has been corrected for normal aging effects by adjusting each of the test results to equivalent values for 45-year-olds. A similar adjustment is made to an individual's results before comparing them with the normative database. For each location, a determination is made as to whether the individual's results are within normal limits or are worse than the lower 5%, 2%, 1% or 0.5% normal probability values and a different shading is used to denote this on the printed results. This determination is called the total deviation probability plot. Next, a pattern deviation probability plot is obtained by adjusting the individual's results for any generalized or average loss and then comparing them with the normative database. In this manner, it is possible to determine the degree of widespread versus localized sensitivity loss. Two summary statistics are also calculated, the mean deviation (*MD*) from normal values (average deviation from normal for all locations), and the pattern standard deviation (*PSD*), which represents the amount of departure from the normal contour of the visual field. These values are also intended to reflect the degree of widespread versus localized sensitivity loss. The left panel of Figure 5.5 presents the printed output resulting from the test procedure and data analysis.

Two rapid screening tests are also available for FDT perimetry. One of the tests (C-20-1) presents stimuli corresponding to the normal 1% probability level. If a stimulus is not detected, it is presented again later in the test. If it is still not detected, the visual field location is considered to have mild sensitivity loss, and a stimulus corresponding to the .5% normal probability level is presented. If this stimulus is not detected, the visual field location is con-

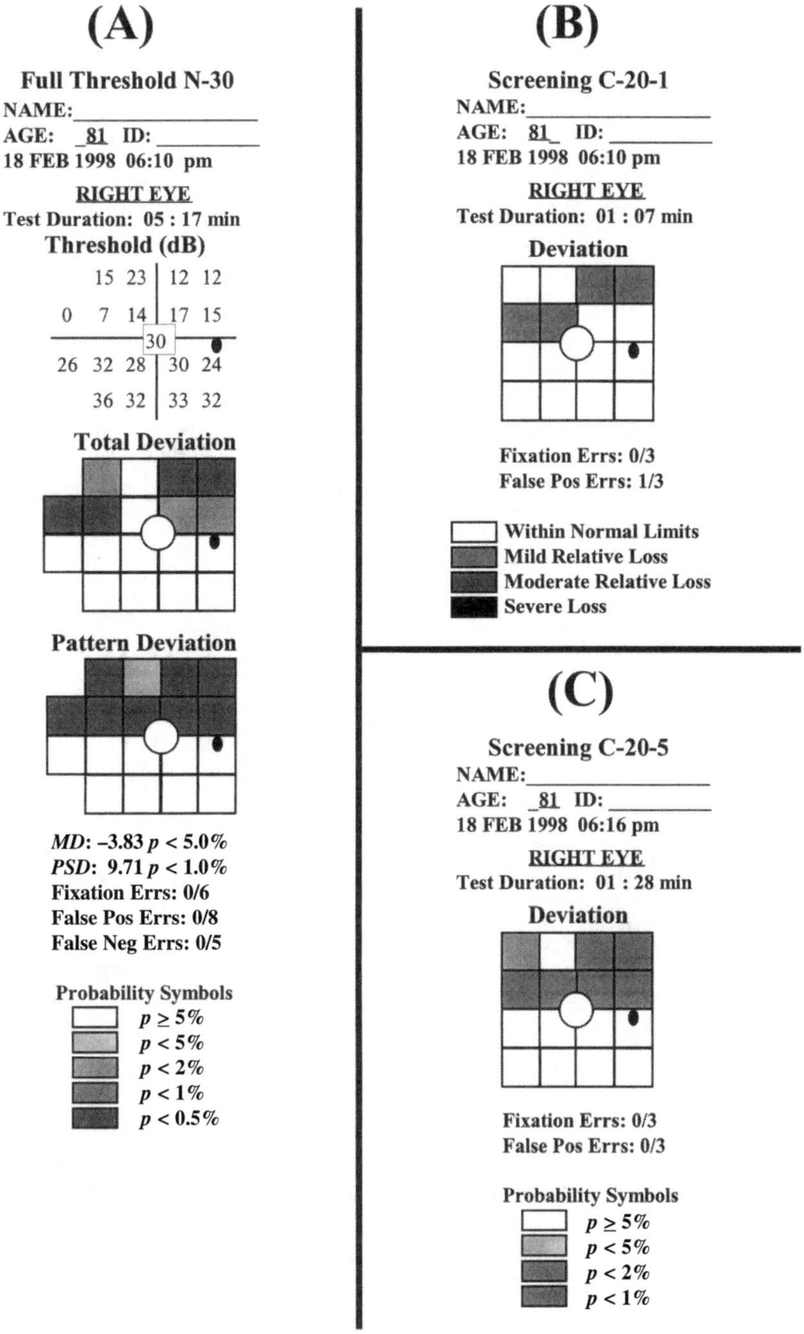

(A)

Full Threshold N-30

NAME:_____
AGE: __81__ ID:_____
18 FEB 1998 06:10 pm

RIGHT EYE

Test Duration: 05 : 17 min

Threshold (dB)

```
      15  23 | 12  12
  0   7  14 | 17  15
        ┌──30──┐    ●
  26 32 28 | 30  24
     36 32 | 33  32
```

Total Deviation

Pattern Deviation

MD: –3.83 $p < 5.0\%$
PSD: 9.71 $p < 1.0\%$
Fixation Errs: 0/6
False Pos Errs: 0/8
False Neg Errs: 0/5

Probability Symbols
$p \geq 5\%$
$p < 5\%$
$p < 2\%$
$p < 1\%$
$p < 0.5\%$

(B)

Screening C-20-1

NAME:_____
AGE: __81__ ID:_____
18 FEB 1998 06:10 pm

RIGHT EYE

Test Duration: 01 : 07 min

Deviation

Fixation Errs: 0/3
False Pos Errs: 1/3

Within Normal Limits
Mild Relative Loss
Moderate Relative Loss
Severe Loss

(C)

Screening C-20-5

NAME:_____
AGE: __81__ ID:_____
18 FEB 1998 06:16 pm

RIGHT EYE

Test Duration: 01 : 28 min

Deviation

Fixation Errs: 0/3
False Pos Errs: 0/3

Probability Symbols
$p \geq 5\%$
$p < 5\%$
$p < 2\%$
$p < 1\%$

Figure 5.5. (A) An example of the printout of test results for the Full Threshold FDT test. (B) An example of the printout for the C-20-1 (1% probability level) screening test. (C) An example of the printout for the C-20-5 (5% probability level) screening test. All three examples were obtained from the same eye, which has moderate glaucomatous visual field loss.

sidered to have moderate relative sensitivity loss and a stimulus of 100% contrast is presented. If the 100% contrast stimulus is not detected, the visual field location is considered to have severe sensitivity loss. The top right panel of Figure 5.5 illustrates the printed output for this test for the same eye that was tested using the full threshold procedure shown in the left panel.

The second screening procedure (C-20-5) is similar, except that it initially presents stimuli corresponding to the normal 5% probability level. If the stimulus is not detected, it is repeated later in the test. If it is still not detected, a stimulus corresponding to the normal 2% probability level is presented, and if this is not detected, then a stimulus at the 1% probability level is presented.

Both screening tests take about 45 to 55 s per eye for a normal visual field and about 50 to 100 s per eye if areas of sensitivity loss are present. Both procedures have good sensitivity and specificity. The screening procedure that presents stimuli at the 1% probability level has moderately higher specificity (> 98%) and moderately lower sensitivity (85%) than the screening test that presents stimuli at the 5% probability level (sensitivity and specificity of about 90% to 92%). The 1% probability level screening test is therefore probably best suited for screening the general population because specificity is high. Conversely, the 5% probability level screening test is probably best suited for screening "at risk" populations or groups in which glaucoma is highly suspected because it has higher sensitivity for detecting early, subtle losses.

Conclusion

In summary, Frequency Doubling Technology perimetry, using either full threshold or rapid screening tests, has now been shown by many investigators to be an efficient and effective method of screening for glaucoma (Cello et al., 2000; Johnson, Cioffi, & Van Buskirk, 1999a, 1999b; Johnson & Samuels, 1997; Kondo, Yamamoto, Sato, Matsubara, & Kitazawa, 1998; Quigley, 1998; Sponsel, Arango, Trigo, & Menash, 1998). Although this technique was primarily intended for detecting glaucoma, subsequent investigations have found that it is also able to detect retinal and neuroophthalmologic disorders as well (Johnson et al., 1998; Nearhing, Wall, & Withrow, 1997). More than 4,000 FDT devices are currently in use in optometry and ophthalmology since the instrument was introduced in 1997, and several groups (Prevent Blindness America, The Glaucoma Foundation, and Discoveries in Sight) are using FDT perimetry to perform an ongoing series of screenings in the general population. FDT perimetry appears to be filling an important need in glaucoma screening.

References

Adams, C. W., Bullimore, M. A., Wall, M., Fingeret, M., & Johnson, C. A. (1999). Normal aging effects for frequency doubling technology perimetry. *Optometry and Vision Science, 76*, 582–587.

Cello, K. E., Nelson-Quigg, J. M., & Johnson, C. A. (2000). Frequency doubling technology perimetry for detection of glaucomatous visual field loss. *American Journal of Ophthalmology, 129,* 314–322.

Chaturvedi, N., Hedley-Whyte, T., & Dreyer, E. B. (1993). Lateral geniculate nucleus in glaucoma. *American Journal of Ophthalmology, 116*, 182–188.

Chauhan, B. C., & Johnson, C. A. (1999). Test-retest variability characteristics of Frequency Doubling Perimetry and conventional perimetry in glaucoma patients and normal controls. *Investigative Ophthalmology and Vision Science, 40*, 648–656.

Cohn, T. E., & Lasley, D. J. (1985). Visual depth illusion and falls in the elderly. *Clinics Geriatric Medicine, 1*, 601–620.

Cohn, T. E., & Lasley D. J. (1990). Wallpaper illusion: Cause of disorientation and falls on escalators. *Perception, 19*, 573–580.

Daffner, R. H. (1989). Visual illusions in the interpretation of the radiographic image. *Current Problems in Diagnostic Radiology, 18*, 62–87.

Dandona, L., Hendrickson, A., & Quigley, H. A. (1991). Selective effects of experimental glaucoma on axonal transport by retinal ganglion cells to the dorsal lateral geniculate nucleus. *Investigative Ophthalmology and Vision Science, 32*, 1593–1599.

Gregory, R. L. (1997). Knowledge in perception and illusion. *Philosophical Transactions of the Royal Society of London. Series B: Biological Sciences, 352*, 1121–1127.

Harper, R. A., & Reeves, B. C. (1999). Glaucoma screening: The importance of combining test data. *Optommetry and Vision Science, 76*, 537–543.

Hochberg, J. (1971). Perception: I. Color and shape. In J. W. Kling & L. A. Riggs (Eds.), *Woodworth and Schlossberg's experimental psychology* (pp. 456–474). New York: Holt, Reinhart and Winston.

Jaffe, C. C. (1984). Medical imaging, vision and visual psychophysics. *Medical Radiography and Photography, 60*, 1–48.

Johnson, C. A. (1995). The Glenn A. Fry Award Lecture. Early losses of visual function in glaucoma. *Optometry and Vision Science, 72*, 359–370.

Johnson, C. A., Cioffi, G. A., & Van Buskirk, E. M. (1999a). Evaluation of two screening tests for frequency doubling technology perimetry. In M. Wall & J. M. Wild (Eds.), *Perimetry Update 1998/1999* (pp. 103–109). Amsterdam: Kugler.

Johnson, C. A., Cioffi, G. A., & Van Buskirk, E. M. (1999b). Frequency doubling technology perimetry using a 24-2 stimulus presentation pattern. *Optometry and Vision Science, 76*, 571–581.

Johnson, C. A., & Demirel, S. (1997). The role of spatial and temporal factors in frequency doubling perimetry. *Perimetry Update 1996/1997* (pp. 13–19), Amsterdam: Kugler.

Johnson, C. A., & Samuels, S. J. (1997). Screening for glaucomatous visual field loss with frequency doubling perimetry. *Investigative Ophthalmology and Vision Science, 28*, 413–425.

Johnson, C. A., Wall, M., Fingeret, M., & Lalle, P. (1998). *A primer for Frequency Doubling Technology perimetry*. Skaneateles, NY: Welch Allyn.

Kass, M. A. (1994). The ocular hypertension treatment study [Editorial]. *Journal of Glaucoma, 3*, 97–100.

Katz, J., Sommer, A., Gaasterland, D. E., & Anderson, D. R. (1991). Comparison of analytic algorithms for detecting glaucomatous visual field loss. *Archives of Ophthalmology, 109*, 1684–1689.

Kelly D. H. (1966). Frequency doubling in visual responses. *Journal of the Optical Society of America, 56*, 1628–1633.

Kelly D. H. (1981). Nonlinear visual responses to flickering sinusoidal gratings. *Journal of the Optical Society of America, 71*, 1051–1055.

Kondo, Y., Yamamoto, T., Sato, Y., Matsubara, M., & Kitazawa, Y. (1998). A frequency-doubling perimetric study in normal-tension glaucoma with hemifield defect. *Journal of Glaucoma, 7*, 261–265.

Lackner, J. R. (1992a). Multimodal and motor influences on orientation: Implications for adapting to weightless and virtual environments. *Journal of Vestibular Research: Equilibrium and Orientation, 2*, 307–322.

Lackner, J. R. (1992b). Spatial orientation in weightless environments. *Perception, 21*, 803–812.

Lackner, J. R., & DiZio, P. (1993). Multisensory, cognitive, and motor influences on human spatial orientation in weightlessness. *Journal of Vestibular Research, 3*, 361–372.

Leibowitz, H. W. (1965). *Visual perception*. London: Macmillan.

Livingston, M., & Hubel, D. (1987). Psychophysical evidence for separate channels for the perception of form, color movement and depth. *Journal of Neuroscience, 7*, 3416–3468.

Livingston, M., & Hubel, D. (1988). Segregation of form, color, movement and depth: Anatomy, physiology and perception. *Science, 240*, 740–749.

Maddess, T., & Henry, G. H. (1992). Performance of nonlinear visual units in ocular hypertension and glaucoma. *Clinical Vision Science, 7*, 371–383.

Mertens, H. W., & Lewis, M. F. (1981). Perception of runway image shape and approach angle magnitude by pilots in simulated night landing approaches. *Aviation, Space, and Environmental Medicine, 52*, 373–386.

Mertens, H. W., & Lewis, M. F. (1982). Effect of different runway sizes on pilot performance during simulated night landing approaches. *Aviation, Space, and Environmental Medicine, 53*, 463–471.

Mertens, H. W., & Lewis, M. F. (1983). Effects of approach lighting and variation in visible runway length on perception of approach angle in simulated night landings. *Aviation, Space, and Environmental Medicine, 54*, 500–506.

Nearhing, R. K., Wall, M., & Withrow, K. (1997). Sensitivity and specificity of frequency doubling perimetry in neuro-ophthalmologic disorders. *Investigative Ophthalmology and Vision Science, 38*(Suppl.), S390.

Quigley, H. A. (1998). Identification of glaucoma-related visual field abnormality with the screening protocol of frequency doubling technology. *American Journal of Ophthalmology, 125*, 819–829.

Quigley, H. A., Dunkelberger, G. R., & Green, W. R. (1988). Chronic human glaucoma causing selectively greater loss of large optic nerve fibers. *Ophthalmology, 95*, 357–363.

Quigley, H. A., Dunkelberger, G. R., & Green, W. R. (1989). Retinal ganglion cell atrophy correlated with automated perimetry in human eyes with glaucoma. *American Journal of Ophthalmology, 107*, 453–464.

Quigley, H. A., Sanchez, R. M., Dunkelberger, G. R., L'Hernault, N. L., & Baginski, T. A. (1987). Chronic glaucoma selectively damages large optic nerve fibres. *Investigative Ophthalmology and Vision Science, 28*, 913–920.

Sponsel, W. E., Arango, S., Trigo, Y., & Menash, J. (1998). Clinical classification of glaucomatous visual field loss by frequency doubling perimetry. *American Journal of Ophthalmology, 125*, 830–836.

Tielsch, J. M., Sommer, A., Katz, J., Royall, R. M., Quigley, H. A., & Javitt, J. (1991). Racial variations in the prevalence of primary open-angle glaucoma. The Baltimore Eye Survey. *Journal of the American Medical Association, 266*, 369–374.

Tolansky, S. (1964). *Optical illusions.* London: Pergamon Press.

Tyler, C. W. (1974). Observations on spatial frequency doubling. *Perception, 3*, 81–86.

Tyrrell, R. A., & Owens, D. A. (1988). A rapid technique to assess the resting states of the eyes and other threshold phenomena: The Modified Binary Search (MOBS). *Behavior Research Methods, Instruments and Computers, 20*, 137–141.

United States Department of Health, Education and Welfare (USDHEW). (1973). Statistics on blindness in the model reporting area 1969–1970. Washington, DC: Author.

6

On the Earliest Known Lenses

Jay M. Enoch

I met Herschel Leibowitz in the early 1950s at one of the annual Sam Renshaw Vision Research Meetings at Ohio State University. Since then, we have become close friends. We have shared ideas and very able students and have helped each other with seemingly endless committee, government, and standards assignments. He has taken sabbaticals with me, often shared my lab, and he and Eileen visited with us in Florida and, later, in the Bay Area.

Hersh is one of the gentlest, most thoughtful, and kindest individuals I have ever known. His friendship has provided me good fun, good companionship, and fine science. I have known no individual who has so put me at ease. Our relationship has been a continuing delight.

There are endless Hersh stories. At one of our many standards meetings on visual acuity, Louise Sloan, Glenn Fry, and others had been debating whether to include serifs on standard letters of the alphabet used in visual acuity tests. Serifs are the little tags at the ends of certain letters found in some print fonts. The interminable discussion/debate/argument had been going on for many hours. Hersh was chairing the meeting, and he came over to me at a coffee break and asked quietly, "Jay, what the hell is a serif?" I told him, and he looked me in the eye and said, "Jay, you have to be kidding; they can't have been arguing about that issue all day!"

Hersh always puts current science into a historical context. His fascination with optics, visual illusions, and visual perception combined with the enthusiasm he has always shown toward learning and solving mysteries makes it fitting that I dedicate this chapter on the origin of the first known lenses to him. I think he will enjoy it as much as I have in preparing it.

The Earliest Known Lenses

The first known lenses were fabricated about 4,600 years ago. They appeared between 2620 and 2400 B.C., that is, at the very end of the Egyptian Early Kingdom Period (Dynasty III) and during the beginning of the Old Kingdom Period (mainly during Dynasties IV and V). Existing examples of these lenses are found in the Louvre Museum in Paris and the Egyptian Museum in

The author wishes to express his thanks to the many individuals who have aided him in the preparation of this manuscript. These included (alphabetically): Stacey Choi, Robert Heitz, Patrick Hunt, Kathleen Keller, Vasudevan Lakshminarayanan, Zenab Osman, R. B. Parkinson, Carol Redmount, Jean Royer, Elisabetta Strada, My Trad and her associate Hanná, and Tareq Youssef. Correspondence concerning this chapter should be addressed to Jay M. Enoch, School of Optometry, University of California at Berkeley, Berkeley, CA 94720-2020.

Cairo. They were components of eyes inserted into elegant statues and had the unique property of appearing to follow the viewer as he or she moved about the statues. This intended illusion or perceptual effect can be readily photographed because it is based on the optical properties of the statuary eyes.

These early lenses were ground from very high quality rock crystal, a transparent form of quartz. Their front surface was convex and highly polished. On the approximately flat or plano rear surface of the lens, an "iris" was painted. Centered in the dark-appearing pupil zone was an approximately hemispheric negative-ground, high-power, concave lens surface. Thus, these earliest known lenses were multifocals with two different optical areas (iris area and pupil area) and had dual optical surfaces in the pupillary zone. It is this dual optical zone that results in the apparent following action by the eyes of these statues, illustrated in Figures 6.1 and 6.2. For more information on this entire subject, consult the *Egyptian Museum Cairo: Official Catalogue* (Saleh & Sourouzian, 1987), the special catalogue published by the Louvre (Ziegler, 1997), as well as Lucas and Harris (1962), Royer (1997), and Enoch (1998a).

The pupil aperture of these eyes probably opened into a sizeable posterior cavity formed by curved copper plates that extended forward from the rear of the eye to form the eyelid structures. Figure 6.3B is modified from a small drawing that appeared in Bouquillon and Quéré (1997). Although Figure 6.3B

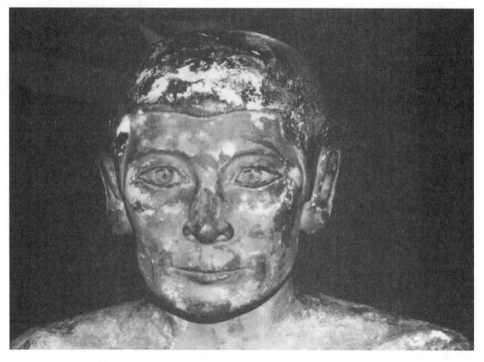

Figure 6.1. This is a photograph of the face of the magnificent Egyptian statue "Le Scribe Accroupi" (the Seated Scribe). This elegant work of art was found at Saqqara (near Memphis). The face was photographed from a straight-ahead position. A flashlight was employed to enhance visibility. This statue was chosen to demonstrate the apparent eye movement effect present in this group of statues. Photograph taken by Jay M. Enoch at the Louvre, Paris, France, in October 1997.

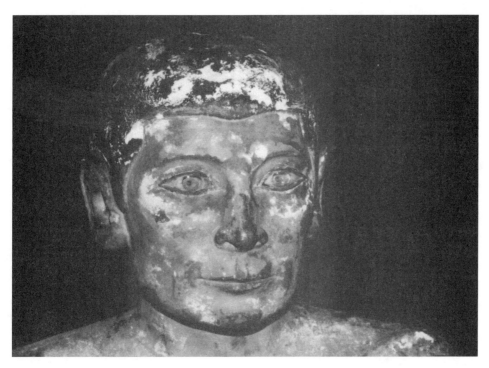

Figure 6.2. Photograph of the "Le Scribe Accroupi" statue rotated to the left side. Notice how the pupils of both eyes appear displaced toward the position of the author. Also observe the shadows of lid structures resulting from the flashlight beam. Photograph taken by Jay M. Enoch at the Louvre, Paris, France, in October 1997.

may not be quite accurate, an attempt has been made to correct some errors in the referenced published drawing: the location of the sclera-equivalent component relative to the lens, the aperture treatment, and the attachment of the lens unit to a substrate. That is, the sclera is visible at the top and bottom of the lens unit on some of these statues, and the lens is supported structurally. The pupillary aperture was open, partly occluded by resin in others, and occluded by resin in some (Lucas & Harris, 1962; Ziegler, 1997). In some statues, the scleral portions were made of white marble that had fine red-veined impurities which simulated conjunctival capillaries, and delicate vessels were added by overpainting (Bouquillon & Quéré, 1997).

The structure of these eyes indicates an advanced understanding of ocular anatomy (Enoch, 1998a). The statues with these eye structures appeared and flourished for a 200-year period from 2620 to 2400 B.C. and then disappeared. These lenses reappeared in Egypt 700 years later, during Dynasty XIII (ca. 1700 B.C.) and then disappeared forever from Egyptian art (Enoch, 1998a). A fine lens, shown in Figure 6.3A, did appear 200 years later (ca. 1550–1500 B.C.) at the Little Palace of Knossos in Crete during the Minoan period, but the design was different from that of the older Egyptian lenses. This lens and its significance are also of special interest (Andronicos, 1981; Enoch, 1987, 1996, 1998b; Higgins, 1981; Papapostolou, 1981; Sakellarakis, 1983).

The existence of these lenses raises more questions than answers. Were the Egyptian lenses built upon the hard rock technology of the Early Kingdom, or

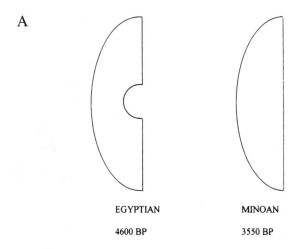

A

EGYPTIAN

4600 BP

MINOAN

3550 BP

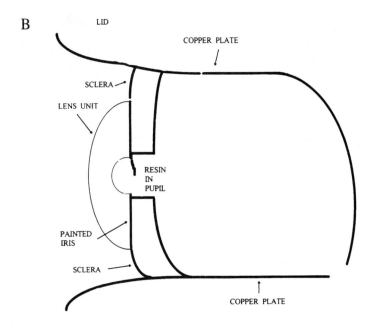

B

LID

COPPER PLATE

SCLERA

LENS UNIT

RESIN
IN
PUPIL

PAINTED
IRIS

SCLERA

COPPER PLATE

Figure 6.3. (A) The designs of lenses found in Egypt (and associated with the unique statues and eye structures described) are compared with those found in Crete (Minoan civilization). The Minoan design (convex-plano) was used over long time periods in Greece and later in many Roman lenses. (B) Shown is an assumed schematic cut through the lens-eye structures found in the Egyptian statues. These eye structures were manufactured by teams of artisans and were inserted en bloc in the statues. The author has no information about the extent of the copper plates at the rear of the eye structures, nor the details of the "scleral" support structure for the lens, that is, the structure behind the exposed scleral surface that one ordinarily sees. The resin "tag" in the pupillary aperture is symbolic of the material seen in some statues. The author assumes that the volume posterior to the pupillary aperture simulates the vitreous and retina of the eye. Eye physicians may have been already displacing cataractous lenses at that time.

were the design and technology imported from abroad through trade or war, or was there a bit of both? What was used to grind and polish the lenses? Patrick N. Hunt at Stanford (personal communication, December 1998) describes early silicon carbide (carborundum) mines in Naxos in the Greek Cyclades island group. Was this abrasive mineral used to grind and polish the lenses?

Egyptian Technology

It is helpful to review the development of Egyptian technology in order to gain some understanding of the processes required to produce lens systems of the amazing quality of these first known ones.

Predynastic Egypt (Earlier Than 3000 B.C.)

Intermittent trade, including that in hard stones (obsidian and flint used for weapons and scrapers), was already established before 3000 B.C. between Egypt and Mesopotamia, Turkey, Syria and the Levant, Palestine, Lebanon, and possibly other locations. Writing and cylinder seals came into use in Sumer (ca. 3500–3000 B.C.), which is located in modern Iraq (Collon, 1995; Kramer, 1958; Richman, 1987). By the time Na'rmer united Upper and Lower Egypt around 2900 B.C., mining of hard stones had begun in the desert of eastern Egypt.

Early Dynastic Period: Dynasties I–III (ca. 2920–2575 B.C.)

Technologies for mining, grinding, and fabricating hard stone objects were developed to an advanced state during Dynasties I and II. Work with rock crystal, the form of quartz later used for lenses, which has hardness of 7 on the Mohs scale, however, was still quite limited (Andrews, 1991; Collon, 1995).

At the time that these earliest known lenses appeared, "ka" statues were developed as funerary substitutes for the deceased (Dynasty III onward). They served as representations of the individual's essence and were intended to be long lasting. Some of the techniques needed for working with hard stone were used to create these ka statues.

King Djoser (Dynasty III) built the distinctive step pyramid at Saqqara. A number of statues containing the special lens-eye constructs (see Figure 6.3B) were located in mastaba burial chambers at Saqqara (these were constructed later), and some of the lens-eye constructs were part of ka statues. For example, the King Djoser statue, now at the Egyptian Museum, has peg holes for eye inserts and evidence of copper rimming of the lids. The eye sockets, however, were too small for the later elegant lens-eye units.

Old Kingdom, Dynasties IV to VIII (2575–2134 B.C.)

Between about 2620 and 2400 B.C., the lens-eye constructs now displayed at the Egyptian Museum and the Louvre were created. The painted limestone statues of Prince Ra-Hotep and his wife, Nofert, discovered near the pyramid of Snerfu at Mejdum, were made around 2620 B.C. (Saleh & Sourouzian, 1987). These are the first statues containing the unique eye and lens structures. Peak production of these lens-eye units occurred around 2475 B.C., based on dates listed with each statue at the two museums.

Just a short time later, however, the quality of the lens systems used in the eyes of statues declined. During Dynasty V (2465–2323 B.C.), the statue of the funerary priest Ka-em-ked was created (ca. 2400 B.C.). This statue had the eye structures, but not the rock crystal lenses. The black, opaque volcanic glass, obsidian, had been used in place of the high-quality rock crystal (Saleh & Sourouzian, 1987). By the time of the reign of King Pepi I (ca. 2281–2241 B.C.) during Dynasty VI, an altogether different eye structure was being employed in statues. Limestone and obsidian were used (Saleh & Sourouzian, 1987).

Middle Kingdom: Dynasties XI to XIII (2040–1640 B.C.)

During Dynasty XII (1937–1759 B.C.) an odd set of occurrences was recorded. The Lady Khnumet was buried around 1895 B.C. at Dahshur; she was called the "Lady from Crete" (Andrews, 1991). On a pendant of one of her necklaces, a figure of a bull is found (this item was not on display at the Egyptian Museum during the author's visit in 1998). The design of this piece of jewelry was covered with rock crystal (Andrews, 1991). Perhaps this was a convex-plano lens. Such lenses were found later in Crete and Greece and an earlier plano-convex lens is illustrated in Figure 6.3A (Enoch, 1987, 1996, 1998b; Higgins, 1981; Williams & Ogden, 1994). Included in this jewelry were fine gold granulations that had already been in use in Mesopotamia for about 500 years (Andrews, 1991). The appellation Lady from Crete was given to her because the bull pattern was a religious symbol in the Minoan civilization in Crete. Khnumet, however, did come from the Greek Islands. It is possible that lenses were reintroduced into Egypt through items brought there by her or others.

During Dynasty XIII one encounters the ka statue of King Auib-rê Hor (ca. 1700 B.C.) (Saleh & Sourouzian, 1987). In this statue, the high-quality lens-eye structures seen in Dynasties IV and V reappear. The eye was rimmed with bronze, the lenses were of rock crystal and the sclera-equivalent utilized white quartz (Saleh & Sourouzian, 1987). The eye-following illusion is readily observed in this statue.

After the appearance of the King Hor statue in 1700 B.C., there is little evidence of comparable lens-eye structures in Egypt, nor, to the author's knowledge, other lenses prior to a discovery by the distinguished British archaeologist Flinders Petrie (Petrie, 1889) of two convex-plano (Figure 6.3A, earlier Minoan or Greek-style lenses) probable magnifying lenses at Tanis in the Nile Delta in the home of an artist. These items had origin in about A.D. 50 and are now at the British Museum. An elegant Hellenistic or Roman-style bronze head, fabricated about the same time in Alexandria, Egypt (ca. 27 B.C.–A.D. 14) was found in Meroe, Sudan. The eyes in this bronze head incorporate Greek-style lenses (Figure 6.3A) covering a brightly painted iris and dark pupil (Caleca, Gioseffi, Mellini, & Collobi, 1967). This item is also at the British Museum.

The Minoan Civilization in Crete

Lenses created by the Minoan civilization on the island of Crete seem to be quite a bit younger than the first known Egyptian lenses that appeared around 2620 to 2400 B.C. The earliest comparable Minoan lenses were made around 1550 to 1500 B.C., 900 years later.

Pre-Palace Period (2600–2000 B.C.)

Bronze working, art objects, pottery, stone carving, metal and gold work, and fine seal engraving were developed. Fine work with rock crystal was found in jewelry. There was an enhancement of society and culture in general (Higgins, 1981).

Old Palace Period (2000–1700 B.C.)

The earliest Minoan palace was built at Knossos, Crete, by King Minos. Extensive trade developed with Egypt, the Levant, Lebanon, the Cyclades, and Israel. Perhaps it was through this trade that lenses were reintroduced to Egypt from Crete.

The Golden Age of Crete: The New Palace Period (1700–1450 B.C.)

The Bull's Head Rhyton, discovered at the Little Palace of Knossos by Sir Arthur Evans, was created between 1550 and 1500 B.C. This libation vessel had a right eye with a rock crystal lens. It was convex-plano and was painted with a human face in silhouette on the plano side. This was backed with a blood red "pupil" surrounded by a black "iris." The left "eye" is a replica of the missing original. The Minoan palaces were destroyed by the eruption of the volcano at Thera (Santorini) about 1450 B.C. The author has discussed the Minoan lens in the Bull's Head Rhyton and its unique properties in detail elsewhere, and refers the interested reader to those sources (Andronicos, 1981; Enoch, 1987, 1996, 1998b; Higgins, 1981; Papapostolou, 1981; Sakellarakis, 1983). This is an equally fascinating matter.

400 B.C.

Magnifying lenses appeared in Greece, later Rome. They were used in jewelry and in decorative settings. Lenses were also placed in a number of eyes of statues (ca. 400 B.C. onward). These lenses had a convex-plano design (Figure 6.3A) (Williams & Ogden, 1994) as do other statues in the National Archaeological Museum in Athens and in the Archaeological Museum in Delos.

The Optics of the Egyptian Lenses

The main optical features of the Egyptian lenses, as well as their eye-following action, have been modeled by the author (see Figures 6.1, 6.2). A metal washer was placed on a sheet of white paper to simulate the iris-pupil plane. In the model, *no* distinction was made between the iris and pupillary zones of the construct. A strong negative or concave lens (a –20 diopter spherical trial case lens) was used as the rear lens element, and a moderate plus or convex lens was used for the front lens element (simulating the corneal front surface of the Egyptian lens). As in the statues, the plus lens had less positive power than the negative lens had minus power. A +8 diopter spherical lens was used. The higher power minus lens was separated from the washer by a plastic tube, and the positive lens was further separated from the washer and the negative lens. Essentially the two lenses and washer, separated, were formed into a concentric stack. The primary focal plane of the negative lens lay behind the washer plane, and the secondary focal point of the plus lens was also located behind the plane of the washer. The image of the washer was seen magnified through the whole construct. As one rotated about the construct in any direction, the image of the washer clearly followed (moved with) the observer (Figures 6.4, 6.5, and 6.6). Adjusting the height of the plus lens a bit varies the speed of the apparent rate of movement of the "pupil."

It does not seem likely that these sophisticated lens systems, having a convex lens front coupled with a plano rear surface with a small-high power concave surface ground in its middle, could be the first lenses. The quality of the rock crystal chosen for the lenses and fine polish of the product also speak against these as the first constructs. To achieve the apparent perceived movement of the pupillary aperture, the illusion, considerable experimentation by the artisans fabricating the lenses must have preceded these final results.

Figure 6.4. These components were used by the author to simulate the optical features of the Egyptian lens unit. The elements have been partly disassembled for observation.

Figure 6.5. Here the camera is oriented directly above the lenses, simulating Egyptian lens design. As noted in the text, the iris plane was not separated from the pupillary plane in this simulation. The iris-pupil represented by the washer is approximately centered in the field of view.

Figure 6.6. The photographer/observer rotated to the left about the model (as was done in Figure 6.2). The washer has apparently translated to follow the camera and the observer. Any direction of displacement resulted in the apparent following motion, an illusion.

The lenses must have created a stunning impact on an individual entering a tomb to view one of these statues by candlelight. Assume that the copper plates lining at least part of the back of these eye structures had not yet corroded. If the observer gazed at the reflected reddish coppery glow in the pupillary aperture, and this pupillary reflex seemed to follow him or her with movement about the statue, it would indeed have been an impressive sight and experience. These advanced lens systems are remarkable achievements, especially because they are the first known lenses.

References

Andrews, C. (1991). *Ancient Egyptian jewelry*. New York: H. N. Abrams.

Andronicos, M. (1981). *Herakleion Museum and archeological sites of Crete*. Athens, Greece: Ekdotike Athenon, SA.

Bouquillon, A., & Quéré, G. (1997). Le regard du scribe. *Pour La Science, 232*, February 27.

Caleca, A., Gioseffi, G. L., Mellini, G. L., & Collobi, L. R. (1967). *British Museum, London*. New York: Simon and Shuster.

Collon, D. (1995). *Ancient Near Eastern art*. Berkeley, CA: University of California Press.

Enoch, J. M. (1987). It is proposed that the cornea of the eye of the Bull's Head Rhyton from the Little Palace of Knossos (artifact dated 1550–1500 B.C.) is a true lens. In A. Fiorentini, D. L. Guyton, & I. M. Siegel (Eds.), *Advances in diagnostic visual optics* (pp. 15–18). New York: Springer-Verlag.

Enoch, J. M. (1996). Early lens use: Lenses found in context with their original optics. *Optometry and Vision Science, 73*, 707–715.

Enoch, J. M. (1998a). Ancient lenses in art and sculpture and the objects viewed through them. In B. E. Rogowitz & T. N. Pappas (Eds.), *Human vision and electronic imaging III: 26–29 January, 1998, San Jose, California* (Vol. 3299, pp. 424–430). Bellingham, WA: Society of Photo-optical Instrumentation Engineers.

Enoch, J. M. (1998b). The cover design: The enigma of early lens use. *Technology and Culture, 39*(2), 273–291.

Higgins, R. A. (1981). *Minoan and Mycenaean art* (Rev. ed.). New York: Oxford University Press.

Kramer, S. N. (1958). *History begins at Sumer*. London: Thames & Hudson.

Lucas, A., & Harris, J. R. (1962). *Ancient Egyptian materials and industries* (4th, rev. and enl. ed.). London: E. Arnold.

Papapostolou, I. A. (1981). *Crete*. Athens, Greece: Clio Editions.

Petrie, W. M. F. (1889). *Tanis: Part 1*. London: Trübner & Sons.

Richman, R. (Ed.). (1987). *Age of god-kings: Timeframe—3000–1500 B.C.* Alexandria, VA: Time-Life Books.

Royer, J. (1997). Les ocularistes de la statuaire égyptienne. *Bulletin Société Francophone d'Histoire de l'Ophtalmologie, 4*, 49–52.

Sakellarakis, J. A. (1983). *Herakleion Museum*. Athens, Greece: Ekdotike Athenon.

Saleh, M., & Sourouzian, H. (1987). *The Egyptian Museum Cairo : Official catalogue*. Cairo, Egypt, and Mainz, Germany: Organization of Egyptian Antiquities and Verlag Philipp von Zabern.

Williams, D., & Ogden, J. (1994). *Greek gold: Jewellry of the classical world*. New York: Abrams.

Ziegler, C. (1997). *Catalogue Louvre: Les statues Égyptiennes de L'Ancien Empire*. Paris: Éditions de la Réunion des Musées Nationaux.

Part IV

Accommodations

7

Controversies Concerning the Resting State of Accommodation

Focusing on Leibowitz

Jeffrey Andre

As Hersh Leibowitz's last graduate student, I had the advantage of having heard the entire story about the *resting state* of accommodation (also called the *dark focus*) before I ever set foot on the Penn State campus. The story about the origins of the dark focus measurement was passed down to me in the same manner as accounts of my family's ancestors. It was the topic of the first article that I read when I arrived at graduate school (Owens: *The Resting State of the Eyes*, 1984), and as it turns out, it was the topic of some of the final research I completed for my postdoctoral studies before moving on to an assistant professorship.

The Penn State dark focus story began simply with the purchase of a laser in 1969, and the development of the laser optometer can be added to other serendipitous discoveries in vision science. The following story was related to me by Bob Hennessy (personal communication, May 1999).

> Toward the end of every fiscal year, Hersh would ask his graduate students for suggestions on how to spend any leftover grant funds. In 1969, he asked Bob Hennessy, who suggested that they purchase a helium/neon laser, which had recently become somewhat affordable (approximately $300). Hersh's next question was, "How could it be used?" Bob said he didn't know, but at the time lasers were part of the zeitgeist and he argued that the lab should at least have one around. At the same time, Bob was thinking about how to measure accommodation while a person is performing a visual task without having to stand in front of the person with a retinoscope. After the laser arrived, Bob and other graduate students began playing with it and noticed that placing a lens in front of the laser spread out the beam and made the laser speckle pattern obvious. The story goes that (farsighted) Bob and (nearsighted) Charles Graham were looking at the speckle pattern when Professor Bob Freeman stuck his head into the lab and noted that the speckles moved when you move your head. Charles stated that the speckle motion was opposite to the direction of the head movement, whereas Bob argued that the motion was in the same direction. The "with" and "against" movement suggested to Bob the same phenomena seen during a retinoscopic examination. After placing plus and minus lenses in front of their eyes, they confirmed that the speckle movement was related to the distance their eyes were focused.

This idea was by no means novel; a researcher at Bausch & Lomb named Henry Knoll had reported on the phenomenon a few years before (Knoll, 1966), and Bausch & Lomb was actually selling a laser and drum kit to optometrists. But for the researchers at Penn State, using a laser to measure visual accommodation was a new idea, and because the laser speckles are produced by interference at the plane of the retina, they do not appear blurred and therefore do not provide any feedback information that would stimulate accommodation. Thus, the researchers now had a way to measure accommodation without stimulating accommodation. By projecting the laser on a moving drum, the speckle pattern appeared to flow without requiring head movements. By using the drum, seen through a beam splitter, and placing lenses between the drum and the beam splitter, it was possible to measure accommodative state while the observer was performing a visual task. The lenses served to alter the distance of the image of the drum from the observer. When an observer reported seeing speckle movement in random directions, the image distance of the drum was taken as the accommodation distance. Further refinements led to the laser optometer. Figure 7.1 shows a photo of Hersh Leibowitz and a laser optometer. (See Hennessy & Leibowitz, 1970, 1972, or Owens, 1984 for a complete review of measuring accommodation with the laser optometer.)

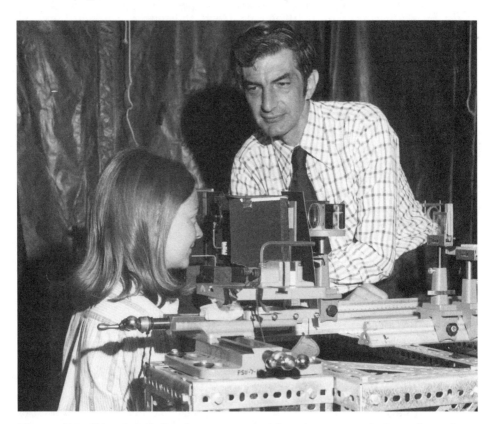

Figure 7.1. Herschel Leibowitz tests a participant's accommodation using a laser optometer. From the personal collection of Professor and Mrs. Herschel W. Leibowitz. Reprinted with permission.

By the time I arrived at Penn State in the fall of 1990, however, all the laser optometers had been retired and research concerning the dark focus had ended in the Leibowitz lab—replaced by work on the persistence of visual guidance information (Tyrrell, Rudolph, Eggers, & Leibowitz, 1993) and contrast sensitivity (Andre, 1996). Having arrived too late to do accommodation work with Hersh, I thought that the studies on accommodation would remain only story to me. It was not until I had left Penn State and was working in my postdoctoral position that I was able to do my first work on the dark focus of accommodation (more than a quarter century after the invention of the laser optometer).

One of the first things students notice when researching the resting state of accommodation is that the literature on accommodation, similar to that on other topics in vision science, is filled with controversies about many aspects and characteristics of the so-called resting state. This chapter will outline some of the more salient controversies concerning the dark focus that began in the late 1970s and conclude with some more recent findings that will, I hope, put an end to a controversy or two.

Defining the Resting State of Accommodation

Students and researchers reading about the resting state of accommodation are immediately confronted with the first controversy, which is what to call the resting state of accommodation. When submitting their paper to *Science* in 1975, Leibowitz and Owens used the term *resting position of accommodation*. This phrase was inspired by Schober's (1954) term *die Akkommodationsruhe-lage*, which translates to "the resting place of accommodation." The editor of *Science* informed them (correctly) that because they did not measure ciliary muscle activity directly, they did not know whether the muscle was indeed at rest, and therefore they would have to use a different name to describe what they measured. Because they measured the distance at which the eye was focusing in the dark, they named it the *dark focus of accommodation*. This operational definition has since been used by various authors (e.g., Jaschinski-Kruza, 1988; Simonelli, 1983; Temme, Ricks, & Morris, 1988) as a way to define the conditions under which accommodation was manipulated and measured.

Other researchers have used the term *tonic accommodation* to describe the resting state (e.g., McBrien & Millodot, 1987; Rosenfield & Ciuffreda, 1991; Rosner & Rosner, 1989). This definition derives from the assumption that the resting state position reflects the tonic intervention of the ciliary muscle (Rosenfield, Ciuffreda, Hung, & Gilmartin, 1993). A second argument for the use of tonic accommodation is the fact that the accommodative system approaches the resting state when the observer is viewing an empty but bright visual field, or *Ganzfeld* (e.g., Leibowitz & Owens, 1975; Post, Owens, Owens, & Leibowitz, 1979). Hence, the term *dark* focus could be misleading. Other terms such as *dark accommodation* (e.g., Rosenfield, Ciuffreda, & Gilmartin, 1992) and "ABIAS" (e.g., Hung, Ciuffreda, & Rosenfield, 1995) have also been used to describe the resting state; the reader is directed to Rosenfield et al. (1993), who provide an additional review of these different definitions.

Another approach to describing the resting state is by equating it to the *pivot point of accommodative behavior*. Accommodation response functions (ARFs) are obtained from observers by measuring accommodative responses to stimuli presented at different optical distances. When ARFs are measured under bright light and degraded (low-light) conditions, the slopes of the functions differ. Specifically, the ARF flattens out as luminance decreases. As Figure 7.2 illustrates, when the two such ARFs are superimposed on the same graph, a pivot point is created at which the accommodation is equivalent for both stimulus conditions.

The first researcher to demonstrate this pivot point of accommodation was Johnson (1976). Using luminances ranging between 0.051 and 51 cd/m², Johnson demonstrated that as luminance decreased, accommodative responses became less and less accurate. As shown in Figure 7.3, when luminance was decreased, subjects tended to over-accommodate near stimuli and under-accommodate far stimuli. The result was a pivoting of accommodative response functions around a point (optical distance) at which accommodation was accurate no matter what luminance was being used. More important, Johnson noted that this point seemed to be related to the participant's accommodated individual dark focus.

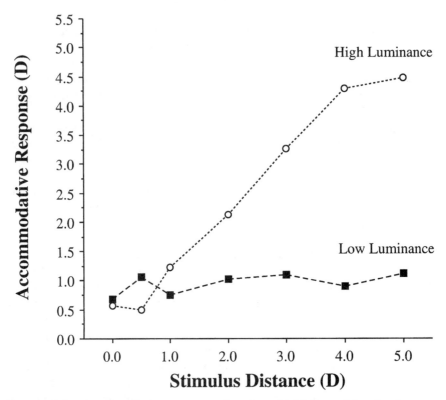

Figure 7.2. Accommodative response functions in high- and low-luminance conditions for a hypothetical participant. The pivot point of accommodation is defined where the two functions cross.

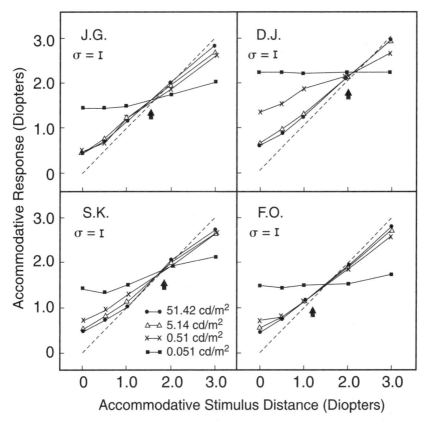

Figure 7.3. Accommodative response functions measured under different luminances from four participants. Arrows indicate the position of the dark focus. From "Effects of Luminance and Stimulus Distance on Accommodation and Visual Resolution," by C. A. Johnson, 1976, *Journal of the Optical Society of America, 66,* p. 140. Copyright 1976 by the Optical Society of America. Reprinted with permission.

Ebenholtz (1992) defined this pivot point in slightly different terms. After measuring an individual's dark focus, he had participants focus on stimuli that were nearer, farther, or at their dark focus distance for approximately 8 min. He then obtained post-fixation dark focus measures in an attempt to quantify accommodative adaptation caused by the fixation task. He found that accommodative adaptation pivoted around the dark focus distance, at which adaptation was minimal. Fixation on far stimuli resulted in an outward shift of the dark focus, whereas fixation on near stimuli caused an inward shift from the dark focus distance.

Investigating the effects of visual fatigue on the dark focus, Miller, Pigion, Wesner, and Patterson (1983) reported that no adaptation of participants' dark focus occurred following a 3-hr task during which accommodation was measured continuously with a laser optometer. Thus, these researchers are in agreement with Ebenholtz: Visual tasks located at an individual's dark focus do not produce adaptation of the dark focus.

Where Is the Resting State of Accommodation?

No matter what the resting state was called, Leibowitz's research in the mid-1970s was at the heart of another controversy, namely, just where indeed did the accommodative system rest? That is, at what optical distance does the eye focus when accommodation is at rest? This controversy probably began in the mid-19th century, when researchers such as Weber (1855, cited in Cornelius, 1861) proposed that the accommodative system rests at an intermediate distance. This viewpoint was contrary to what later become the established theory that accommodation rests at the far point of the accommodative range (optical infinity). Donders (1864) stated that "we call the structure of the eye normal, when, in the state of rest, it brings the rays derived from infinitely distant objects to a focus on the anterior surface. . . ." (p. 81). Later, Helmholtz (1909/1962) echoed what Donders had said, and although this theory suggests that accommodation works contrary to most other muscular systems in the body, which have an "intermediate" resting position (neither fully contracted nor fully extended), it became widely accepted by the early part of the 20th century.

Although other researchers in the mid 20th century also proposed an intermediate resting state for accommodation (see, for example, Cogan, 1937; Morgan, 1946; and Schober, 1954), perhaps the largest problem for the established far resting point theory was its inability to explain what have come to be known as *anomalous myopias,* unexplained transient situations in which observers become myopic (nearsighted). The first anomalous myopia was reported in 1789 by Astronomer Royal Lord Maskelyne, who observed that his nighttime vision was facilitated by a negative lens—a lens that had no beneficial effects during daylight (see Levene, 1965; see also chapter 3, "The Symbiosis Between Basic and Applied Research," by Herschel W. Leibowitz). This phenomenon, now known as *twilight or night myopia,* is defined as the tendency for the eye to become nearsighted in low-light conditions. The far resting point theory would state that when the eye was presented with a degraded stimulus (e.g., in near-darkness), the individual should if anything become hyperopic, and therefore focusing on distant objects should cause no problem. This is exact opposite to what Lord Maskelyne reported.

Following World War II, some 160 years after Maskelyne's observations, two other reports of anomalous myopias surfaced. Whiteside (1952) reported that *empty-field myopia* occurs for some pilots flying at high altitude while viewing a uniform visual field. Schober (1954) found that participants became myopic when using optical instruments that have small exit pupils, thus increasing depth of field and reducing the need for the participant to actively accommodate for clear vision. He called this condition *instrument myopia.* As with night myopia, the far resting point theory could not explain these myopias, and because both occurred at higher luminances (than night myopia), they could not be explained by increased optical aberrations found at night. At the time, Schober proposed that accommodation had the natural tendency to drift to an intermediate resting position, *die Akkommodationsruhelage,* in a paper that later motivated Leibowitz and his students to reexamine these phenomena.

Empirical evidence for the intermediate resting state was scarce until the laser optometer was developed at Penn State in the early 1970s. In 1975, Leibowitz and Owens reported the first large sample of dark focus values measured with a laser optometer. As illustrated in Figure 7.4, they found that the mean dark focus was 1.71 diopters (D), or ≈ 58 cm (23 in.), and that large individual differences were present among their sample of 124 college students. More important, they found that individual dark focus measures were significantly correlated with magnitudes of night, empty-field, and instrument myopia. The large individual differences in dark focus values seemed to explain why some individuals experienced anomalous myopias, whereas others did not: individuals with far dark focus values were less prone to exhibit these transient myopias.

This study served as the catalyst for many other research endeavors investigating the true resting position of the accommodative system. Now, there is considerable evidence to suggest that the intermediate resting state theory is correct because researchers have found a variety of situations in which accommodation is biased toward an *intermediate* resting position (see Owens, Andre, & Owens, 2000, for a listing). In addition to low light, empty field, and working with optical instruments, some of these situations are as follows: viewing a simple fixation point (Owens & Leibowitz, 1975); the presence of iso-luminant contours (Wolfe & Owens, 1981) or low and high spatial frequencies (e.g., Mathews & Kruger, 1994); with the presence of intervening surfaces (Adams & Johnson, 1991; Owens, 1979) and viewing with pinhole pupils (e.g., Hennessy, Iida, Shiina, & Leibowitz, 1976; Ward & Charman, 1985).

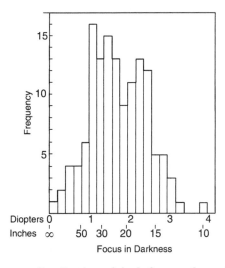

Figure 7.4. Frequency distribution of dark focus values obtained from 124 college-aged observers. Reprinted with permission from "Anomalous Myopias and the Intermediate Dark Focus of Accommodation," by H. W. Leibowitz and D. A. Owens, 1975, *Science, 189,* p. 646. Copyright 1975 American Association for the Advancement of Science.

How Many Resting States Does Each Individual Have?

One would have thought that the controversies would have ended once the intermediate resting state hypothesis gained support, but this was not the case. Advances in technology brought the development of new methods to measure accommodation and yet another controversy about the resting state—one that led to questioning the utility of the dark focus. In the mid-1980s, researchers began to notice discrepancies between dark focus values obtained with a laser optometer and those measured with infrared (IR) optometers (e.g., Post, Johnson, & Owens, 1985; Post, Johnson, & Tsuetaki, 1984). The latter were developed as a clinical tool to measure refractive error without subjective judgments, but vision researchers welcomed the use of IR optometers as a new technique to measure accommodation while observers sat passively in darkness. This passive procedure was quite different from measuring accommodation with a laser optometer, during which the participant is making active direction discriminations of laser speckle patterns.

Typically, laser optometers yield dark focus values that are more myopic (closer to the individual) than IR measures. Post, Johnson, and Owens (1985) found differences as large as 2 D between dark focus measures when participants sat passively or were engaged in a laser optometer procedure (mean accommodative states for 16 subjects were 0.7 and 1.04 D, respectively). In another study, Rosenfield (1989) found that participants' dark focus values measured with an IR optometer had a mean of 1.28 D, whereas those from the same participants measured with a laser optometer averaged $\approx$ 2 D. Various explanations have been proposed to account for these discrepancies, including effects of a perception of nearness ("propinquity"; Rosenfield & Ciuffreda, 1991) and visual attention or "effort to see" (Francis, Jiang, Owens, Tyrrell, & Leibowitz, 1989; Post, Johnson, & Owens, 1985).

Andre and Owens (1999) took a slightly different approach to the discrepant dark focus controversy. Conceding that multiple dark focus values were likely for each individual, they sought to determine which measure better predicts optimal accommodative performance: an "active" one measured during a laser optometer procedure or a "passive" one measured while observers sat staring at total darkness. Andre and Owens defined the optimal accommodation distance as the pivot point of accommodation (defined previously) because accommodation is always accurate at this distance. Active and passive dark focus values along with ARFs in bright and dim conditions were obtained from 10 observers. Pivot points were calculated using the two ARFs. Mean ARFs and dark foci are presented in Figure 7.5. Active dark focus measures were located closer to the optimal accommodation distance. More important, there was a strong positive correlation between active dark focus values and optimal accommodation distances; no relationship was found between this distance and passive dark focus. Given this finding and the fact that grating acuity and accommodative response are most accurate (Johnson, 1976) and accommodative adaptation is minimal (Ebenholtz, 1992) at the dark focus distance, Andre and Owens concluded that the active dark focus value could be considered a resting state from which all active accommodation and viewing commence.

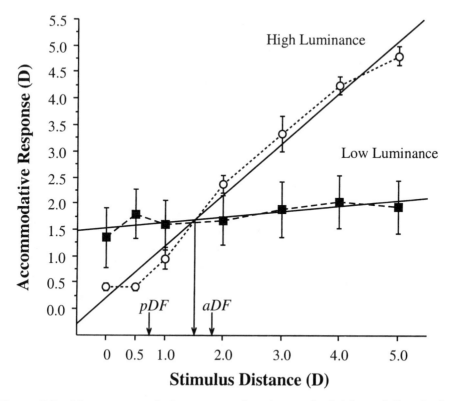

Figure 7.5. Mean accommodative response functions under bright and dim viewing conditions. Mean optimal accommodation distance and active (*aDF*) and passive (*pDF*) dark focus values are plotted on the *x*-axis.

Conclusion

I believe that some of these controversies over accommodation have now been settled. First, no matter what it is called, it seems that the eye's resting state of accommodation, like that of other muscular systems in the human body, is located at an intermediate distance and not optical infinity as was previously thought. Second, where exactly that distance is located is variable and may be influenced by factors such as effort to see, mental activity, and perhaps a perception of nearness. Finally, dark focus measured during active viewing (as with the laser optometer procedure) is significantly related to the optimal accommodation distance at which accommodative responses are always accurate. Much more research, however, remains to be done on the dark focus of accommodation, and this future research will help us further clarify and understand the role of the dark focus in accommodative behavior under a variety of conditions.

A Personal Note About Hersh

Although it will be mentioned by other authors in this volume, I would be remiss if I did not mention what Hersh's guidance and mentoring have meant to me during the early years of my professional career. Perhaps Hersh's greatest lesson was to teach me how to think independently. For any project I worked on in graduate school, Hersh's deceptively simple question, "Why is that important?" always forced me to think about the "big" picture from my own individual perspective. My views of the big picture were also influenced by Hersh's lesson concerning the integration of basic and applied research: They are symbiotic, feeding off each other in the progress of science.

In this chapter, I had the pleasure of telling one of Hersh's best stories— in the form of some of his best known research. His (and his colleagues') dark focus research was the catalyst for countless other studies about the human eye's accommodative processes. It is quite an honor to have been able to work with Hersh and to be in the company of the other students and collaborators on his "class roll." The diversity and excellence of the students who worked with Hersh before me is truly astounding.

Finally, I would like to thank Hersh and his wife, Eileen, for their patience and support, for the intellectual freedom, and for the love they have shown me throughout our relationship. I consider myself very fortunate that I should have two most excellent families—one biological and the other academic.

References

Adams, C. W., & Johnson, C. A. (1991). Steady-state and dynamic response properties of the Mandelbaum effect. *Vision Research, 31*(4), 751–760.

Andre, J. T. (1996). Visual functioning in challenging conditions: Effects of alcohol consumption, luminance, stimulus motion, and glare on contrast sensitivity. *Journal of Experimental Psychology: Applied, 2*, 250–269.

Andre, J. T., & Owens, D. A. (1999). Predicting optimal accommodative performance from measures of the dark focus of accommodation. *Human Factors, 41*, 139–145

Cogan, D. G. (1937). Accommodation and the autonomic nervous system. *Archives of Ophthalmology, 18*, 739–766.

Cornelius, C. S. (1861). *Die Theorie des Sehens und raümlichen Vorstellens* (pp. 283–285). Halle: H. W. Schmidt.

Donders, F. C. (1864). *On the anomalies of accommodation and refraction of the eye.* London: The Sydenham Society.

Ebenholtz, S. M. (1992). Accommodative hysteresis as a function of target-dark focus separation. *Vision Research, 32*(5), 925–929.

Francis, E. L., Jiang, B. C., Owens, D. A., Tyrrell, R. A., & Leibowitz, H. W. (1989). "Effort to see" affects accommodation and vergence but not their interactions. *Investigative Ophthalmology and Visual Science, 30*(3), 135.

Helmholtz, H. (1962). *Handbook of physiological optics* (3rd ed., Vol. 1). (J. P. C. Southall, Trans.). New York: Voss. (Original work published 1909)

Hennessy, R. T., Iida, T., Shiina, K., & Leibowitz, H. W. (1976). The effect of pupil size on accommodation. *Vision Research, 16*, 587–589.

Hennessy, R. T., & Leibowitz, H. (1970). Subjective measurement of accommodation with laser light. *Journal of the Optical Society of America, 60*, 1700–1701.

Hennessy, R. T., & Leibowitz, H. (1972). Laser optometer incorporating the Badal principle. *Behavioral Research Methods and Instrumentation, 4*, 237–239.

Hung, G. K., Ciuffreda, K. J., & Rosenfield, M. (1996). Proximal contribution to a linear static model of accommodation and vergence. *Ophthalmic and Physiological Optics, 16*, 31–41.

Jaschinski-Kruza, W. (1988). Visual strain during VDU work: The effect of viewing distance and dark focus. *Ergonomics, 31*(10), 1449–1465.

Johnson, C. A. (1976). Effects of luminance and stimulus distance on accommodation and visual resolution. *Journal of the Optical Society of America, 66*, 138–142.

Knoll, H. A. (1966). Measuring ametropia with a gas laser: A preliminary report. *American Journal of Optometry, 43*, 415–418.

Leibowitz, H. W., & Owens, D. A. (1975). Anomalous myopias and the intermediate dark focus of accommodation. *Science, 189*, 646–648.

Levene, J. R. (1965). Nevil Maskelyne, F.R.S. and the discovery of night myopia. *Notes and Records of the Royal Society of London, 20*, 100–108.

Maskelyne, N. (1789). An attempt to explain a difficulty in the theory of vision, depending on the different refrangibility of light. *Philosophical Transactions of the Royal Society, 19*, 256–264.

Mathews, S., & Kruger, P. B. (1994). Spatiotemporal transfer function of human accommodation. *Vision Research, 34*(15), 1965–1980.

McBrien, N. A., & Millodot, M. (1987). The relationship between tonic accommodation and refractive error. *Investigative Ophthalmology and Visual Science, 28*, 997–1004.

Miller, R. J., Pigion, R. G, Wesner, M. F., & Patterson, J. G. (1983). Accommodation fatigue and dark focus: The effects of accommodation-free visual work as assessed by two psychophysical methods. *Perception and Psychophysics, 34*, 532–540.

Morgan, M. W. (1946). A new theory for the control of accommodation. *American Journal of Optometry and Archives of American Academy of Optometry, 23*, 99–110.

Owens, D. A. (1979). The Mandelbaum Effect: Evidence for an accommodative bias toward intermediate viewing distances. *Journal of the Optical Society of America, 69*, 646–652.

Owens, D. A. (1984). The resting state of the eyes. *American Scientist, 72*, 378–387.

Owens, D. A., Andre, J. T., & Owens, R. L. (2000). Predicting accommodative performance in difficult conditions: A behavioral analysis. In O. Franzén, H. Richter, & L. Stark (Eds.), *Accommodation and vergence mechanisms in the visual system* (pp. 273–284). Basel, Switzerland: Birkhäuser.

Owens, D. A., & Leibowitz, H. W. (1975). The fixation point as a stimulus for accommodation. *Vision Research, 15*, 1161–1163.

Post, R. B., Johnson, C. A., & Owens, D. A. (1985). Does performance of tasks affect the resting focus of accommodation? *American Journal of Optometry and Physiological Optics, 62*, 533–537.

Post, R. B., Johnson, C. A., & Tsuetaki, T. K. (1984). Comparison of laser and infrared techniques for measurement of the resting state of accommodation: Mean differences and long-term variability. *Ophthalmic and Physiological Optics, 4*, 327–332.

Post, R. B., Owens, R. L., Owens, D. A., & Leibowitz, H. W. (1979). Correction of empty-field myopia on the basis of the dark focus of accommodation. *Journal of the Optical Society of America, 69*, 89–92.

Rosenfield, M., (1989). Comparison of accommodative adaptation using laser and infrared optometers. *Ophthalmic and Physiological Optics, 9*, 431–436.

Rosenfield, M., & Ciuffreda, K. J. (1991). Effect of surround propinquity on the open-loop accommodative response. *Investigative Ophthalmology and Visual Science, 32*, 142–147.

Rosenfield, M., Ciuffreda, K. J., & Gilmartin, B. (1992). Factors influencing accommodative adaptation. *Optometry and Vision Science, 69*, 270–275.

Rosenfield, M., Ciuffreda, K. J., Hung, G. K., & Gilmartin, B. (1993). Tonic accommodation: A review. I. Basic aspects. *Ophthalmic and Physiological Optics, 13*, 266–284.

Rosner, J., & Rosner, J. (1989). Relation between clinically measured tonic accommodation and refractive status in 6- to 14-year-old children. *Optometry and Visual Science, 66*(7), 436–439.

Schober, H. (1954). Über die Akkommodationsruhelage. *Optik, 6*, 282–290.

Simonelli, N. M. (1983). The dark focus of the human eye and its relationship to age and visual defect. *Human Factors, 25*, 85–92.

Temme, L. A., Ricks, E., & Morris, A. (1988). Dark focus measured in Navy jet tactical fighter pilots. *Aviation, Space, and Environmental Medicine, 59*(3), 138–141.

Tyrrell, R. A., Rudolph, K. K., Eggers, B. G., & Leibowitz, H. W. (1993). Evidence for the persistence of visual guidance information. *Perception and Psychophysics, 54*, 431–438.

Ward, P. A., & Charman, W. N. (1985). Effect of pupil size on steady state accommodation. *Vision Research, 25*(9), 1317–1326.

Whiteside, T. C. D. (1952). Accommodation of the human eye in a bright and empty visual field. *Journal of Physiology (London), 118*, 65–66.

Wolfe, J., & Owens, D. A. (1981). Is accommodation colorblind? Focusing chromatic contours. *Perception, 10*, 53–62.

8

Early Astigmatism Contributes to the Oblique Effect and Creates Its Chinese–Caucasian Difference

Richard Held, Frank Thorn, James McLellan, Kenneth Grice, and Jane Gwiazda

Early research by Herschel Leibowitz (1953, 1955) played an important role in bringing the oblique effect into the orbit of visual psychophysics designed to elucidate the determinants of perceptual phenomena. By studying the consequences of varying basic parameters of stimulation such as illumination level, pupillary size, and contrast, Leibowitz could argue that although part of the effect may arise optically, a neural component is inevitably involved. By introducing these procedures, he set the stage for further progress.

Many investigators (Charman & Voisin, 1993; Coppola, Purves, McCoy, & Purves, 1998; Daugman, 1983; Freeman & Thibos, 1975; Gwiazda, Scheiman, & Held, 1984; Gwiazda, Scheiman, Mohindra, & Held, 1984; Harwerth, Smith, & Boltz, 1980; Held, 1978; Mitchell & Wilkinson, 1974) have suggested that meridional amblyopia (MA), often an accompaniment of astigmatism, is related to the more familiar oblique effect (OE). The OE refers here to the finding that visual acuity for targets with edges oriented obliquely on the retina is, on average, less than that for vertical- and horizontal-edged ones as imaged on the retina. Consequently, when measured at different meridia, acuity varies with a period of 90 deg. The less well known MA is marked by acuity maxima and minima for edges on orthogonal meridia, with a period of 180 deg. Idealized representations of these variations in sensitivity are shown in Figure 8.1. In this paper we propose to reexamine the relationship between OE and MA.

Meridional amblyopia was first reported by the French ophthalmologist G. Martin (1890), who found large variations in acuity on orthogonal axes in astigmatic adults despite their wearing full optical correction. More recently, a number of investigators, riding the tide of discoveries of the neuronal and visual consequences of aberrant early rearing (Daw, 1995), have reexamined MA in astigmatic adults (Mitchell, Freeman, Millodot, & Haegerstrom, 1973).

This chapter is dedicated to Herschel Leibowitz, who introduced the first author of this chapter, R. Held, to the oblique effect when he presented his incisive work on the topic (Leibowitz, 1953, 1955) to an audience including the author. Hersh went on to become a major figure in a number of different fields of psychological research. Even more significant, he has become a much loved mentor of his many devoted students and a much appreciated friend to his colleagues. The production of this manuscript and collection of some of the data reported in it were supported by grant NEI R01 EY01191.

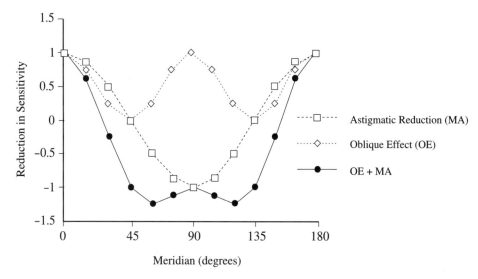

Figure 8.1. Idealized meridional reductions in sensitivity as in main axis astigmatism–induced meridional amblyopia (MA), in the oblique effect (OE), and in their combination.

Once a purely optical explanation was conclusively ruled out by bypassing the optics using laser-produced interference fringes, the meridionally selective reduction of acuity was necessarily attributed to pathological development in the visual nervous system (a type of amblyopia). Since the most and least sensitive meridia correspond to the principal axes of cylinder correction in many cases of adult astigmatism, the loss of acuity has generally been attributed to the desensitizing effects of the chronic optical blurring produced by uncorrected astigmatism, a type of visual form deprivation. In other words, the modulation transfer function produced by a spherocylindrical lens of fixed power has 180-deg meridional periodicities with sharp focus simultaneously possible for an edge parallel to only one of its two orthogonal principal axes. This blur bias could, in principle, be the source of amblyopia. If edges aligned with one of the two orthogonal foci are chronically kept in focus, edges aligned with the other focus will suffer from chronic blur. Such blur occurring during an early susceptible period results in degraded acuity. Parenthetically, it has been argued that degraded acuity may result from a failure of development caused by early deprivation of adequate form vision rather than a loss as in amblyopia. For present purposes this difference in interpretation does not seem important.

A Paradox and Its Resolution

The explanation of MA as the outcome of chronic astigmatism would be satisfactory at least in theory but for the fact that many sets of acuity measurements on nonastigmatic older children and adults show substantial differences between orthogonal meridia (MA) indistinguishable from those of astigmatic individuals (e.g., see Gwiazda, Scheiman, Mohindra, & Held, 1984). One case of MA, in the absence of accompanying astigmatism, has been elegantly portrayed by contrast sensitivity functions and attributed to a childhood astigmatism for which there was no evidence whatever (Daugman, 1983). The resolution of this apparent paradox begins with the rediscovery of the surprisingly high prevalence of astigmatism in infancy. Increasing interest in astigmatism at the time had led investigators from several laboratories (Fulton et al., 1980; Howland, Atkinson, Braddick, & French, 1978; Mohindra, Held, Gwiazda, & Brill, 1978) to discover this prevalence among infants, although it had been previously reported by the Italian ophthalmologist Santonastaso (1930) but had been overlooked and even denied by several ophthalmologists when first presented at vision meetings of the time (personal experience). Estimates of prevalence (1 or more diopters of cylinder) ranged between 20% and 60%, with the principal axis primarily at either horizontal or vertical orientations with a small fraction at an oblique orientation.

In the majority of cases of early astigmatism, its magnitude begins to decline during the 1st year, and within a few years the frequency of occurrence drops to the (< 10%) level of young adults (Atkinson, Braddick, & French, 1980; Mohindra et al., 1978; Gwiazda, Grice, Held, McLellan, & Thorn, 2000). This reduction of refractive error is one form of the naturally occurring process of adaptive correction called *emmetropization*, with emmetropia being the state of having eyes capable of accurate focus without either optical correction, as in myopia, or excessive accommodation, as in hyperopia. The apparent paradox of MA in emmetropes having no astigmatism could be explained if the MA that developed in an astigmatic infant persisted despite the emmetropization that eliminates the astigmatism. Then a substantial proportion of older children and adults who had lost their early astigmatism would bear its marks in the form of sensitivity differences between orthogonal axes. This account was confirmed by Gwiazda, Scheiman, and Held, (1984) and by Gwiazda, Bauer, Thorn, and Held (1986) in prospective studies of the development of refraction and visuospatial sensitivity (vernier acuity) beginning in infancy and extending into adolescence. Whereas most previous investigators had studied currently astigmatic observers, Gwiazda and colleagues were able to show in prospective studies that emmetropes who had lost their early astigmatism exhibited its consequences years later in the form of a predictable MA. There appeared to be a particularly susceptible period between 6 months and 2 years of age during which the child with early astigmatism had developed meridional acuity differences that were measured years later. The precise degree of susceptibility as a function of age remains uncertain. So also is the possibility of some recovery from MA as emmetropization proceeds. In addition, the effect of increased acuity with growth during infancy and beyond on measuring MA is not clear. A summary of relevant evidence follows.

Measuring grating acuity, Gwiazda, Mohindra, Brill, and Held (1985) found no evidence for development of MA in astigmatic infants during the 1st year, although some years later evidence of MA appeared in infants who had lost their astigmatism by the end of that 1st year. Relevant but fragmentary data have been published by several authors. Cobb and MacDonald (1978) found less MA in a few children with astigmatism optically corrected before, but not after, the age of 7 years. They interpret their results as demonstrating recovery from early MA when astigmatism is corrected early enough. Mitchell et al. (1973) reported that an astigmatic child corrected at 3 years of age had no MA, whereas others corrected after age 6 all showed MA. Daugman (1983) reported on a child with severe MA who was first refracted at 5 years of age and found to be emmetropic. In light of these reports and their shortcomings, perhaps the most reasonable generalization is that susceptibility to both increase of MA and recovery from MA becomes high during the latter part of the first year, plateaus in the 2nd year, and steadily reduces after that for 4 or 5 years. This susceptible period clearly overlaps the period of high prevalence of ocular astigmatism. Moreover, the distribution of orientations yielding maximal orthogonal differences of acuity is not unlike the distribution of axes of early astigmatism, mostly either vertical or horizontal and occasionally oblique.

Amblyopia on the Obliques?

So far this account of the production of MA as a result of the blurring effects of astigmatism has assumed chronic focus along one axis (usually either hori-zontal or vertical), with increasing amounts of defocus peaking at a meridional deviation of 90 deg. More realistically, varied accommodation can optimize a hyperopic focus in any meridian, and varied object distances can alter image clarity, particularly with myopic foci. But even with optimal focus, maximal clarity can occur only for edges parallel to the principal astigmatic axes. Best focused edges are increasingly blurred as they deviate from those meridia toward the obliques (see Charman & Voisin, 1993, for a detailed account of the optics). This blur increases in magnitude as a function of the sine of twice the angle of deviation yielding the 90-deg meridional periodicity. Blur maxima occur on both obliques with respect to the axes of the cylinder. Because a great majority of those with astigmatism have their cylinder axes near to either vertical or horizontal retinal meridia, the retinal obliques tend to suffer max-imally from the blur that cannot be eliminated by changes in spherical power. We proposed that this condition may contribute to the OE by chronically reducing sensitivity along the oblique meridia, as shown in Figure 8.1 (OE), in addition to that along a main axis (MA) (Held, McLellan, Grice, Thorn, & Gwiazda, 1998). The susceptible period for this development is presumably the same as that for the development of amblyopia on a main axis, namely, the first few years of life, and the reduction of sensitivity on all blurred meridia may well grow proportionately. How can this proposal be tested?

Tests of Proposal

Four tests are formulated in the following discussion.

Test 1. We have access to detailed refractive histories beginning in infancy of a group of participants now past the susceptible period. We know that acuity differences on orthogonal meridia (MA) are greater in those with former astigmatism compared with those not having astigmatism. Will the OE be correspondingly greater in the astigmatic group?

Test 2. In the abovementioned group (Test 1), will the magnitude of the OE be correlated with that of the MA as a common consequence of astigmatic blurring during the earliest years?

Test 3. Among the 10% or so of adults who have significant astigmatism, the great majority appear to have retained it from infancy. Few, if any, children and young adults appear to acquire astigmatism not present in infancy (Gwiazda, Scheiman, Mohindra, et al., 1984; Gwiazda et al., 2000). Consequently, we may treat adults with astigmatism as if they had also been astigmatic during the susceptible period. If so, their OE should show an increase with the magnitude of their MA.

Test 4. If a defined group of adult subjects (Caucasians) exhibits, on the average, greater OE than a different group (Chinese), we might conjecture that the origin of the difference lies in a greater amount of early astigmatism in the former.

In the following, we briefly report the backgrounds, procedures, and outcomes of examples of these four tests. Under the title Infantile Oblique Effect and Meridional Amblyopia, the first three tests deal with the relation between OE and ME as predicted from measured early astigmatism. Under the title The Chinese–Caucasian Difference in Oblique Effect, the fourth test takes a difference in measured OE between adult groups and asks whether its source could be a predicted difference in the magnitude of early astigmatism between these groups.

Infantile Oblique Effect and Meridional Amblyopia

Test 1

Studies of grating acuity along the main and oblique meridia of human infants reveal an OE by a few months of age (Held, 1978; Leehey, Moskowitz-Cook, Brill, & Held, 1975). However, MA in the form of orthogonal differences in grating acuity has not been detected in infants up to an age approaching 1 year (Gwiazda et al., 1985). These results argue for an OE antedating MA. If MA appears only after the earlier OE, it must add to it either by simple summation (as shown in Figure 8.1) or by some more complex combination. However this combination may occur, the most direct test of the hypothesis that early astigmatism contributes to the OE would be to examine the relationship between the magnitude of the early astigmatism and that of current OE.

We have prospectively followed a group of 41 participants from infancy until ages ranging from 5 to 12 years, with a mean of 9 years. Measures of cylindrical power were repeatedly taken on the right eye during the susceptible period from 6 to 24 months and were taken again at the end of the testing period. Measures of vernier acuity on that eye were also taken at the end of the testing period on the four major meridia: horizontal, vertical, and the two obliques. We chose to measure vernier acuity because we had found this measure to be more sensitive to meridional differences than grating acuity. The procedures were essentially the same as reported in Gwiazda et al. (1986). The refraction data allow a division of the group into those with former astigmatism ($\geq$ 1 D, N = 15) and those with no astigmatism (< 1 D, N = 26) and a comparison of the magnitudes of the OE for these two groups. OE is taken as the octaval difference between the geometric mean acuity for horizontal (H)– and vertical (V)–edged targets and the geometric mean acuity for right (R) and left (L) oblique-edged targets calculated for each individual as:

$$\log_2\sqrt{HV} - \log_2\sqrt{RL}$$

The resulting means for the two subgroups are shown in the bar graph of Figure 8.2. A t test of the difference between them yields p = .051. MA for each individual is calculated as

$$|\log_2 V - \log_2 H|$$

using the absolute value of the difference because the expected effect on OE is independent of its sign. In accord with earlier findings (Gwiazda et al., 1986), those with former astigmatism had mean MA of 0.85 octave compared with a mean for those with no astigmatism of 0.54 octave, a difference yielding t = 2.42, p = .021.

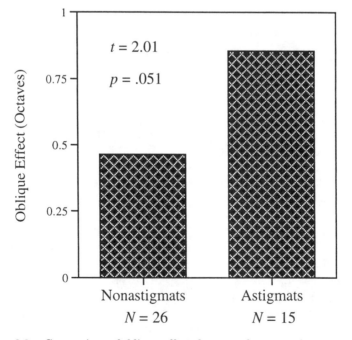

Figure 8.2. Comparison of oblique effects between former astigmats and nonastigmats.

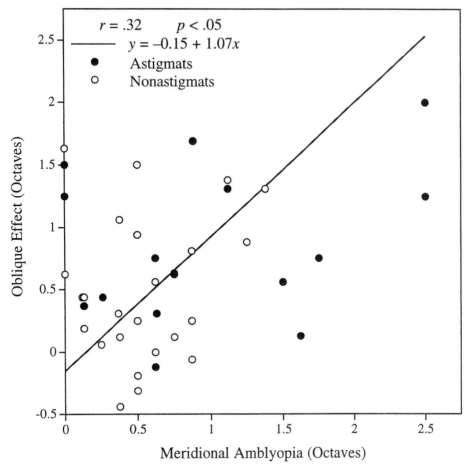

Figure 8.3. Increase of oblique effect with meridional amblyopia in former astigmats and nonastigmats. Octaval measures were based on vernier acuities and calculated by formulas in the text.

Test 2

In addition to the preceding, the values of OE were correlated with those of MA for the 41 participants and are shown in the scatterplot of Figure 8.3. The results show a small but significant correlation (Pearson $r = .32$, $p < .05$). Principal axis analysis suggests that each octave increase of MA is accompanied by an octave increase of OE.

Test 3

The results of Tests 1 and 2 support the hypothesis that infantile astigmatism can result in an enhanced OE. Accordingly, if adults with astigmatism have retained their astigmatism from infancy, we may expect that they have acquired an enhanced OE during their susceptible periods and have retained it since. To test this notion, measurements both of refraction and of acuity in the major meridia are required. The literature contains two such sources of data. Mitchell et al. (1973) report the refractions of 11 astigmatic adults, with cylinder axes close to either horizontal or vertical, and 6 nonastigmatic adults, together with grating acuities measured in the four main meridia. The OE and MA values were calculated from the data according to the previous definitions and plotted in Figure 8.4, with the resulting Pearson $r = .75$. Cobb and Mac-Donald (1978) report the refractions of 12 astigmatic adults who were also tested for grating acuity in the four meridia of which two were aligned with the principal axes of the individual's astigmatism. In addition, 6 adults without astigmatism were tested for acuity in the four main meridia. Values of MA and OE were calculated from the data in accord with acuities measured on the meridia of the principal axes of astigmatism and those 45 deg removed, respectively; the values were then correlated and are plotted in Figure 8.4 with the resulting Pearson $r = .51$, $p = .03$.

Test 4

See p. 85 for a recap of this test.

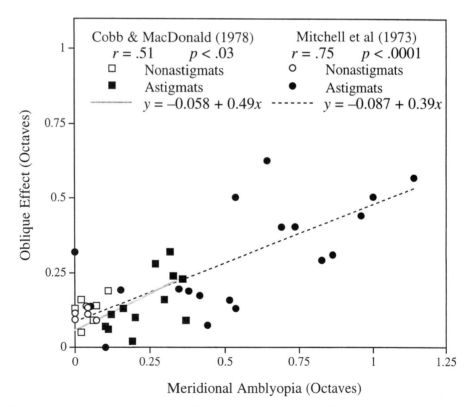

Figure 8.4. Increase of oblique effect with meridional amblyopia in adult astigmats as reported (some in graphs) by authors cited. Octaval measures were based on grating acuities.

The Chinese–Caucasian Difference in Oblique Effect

Visual acuity for oblique-edged targets is, on average, less than that for vertical and horizontal ones. Twenty-five years ago Annis and Frost (1973) published data purporting to show that Cree Indians living in rural Canada have less of this OE than a comparable group of urban Caucasians. At that time, the plasticity of the visual nervous system in response to altered rearing conditions had recently been demonstrated and given broad credence (reviewed by Daw, 1995). In accord with the enthusiasm of the time toward environmental explanations, Annis and Frost attributed their finding to the fact that the Caucasians, unlike the Cree, lived in an urban "carpentered" world. Consequently, the former were more frequently exposed and sensitized to edges more oriented on or near vertical and horizontal than to obliques. The Cree environment was markedly less carpentered.

The reaction was not long in coming. Timney and Muir (1976) recorded the acuities of a large group of Caucasians and a smaller group of Chinese both of whom lived in similar urban settings. The results showed that the Chinese, like the Cree, had significantly less OE than the Caucasians (the means are replotted in Figure 8.5. A later replication by Fang, Bauer, Held, and Gwiazda (1997) produced results rather like the differences found by Annis and Frost. Moreover, some individuals of both races showed either no OE or even a slightly negative one, despite having spent their lives in the carpentered environment. Both of these results embarass any environmental attempt to account completely for the OE. Consequently, their authors favored an ethnic (meaning racial) source of the effect because at least two peoples of Asian origin had been shown to have, on average, less OE than Caucasians. In principle, genetic differences could account for a wide range of differences both within and across populations. See Conclusion for further discussion.

At about the same time as the Timney and Muir report appeared, Leehey et al. (1975) demonstrated that infants tested in a two-alternative forced-choice procedure, beginning at a few weeks of age (6–13 weeks), preferred to look at near-threshold gratings oriented along the main axes rather than at oblique gratings. The gratings were equal in contrast and spatial frequency and at or near their acuity limits, thereby demonstrating an OE. The authors argued that it could hardly be claimed that such infants had experienced much of a carpentered environment. More likely was intrinsic development based on a genetic account. Ethnic and individual differences could readily be understood on that basis. Switkes, Mayer, and Sloan (1978) administered what then appeared to be the coup de grace to the carpentered world hypothesis. They analyzed the frequency of occurrence of main and oblique axis edges in an urban environment and failed to find a bias in favor of main axis edges at the spatial frequencies at which the OE is found. Parenthetically, we note that two recent papers have again raised the issue of a bias in the prevalence of main axis-oriented edges in the environment and speculate about its significance for perception and its neuronal substrate (Coppola et al., 1998; Keil and Cristobal, 2000).

Such was the state of affairs when we undertook to compare the meridional distribution of acuities in groups of Caucasian and Chinese infants. Since the

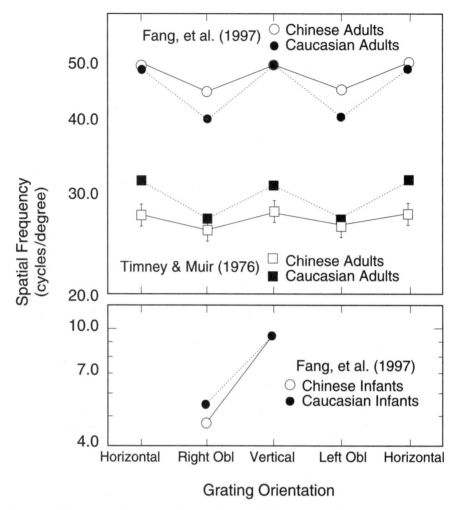

Figure 8.5. Comparison of oblique effects in Chinese and Caucasians. Measures of grating acuity in terms of cutoff spatial frequency are as reported by authors cited.

OE appeared to be present almost as early as we could test and we then favored its genetic origin, we expected it to be accompanied by the ethnic difference. But contrary to our expectations, the results (see bottom of Figure 8.5) showed no such ethnic difference in infants (average age of 10 months), although the OEs showed amplitudes of the order of one octave (Fang et al., 1997).

Failure to detect the ethnic difference in infants suggested that the OE that is already present in early infancy differs in origin from the component that develops later, a suggestion consistent with that of two different mechanisms raised earlier on other grounds (Harwerth et al., 1980). This finding raised the question of what other process could possibly account for the differential ethnic development of the OE. In particular, it should be a process that must largely prevail after infancy. Is it possible that in our haste to criticize one environmental explanation for the OE we have overlooked another and, speaking metaphorically, have thrown the baby out with the bath water?

Obviously, we suspected by now that the ethnic difference may result from greater amounts of astigmatism in the infant Caucasians than in the Chinese. If that were true, we might expect that a greater average OE would develop in the Caucasian population. Since both vertical and horizontal orientations of cylinder axes occur in the population during the susceptible period, the consequent mean amblyopia on these axes would tend to equalize out, as is in fact observed. To test this notion, all we had to do was to find comparable refractive data for the two ethnic groups of infants. But that quest proved not as easy as it sounds. Since astigmatism begins to diminish (emmetropize) during infancy, one measures a moving target that changes magnitude with age. Consequently, for meaningful comparisons, the ages of groups must be matched. Moreover, there are numerous techniques and procedures for measuring refraction that may yield different values. The examiner also makes a difference. We found a few sources of data that appear to yield comparable refractions. The first is the set of data collected by one of us and plotted in Figure 8.6 (Thorn, Held, & Fang, 1987). These data were collected on groups of 21 infants of Chinese families and 45 of Caucasian origins. All measurements were taken by near retinoscopy by the same examiner (Frank Thorn) and hence are quite comparable. Although a greater percentage of the Caucasian infants had 1 or more diopters (cylinder) of astigmatism, the small sample size precluded finding a significant difference (Figure 8.6).

The second and major source of data comes from the refraction study of a large number of Hong Kong Chinese infants by Marion Edwards (1991). Her measurements taken on 46 Chinese infants at 6 months of age who had been administered 1% cyclopentalate are comparable with those of Hopkisson, Arnold, Billingham, McGarrigle, and Shribman (1992) taken on 55 Caucasian infants under otherwise similar conditions. As plotted in Figure 8.6, 30% of the Chinese infants compared with 42% of the Caucasian infants showed astigmatism of 1 or more diopters (≥ 1 D), a difference in the expected direction but not statistically significant. Edwards measured 50 Chinese infants 9 months of age in a procedure matching that of Ehrlich, Braddick, Atkinson, Anker, Weeks, and Hartley (1997), who took measurements with the same method on 254 Caucasian English infants, also 9 months of age. Compared with 26% of the English infants, 16% of the Chinese infants showed ≥ 1 D, a difference of proportions significant at $p = .004$. Within the limitations of these studies, the weight of evidence suggests that Chinese infants do indeed have less astigmatism at least during the 2nd semester of infancy.

A curious paradox remains. The original finding of difference in the OE between people of Caucasian and Asian origin was made on members of the Cree Indian tribe in Canada, as discussed earlier. However, any general claim that Native American children have less astigmatism than Caucasians is contradicted by the findings of Dobson, Miller, Harvey, and Sherril (1999) of high degrees of astigmatism in children of the Tohono O'Odham Nation of Native Americans in southern Arizona. No doubt this paradox will not be the only one found in this area of research.

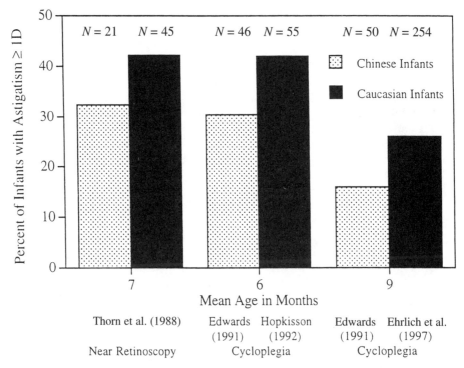

Figure 8.6. Caucasian infants have more astigmatism than do Chinese. Comparisons of percentages of astigmatism in the two groups were made by authors cited.

Conclusion

Much of the detailed evidence presented here is not as convincing as we should like. However, the constellation of results does seem consistent with the conclusion that the blur produced by early astigmatism usually causes the meridionally varied amounts of amblyopia responsible for an enhanced OE as well as the previously recognized MA. The combination is characterized by the summation curve shown in Figure 8.1. The two summating sources of meridional variation appear to have independent origins by a number of criteria; we have previously mentioned their timing of onset, with the OE appearing as early in infancy as has been tested but the MA not before the 2nd year. Harwerth et al. (1980) discuss a difference between the two in suprathreshold compensation at high contrast. That the two effects summate is confirmed by the acuity variations found in a few tested subjects who had had early oblique-axis astigmatism with the consequence of showing reduced and even negative OEs (see Mitchell et al., 1973, results of left eye of subject DH; and Harwerth et al., 1980, results of subject 7721). In these cases the reduction of acuities on the main retinal meridia, caused by the oblique astigmatism, was sufficient to reduce their mean to equal or less than that of the retinal obliques despite the substantial difference in acuities between them: the usual mark of MA. Generalizing from such cases, one can regard combinations of OE with variations of MA as the source of the surprising diversity of shapes of individual meridional variations in acuity even in adult emmetropes (see Cobb & MacDonald, 1978). The neat W-shaped graphs found in the literature of the subject (see Figure 8.5) are usually the averaged data from groups of observers.

Concerning the Chinese–Caucasian difference in magnitude of the OE, two considerations suggest that early visual experience biased by astigmatism contributes to the OE. One is the absence of the difference in early infancy, suggesting that the astigmatism-induced modulation has not yet occurred, even though both groups demonstrate substantial OEs presumably of intrinsic developmental origin. The other is the small ethnic difference in the prevalence and average magnitude of infantile astigmatism. If this blur-induced altered sensitivity thesis is correct, it constitutes an example of the close interaction between a presumedly genetically determined feature (astigmatism) and an environmental interaction codetermining development of function. Demonstration of this early plasticity in response to a property of habitual stimulation gives an empirical basis to the recently renewed speculation that bias in the prevalence of oriented edges in the environment may account for an OE (Coppola et al., 1998; Keil & Cristobal, 2000). One objection to this thesis is that the biased distribution, as imaged on the retinas, is subject to changes in head orientation, which could reduce or even eliminate the bias. But because the blurring effects of astigmatism are largely independent of such changes, their amblyopic consequences strengthen the argument for plasticity and tend to discount the head movement objection. Finally, because the demonstrated plasticity appears to be restricted to an early age, protagonists of the environmental bias must convince us that the biased environment is that to which the young child is exposed.

References

Annis, R. C., & Frost, B. (1973). Human visual ecology and orientation anisotropies in acuity. *Science, 182*, 729–731.

Atkinson, J., Braddick, O., & French, J. (1980). Infant astigmatism: Its disappearance with age. *Vision Research, 20*, 891–893.

Charman, W., & Voisin, L. (1993). Astigmatism, accommodation, the oblique effect and meridional amblyopia. *Ophthalmic and Physiological Optics, 13*(1), 73–81.

Cobb, S. R., & MacDonald, C. F. (1978). Resolution acuity in astigmats: Evidence for a critical period in the human visual system. *British Journal of Physiological Optics, 32*, 38–49.

Coppola, D. A., Purves, H. R., McCoy, A. N., & Purves, D. (1998). The distribution of oriented contours in the real world. *Neurobiology, 95*(7), 4002–4006.

Daugman, J. G. (1983). Visual plasticity as revealed in the two-dimensional modulation transfer function of a meridional amblyope. *Human Neurobiology, 2*, 71–76.

Daw, N. W. (1995). *Visual development.* New York and London: Plenum Press.

Dobson, V., Miller, J. M., Harvey, E. M., & Sherril, D. L. (1999). Prevalence of astigmatism, astigmatic-anisometropia, and glasses wearing among preschool- and school-age Native American children. In *Vision science and its applications* (OSA Technical Digest, pp. 177–184). Washington, DC: Optical Society of America.

Edwards, M. (1991). The refractive status of Hong Kong Chinese infants. *Ophthalmic and Physiological Optics, 11*, 297–303.

Ehrlich, D., Braddick, O., Atkinson, J., Anker, S., Weeks, F., & Hartley, T. (1997). Infant emmetropization: Longitudinal changes in refraction components from nine to twenty months of age. *Optometry and Vision Science, 7* (10), 822–843.

Fang, L.-L., Bauer, J., Held, R., & Gwiazda, J. (1997). The oblique effect in Chinese infants and adults. *Optometry and Vision Science, 74*(10), 816–821.

Freeman, R. D., & Thibos, L. N. (1975). Contrast sensitivity in humans with abnormal visual experience. *Journal of Physiology, 247,* 687–710.

Fulton, A. B., Dobson, V., Salem, D., Mar, C., Peterson, R. A., & Hansen, R. M. (1980). Cycloplegic refractions in infants and young children. *American Journal of Ophthalmology, 90,* 239–245.

Gwiazda, J., Bauer, J., Thorn, F., & Held, R. (1986). Meridional amblyopia *does* result from astigmatism in early childhood. *Clinical Vision Sciences, 1*(2), 145–152.

Gwiazda, J., Grice, K., Held, R., McLellan, J., & Thorn, F. (2000). Astigmatism and the development of myopia in children. *Vision Research, 40*(8), 1019–1026.

Gwiazda, J., Mohindra, I., Brill, S., & Held, R. (1985). Infant astigmatism and meridional amblyopia. *Vision Research, 25*(9), 1269–1276.

Gwiazda, J., Scheiman, M., & Held, R. (1984). Anisotropic resolution in children's vision. *Vision Research, 24,* 527–531.

Gwiazda, J., Scheiman, M., Mohindra, I., & Held, R. (1984). Astigmatism in children: Changes in axis and amount from birth to six years. *Investigative Ophthalmology Vision Science 25*(1), 88–92.

Harwerth, R. S., Smith, E. L., III, & Boltz, R. L. (1980). Meridional amblyopia in monkeys. *Experimental Brain Research, 39,* 351–356.

Held, R. (1978). Development of visual acuity in normal and astigmatic infants. In S. J. Cool & E. L. Smith III (Eds.), *Frontiers in visual science* (pp. 712–719). New York: Springer-Verlag.

Held, R., McLellan, J., Grice, K., Thorn, F., & Gwiazda, J. (1998). Does early astigmatism contribute to the oblique effect? [ARVO Abstract No. 1857]. *Investigative Ophthalmology and Visual Science, 39*(4), S397.

Hopkisson, B., Arnold, P., Billingham, B., McGarrigle, M., & Shribman, S. (1992). Can retinoscopy be used to screen infants for amblyopia? A longitudinal study of refraction in the first year of life. *Eye, 6,* 607–609.

Howland, H. C., Atkinson, J., Braddick, O., & French, J. (1978). Infant astigmatism measured by photorefraction. *Science, 202,* 331–334.

Keil, M. S., & Cristobal, G. (2000). Separating the chaff from the wheat: Possible origins of the oblique effect. *Journal of the Optical Society America, 17*(4), 697–710.

Leehey, S. C., Moskowitz-Cook, A., Brill, S., & Held, R. (1975). Orientational anisotropy in infant vision. *Science, 190,* 900–902.

Leibowitz, H. (1953). Some observations and theory on the variation of visual acuity with the orientation of the test object. *Journal of the Optical Society of America, 43,* 902–905.

Leibowitz, H. (1955). Some factors influencing the variability of vernier adjustments. *American Journal of Psychology, 68,* 266–273.

Martin, G. (1890). De l'amblyopia des astigmates. *Annales D'Oculist, 103,* 5–22.

Mitchell, D. E., Freeman, R. D., Millodot, M., & Haegerstrom, G. (1973). Meridional amblyopia: Evidence for the modification of the human visual system by early visual experience. *Vision Research, 13,* 535–557.

Mitchell, D. E., & Wilkinson, F. (1974). The effect of early astigmatism on the visual resolution of gratings. *Journal of Physiology, 243,* 739–756.

Mohindra, I., Held, R., Gwiazda, J., & Brill, S. (1978). Astigmatism in infants. *Science, 202,* 329–331.

Santonastaso, A. (1930). La refrazione oculare nei primi anni di vita. *Annali di Ottalmologia e Clinica Oculistica, 58,* 852–885.

Switkes, E., Mayer, M. J., & Sloan, J. A. (1978). Spatial frequency analysis of the visual environment: Anisotropy and the carpentered environment hypothesis. *Vision Research, 18,* 1393–1399.

Thorn, F., Held, R., & Fang, L. (1987). Orthogonal astigmatic axes in Chinese and Caucasian infants. *Investigative Ophthalmology and Visual Science, 28,* 191–194.

Timney, B. N., & Muir, D. W. (1976). Orientational anisotropy: Incidence and magnitude in Caucasian and Chinese subjects. *Science, 193,* 699–700.

Part V _____

Interactions With Visual Information

9

Misperceiving Extents in the Medial Plane

The Paradox of Shepard's Tables Illusion

Boris Crassini, Christopher J. Best, and Ross H. Day

Herschel W. Leibowitz's unique symbiotic approach to theoretical and applied research in psychology was elaborated in his 1995 award address after receiving the American Psychological Association Distinguished Scientific Award for the Applications of Psychology (see Leibowitz, 1996). This approach can be summarized as Leibowitz's second law[1]: *Applied research should illuminate basic understanding of visual perception, and basic research should illuminate solution of practical problems.* A fine example of the symbiosis between basic and applied research is the explanation that Hersh proposed to account for the disturbing occurrence of collisions between cars and trains at level crossings under conditions of good visibility (Leibowitz, 1985). Hersh and his colleagues had illuminated our understanding of basic visual processes involved in visual illusions (e.g., Hennessy & Leibowitz, 1973; Leibowitz & Pick, 1972) and perceptual constancy (e.g., Leibowitz, Wilcox, & Post, 1978). Extending the insight that this kind of research provided, Hersh suggested that the mechanisms mediating the size-velocity illusion (i.e., larger objects appearing to move more slowly than smaller objects moving at identical speeds) may be involved in explaining car–train collisions. He proposed that car drivers deciding whether or not to stop at a level crossing may underestimate the speed of an approaching train (a large moving object) and consequently may overestimate the time they have available to cross the tracks, often with tragic results. The research that we report in this chapter was carried out in the spirit of Leibowitz's second law; it also involves a visual illusion, and a practical problem to do with motor traffic. The research was prompted by a seeming inconsistency between the following:

- The proposed explanation of a compelling visual illusion. (The explanation, further on, is based on the assumption of the *presence* of a mechanism producing size constancy during perception of extents lying in the line of sight.)
- The solution to the practical problem of ensuring that traffic signs on road surfaces are maximally visible and therefore maximally effective

---

[1]To remind those who do not know or remember, Leibowitz's first law is, "You can't see a damn thing in the dark."

in minimizing traffic accidents. (The solution, also outlined further on, is based on the assumption of the *absence* of a mechanism producing size constancy during perception of extents lying in the line of sight.)

Clearly, these separate assumptions about a mechanism for producing size constancy with extents lying in the line of sight are contradictory, and the research to be reported was designed to help resolve this paradox.

We begin by presenting the compelling visual illusion that prompted, in part, our research. Figure 9.1 is reproduced from Shepard's (1990) collection of whimsical, humorous, and sometimes bizarre illustrations called *Mind Sights*.[2] The two-dimensional (2-D) representations of the three-dimensional (3-D) tables in Figure 9.1 look a little odd (e.g., the rendering of the 3-D tables seems to be somehow nonrealistic). Despite this, Figure 9.1 is generally seen as representing two tables standing on a surface extending in depth "into" the page. It is difficult to believe that the table on the left shown standing with its *longer* sides in the medial plane approximately parallel to the observer's line of sight (hereafter called the medial table), and the table on the right shown standing with its *longer* sides in the transverse plane approximately orthogonal to the observer's line of sight (hereafter called the transverse table), have identical tabletops: The medial tabletop looks much narrower and longer than

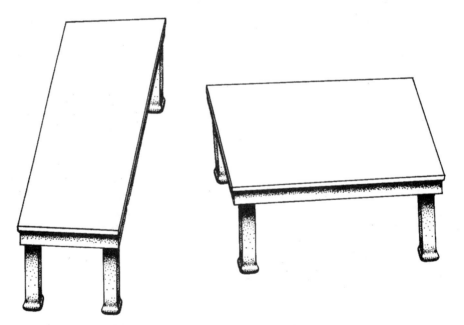

Figure 9.1. Shepard's Tables illusion. Despite appearances, the tops of the two tables are identical in size and shape. From *Mind Sights* by Roger N. Shepard. Copyright 1980 by Roger N. Shepard. Reprinted with permission of Henry Holt and Company, LLC.

---

[2]In *Mind Sights* Shepard called the compelling illusion reproduced in Figure 9.1, "Turning the tables." However, we will refer to the illusion in this chapter as Shepard's Tables.

the transverse tabletop. However, outlining one tabletop on transparent film and rotating the transparency so that the outline lies on the other tabletop dramatically demonstrates their identity. When this is done, the outline of, for example, the transverse tabletop appears to stretch and narrow during rotation to fit the medial tabletop. In summary, the compelling illusion in Figure 9.1 is an illusion of extent; that is, representations of extents in the medial plane appear longer than the representations of the same extents in the transverse plane.

The technique for demonstrating the illusion described above was outlined by Shepard (1981) when he presented an earlier version of the illusion in the form of rectangular boxes rather than tables. Shepard used the illusion to illustrate the nature of what he termed "formational processes" that he proposed were involved in producing internal representations of external objects during visual perception. These internal representations were necessary, argued Shepard, to explain, among other things, perceptual constancy—that is, the unchanging nature of perception of an object despite changes in the pattern of stimulation on receptor surfaces produced by this object (see Walsh & Kulikowski, 1998, for a comprehensive review of perceptual constancy literature). Shepard (1990) explained the illusion as follows:

> Clearly, this illusion arises because our visual system has once again given us depth interpretations of the two-dimensional drawing. The perspective cues [and other depth cues; see further on] indicate that the long axis of the table on the left goes back in depth while the long axis of the table on the right is more nearly at right angles to the line of sight. Now, if the table on the left goes back in depth, its retinal image must be correspondingly fore-shortened. The fact that the retinal images of the two quadrilaterals interpreted as table tops are identical in length then implies that the real length of the table going back in depth must be greater than the real length of the crosswise table (and vice versa for their widths). Because the inferences about orientation, depth, and length are provided automatically by underlying neuronal machinery, any knowledge or understanding of the illusion we may gain at the intellectual level remains virtually powerless to diminish the magnitude of the illusion. (p. 128)

In summary, Shepard's (1981) explanation of the illusion in Figure 9.1 is a version of the misapplied-constancy explanation proposed by Gregory (1990) to explain, for example, the Ponzo illusion. In the case of the Ponzo illusion the constancy mechanism that is taken to be "misapplied" is one designed to compensate for the decrease in visual angle of a transverse object as the viewing distance between object and observer increases. However, the constancy mechanism taken by Shepard to be misapplied when looking at Figure 9.1 is one designed to correct for the differences in visual angle of an object as a function of its orientation-in-depth, with a fixed viewing distance. That is, it may be described as an orientation-in-depth size constancy mechanism: For the sake of brevity, we will use the term *size-depth constancy* when referring to this process/mechanism in the remainder of this chapter. To understand fully the fundamental assumptions inherent in Shepard's size-depth constancy explanation of the Shepard Tables illusion, it is instructive to consider the influence of orientation-in-depth on visual angle/retinal image size.

The same object at the same distance from an observer subtends a different visual angle (and therefore produces retinal images of different sizes in the observer's eyes) depending on the orientation-in-depth of the object relative to the observer's line of sight. This finding is represented schematically in Figure 9.2, which shows the visual angles[3] subtended at the eyes of an observer standing 720 cm from a 270-cm-long object. The object is lying on the ground either orthogonal to the observer's line of sight (transverse object) or parallel to the observer's line of sight (medial object). These values were used because they correspond to the length of the *longer* side (2.7 m) of the table that is presented as a 3-D simulation at a simulated viewing distance of 7.2 m in the displays used in the experiments to be reported. At the 720-cm viewing distance, the visual angle subtended by the transverse object is more than five times larger than that subtended by the same object when in the medial plane. The ratio of visual angle subtended by medial and transverse objects of identical length increases as a function of viewing distance. For example, if the viewing distance in Figure 9.2 was 20 m, then the visual angle of the transverse object (7.0 deg) would now be almost 12 times that of the medial object (0.6 deg). Therefore, to account for veridical perception of the size of an object on the basis of the size of its retinal image, it is necessary to have information not only about the viewing distance but also about the height of the observer's eyes above the ground plane and the orientation-in-depth of the object relative to the observer's line of sight (see Baird & Wagner, 1991).

When an observer views a 2-D representation of 3-D objects (such as the tables in Figure 9.1) from a fixed eye height and a constant viewing distance, the size-depth constancy "neuronal machinery" posited by Shepard (1981, 1990) is applied incorrectly. This results in over compensation for the "assumed" reduced visual angles of medial extents, and these extents look longer than they should. When an observer views 3-D objects in a normal 3-D

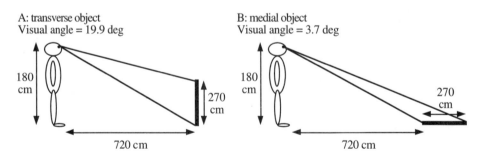

Figure 9.2. Schematic representation of visual angles subtended by a 270-cm object lying in the transverse plane (A) or medial plane (B) relative to an observer who is 180 cm tall and standing 720 cm from the object. The size of the retinal image of the object in the transverse plane is more than 5 times larger than that of the same object in the medial plane. Note that as in Figure 9.1, perspective information is absent from this representation, which is not in scale.

---

[3]The visual angles were calculated using the formula provided by Baird and Wagner (1991) in Appendix A on p. 863. In the remainder of this chapter we will use the term *visual angle* to mean both visual angle subtended by, and size of retinal image of, the object in question.

scene, the same neuronal machinery is applied correctly, and the perceived sizes of the objects remain constant despite the reduction in the sizes of their retinal images as their orientation-in-depth changes from transverse to medial. But does this occur? Loomis and Philbeck (1999) point out that "a number of experimental studies have shown that, even under full-cue viewing, there is clear anisotropy of perceived 3-D shape, with spatial intervals having a significant depth component appearing shorter than equal lengths oriented within a frontoparallel plane" (p. 397). The results of the studies referred to by Loomis and Philbeck suggest that if a size-depth constancy mechanism exists as proposed by Shepard, then its operation is not very effective.

A less formal piece of evidence supporting the conclusion that the size-depth constancy process is not effective is provided in Figure 9.3, which shows three photographs of the same right-turn arrow painted on a road surface in suburban Geelong, Australia. Figures 9.3A and 9.3B show the road sign photographed from a standing position and from viewing distances of about 15 m and 2 m, respectively. In both Figures 9.3A and 9.3B, the initial segment of the arrow shaft lies in the medial plane of the photographer and a driver approaching the sign in a car. The medial segment of the arrow shaft is 200 cm long before it "turns" to the right and lies in the photographer's or driver's transverse plane. The shaft extends 59 cm in the transverse plane before joining the arrowhead pointing to the right. At the 15-m viewing distance (Figure 9.3A) the arrow shaft appears uniform in width from shaft base to arrowhead; the arrowhead itself appears symmetrical about the segment of the shaft to which it is attached. At the 2-m viewing distance (see Figure 9.3B) the arrow shaft appears less uniform; the width of the base segment in the medial plane appears narrower than the width of the transverse segment of shaft joined to the arrowhead.[4] Figure 9.3C shows the arrow viewed from the side; the shaft segment previously viewed in the medial plane is now in the transverse plane, and vice versa. The striking difference in the width of the arrow shaft is now clearly visible, as is the asymmetry of the arrowhead. The width of the transverse base of the initial medial segment of the arrow was 20 cm, whereas the width at the shaft head immediately before the arrowhead (i.e., in the medial plane) was 87 cm.

This road sign, and indeed most signs painted on road surfaces in Australia and elsewhere, are painted with their medial extents greatly elongated relative to their transverse extents. After careful perusal of the Standards Association of Australia Road Signs Code, Macdonald and Hoffmann (1973) concluded that

> No particular basis for this policy . . . of greatly [elongating] letters in the direction of traffic flow . . . is stated, but there appears to be an underlying assumption that the more elongated are the letters, the greater is the distance at which the message can be read. (p. 314)

This rationale seems sensible in terms of minimizing traffic accidents; the longer the distance over which drivers can read a road sign, the more time

---

[4]The medial segment of the shaft appears slightly nonuniform in width along its medial length. This is an artifact of photography; the shaft actually had parallel sides.

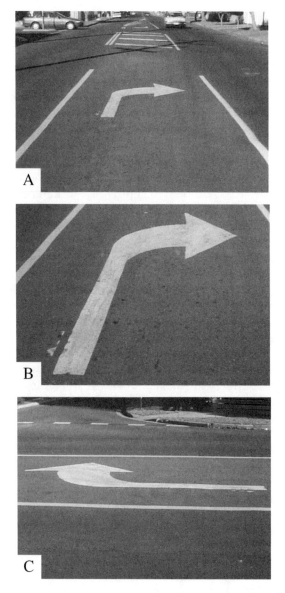

Figure 9.3. (A) Right-turn arrow marked on the surface of a road viewed from a distance of approximately 15 m. Note the uniform appearance of the width of both the medial segment (i.e., "along" the road, parallel to the line of sight) and the transverse segment (i.e., "across" the road, orthogonal to the line of sight) of the arrow shaft. Note also the symmetrical appearance of the arrowhead. (B) The same right-turn arrow viewed from a distance of approximately 2 m. Compared to the view in A, the widths of the medial and transverse segments of the arrow shaft appear less uniform, and the appearance of the arrowhead seems less symmetrical. (C) The same right-turn arrow from a distance of approximately 5 m, but from the side. The width of the transverse segment of the arrow shaft immediately before the arrowhead is clearly greater than the width of the medial segment of the shaft. Note also the asymmetry of the arrowhead. Personal photo: B. C. Reprinted with permission.

they have to take appropriate action in response to the sign. Given the differences in visual angles subtended by medial and transverse objects represented in Figure 9.2, the "medial elongation" policy in relation to road signs could be designed to equate the retinal image sizes of medial and transverse extents of road signs. In this way, all segments of the road sign would become visible at the same time or viewing distance. At an eye height of 180 cm and at a viewing distance of 20 m, the visual angle subtended by the 20-cm transverse shaft base of the arrow is 29.3 min. The visual angle subtended by the 87-cm medial shaft head of the arrow is 12.8 min; if the width of the shaft had been kept uniform at 20 cm, the visual angle subtended would have been 3.0 min. Although the policy of medial elongation of road signs has not produced equivalence of transverse and medial visual angles at a viewing distance at which they should be recognized to enable appropriate action, the differences in these visual angles are significantly less than would be the case if the road signs were uniform in shape.

The appearance of road signs of the type shown in Figure 9.3 in the face of their elongated medial extents is inconsistent with the operation of the size-depth constancy mechanism proposed by Shepard (1981, 1990). If it is the case that visual perception involves "involuntary, automatic, and efficient perceptual machinery" (Shepard, 1981, p. 297) to compensate for the reduced sizes of retinal images of medial extents relative to transverse extents, then there should be no need to paint road signs with elongation of their medial extents. Indeed, by elongating road signs in their medial extent, thereby equating (approximately at least) the visual angles subtended by their medial and transverse extents, a 3-D analogue of Shepard's Tables is, in effect, produced. Operation of the proposed size-depth constancy mechanism should result in the elongated medial extents of the road signs appearing even more greatly distorted than they are. But such distortion does not occur. When road signs of the type shown in Figure 9.3 are observed in situ from an appropriate viewing distance, they look as they are "meant" to look (i.e., uniform in medial and transverse extents), and not as they are actually painted.

We considered two factors that may account for this paradox:

1. The first factor concerned the quality of the 3-D representation of the tables in Figure 9.1. Earlier, we described the 2-D rendering of 3-D objects in Figure 9.1 as nonrealistic. This comment does not apply to the depth cues of shadow (the tabletops cast shadows on the table legs nearer to the observer) and occlusion (the tabletops obscure the table legs farther from the observer), which do appear realistic. It is the perspective information in Figure 9.1 that does not seem realistic; there is very little change in the size and shape of segments of the tables that are represented as being farther away from the point of view. It may be that the Shepard's Tables illusion occurs only with displays that lack realistic perspective depth information. We tested this hypothesis by measuring the Shepard's Tables illusion using 2-D representations of 3-D objects in which there was appropriate and realistic perspective depth information, as well as depth information provided by shadow and occlusion.

2. The second factor concerned the nature of the two different "objects" represented in Figures 9.1 and 9.3. Despite the nonrealistic 3-D rendering, Figure 9.1 does appear to be a representation of two 3-D objects. However, the road sign in Figure 9.3 is not really perceived as a 3-D object, even though it extends from the observer in the medial depth plane. The road sign is perceived as part of the road-ground plane. It may be that the size-depth constancy mechanism that Shepard proposed to explain the Shepard's Tables illusion functions only during perception of objects and not perception of segments of the ground-plane surface. We tested this hypothesis by measuring the Shepard's Tables illusion with 2-D representations of segments of a 3-D ground.

The two hypotheses outlined above were tested using computer-generated 2-D stimuli that realistically simulated 3-D scenes. Figure 9.4 shows examples of the tables displays used, which consisted of pairs of tables standing on a ground plane. In addition, we used displays consisting of quadrilaterals that appeared to be part of the ground-plane surface similar to the way in which the road sign in Figure 9.3 appears to be part of the road surface. To understand more clearly the hypotheses that were tested, some further information is needed about the displays and about the participants' task in the studies to be reported. Data were collected by using the method of constant stimuli to measure

- points of subjective equality (PSEs: A PSE is the value of a comparison stimulus reported by observers to be equal in magnitude to some standard stimulus), and
- corresponding difference thresholds (just noticeable differences, *jnds*: A *jnd* is the value of a comparison stimulus that observers report as just noticeably different from some standard stimulus).

As discussed previously, the Shepard's Tables illusion involves perceptual overestimation of simulated medial extents compared with corresponding (in terms of size of visual angle) transverse extents. For displays of the type shown in Figure 9.4, each 3-D object has both simulated medial and transverse extents. To simplify their judgment task, participants were required to attend to, and compare, the extents of only the *longer* sides of each of the pairs of simultaneously presented stimuli and then to select which one (left or right) had the longer *longer* sides.

The pairs of tables or quadrilaterals (a standard and a comparison) were shown under four display conditions. In two of these the standard and comparison stimuli were both presented with their respective *longer* sides in the transverse plane (T-T; see Figure 9.4A) or in the medial plane (M-M; see Figure 9.4B). These displays formed control conditions in that comparisons of extents across orthogonal orientations-in-depth (as occur in the Shepard's Tables illusion) were not involved. In terms of PSE data, if the *longer* sides of the table on the left of Figures 9.4A and 9.4B were taken as the standard stimulus (100%), and the *longer* sides of the table of the right of these figures were varied as the comparison stimulus, then a PSE > 100% would indicate *overestimation,* and a PSE < 100% would indicate *underestimation* of the

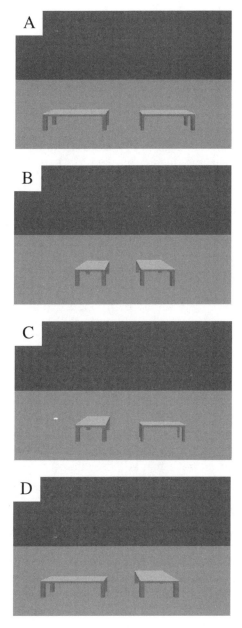

Figure 9.4. (A) T-T display; both tables are in a transverse orientation-in-depth relative to the observer's line of sight. The standard table is on the left, and the smallest comparison table used is on the right. (B) M-M display; both tables are in a medial orientation-in-depth relative to the observer's line of sight. The standard table is on the left, and the largest comparison table used is on the right. (C) M-T display; the table on the left (comparison table) is in a medial orientation-in-depth, and the table on the right (smallest comparison table) is in a transverse orientation-in-depth relative to the observer's line of sight. (D) T-M display; the table on the left (comparison table) is in a transverse orientation-in-depth, and the table on the right (largest comparison table) is in a medial orientation-in-depth relative to the observer's line of sight.

standard stimulus. If *jnd*s were measured under some conditions producing larger values than other conditions, this would indicate that the comparison stimulus needed to be varied by a larger magnitude to be seen as different from the standard stimulus in the former conditions compared with the latter. Examples of the critical displays with respect to testing the hypotheses are shown in Figures 9.4C and 9.4D; these are realistically simulated 3-D versions of the Shepard's Tables illusion containing appropriate perspective, shadow, and occlusion depth information. In Figure 9.4C the standard table is shown on the left with its *longer* sides in the medial plane. It is paired with the smallest of the comparison tables used (see Method section) with its *longer* sides in the transverse plane (M-T). Figure 9.4D shows the reverse orientation-in-depth pairing; the transverse standard is on the left, and the largest medial comparison is on the right (T-M). Inspection of Figures 9.4C and 9.4D shows clearly that as a consequence of the realistic rendering of 3-D tables, the medial extents are foreshortened (e.g., the actual extents of the *longer* sides of the medial tables are shorter than the extents of the corresponding *longer* sides of transverse tables). Details of this foreshortening are presented in the Methods section.

We can now state the previously mentioned hypotheses more formally in terms of PSE and *jnd* scores. The first hypothesis is that if the size-depth constancy mechanism proposed by Shepard (1981, 1990) to explain the Shepard's Tables illusion operates while a realistic rendering of 3-D tables is being viewed, the Shepard's Tables illusion should occur, and medial extents should appear longer than they are (as reflected in terms of visual angles subtended). In terms of PSE scores, the extent of the *longer* sides of medial standard (100%) tables should be overestimated when measured with transverse comparison tables (i.e., in M-T conditions, see Figure 9.4C, PSE > 100%). Conversely, the extent of the *longer* sides of transverse standard (100%) tables should be underestimated when measured with medial comparison tables (i.e., in T-M conditions, see Figure 9.4D, PSE < 100%). If sensitivity to changes in extent is consistent with Weber's law, then *jnd*s should be correlated with PSEs across conditions. The second hypothesis is that if Shepard's (1981, 1990) size-depth constancy mechanism operates with only 2-D representations of 3-D objects, and not with segments of ground planes, then the Shepard's Tables illusion should not occur in displays where, for example, the tables in Figure 9.4 are replaced by quadrilaterals. Perception of medial extents of quadrilaterals should not be overestimated but should be determined by the sizes of their retinal images (as occurs with road signs; see Figure 9.3). In terms of PSE scores, the extents of the *longer* sides of medial standard (100%) quadrilaterals should be underestimated when measured with transverse comparison quadrilaterals (i.e., in M-T conditions analogous to that shown in Figure 9.4C, PSE < 100%). Conversely, the extents of *longer* sides of transverse standard (100%) quadrilaterals should be overestimated (i.e., in T-M conditions analogous to that shown in Figure 9.4D, PSE > 100%) when measured with medial comparison quadrilaterals. If sensitivity to changes in extent is consistent with Weber's law, then *jnd*s should be correlated with PSEs across conditions. These predictions are summarized in Table 9.1. Two experiments were carried out to test these predictions, the second being essentially a replication and extension

Table 9.1.   Predictions for the Perceived Extents of *Longer* Sides of Displays.

	Tables displays[a]		Quadrilaterals displays[b]	
	M-T condition	T-M condition	M-T condition	T-M condition
PSE	> 100%	< 100%	< 100%	> 100%
jnd	Larger	Smaller	Smaller	Larger

Note. Predictions are in terms of PSE and *jnd* scores. The M-T condition involved presentation of the tables and quadrilaterals with their longer axis in the medial plane as the left-hand member of the pair of stimuli; the right-hand member had its longer axis in the transverse plane The T-M condition involved presentation of the tables and quadrilaterals with their longer axes in the transverse plane as the left-hand member of the pair of stimuli; the right-hand member had its longer axis in the medial plane. PSE refers to the point of subjective equality, at which the longer sides of the medial and transverse tables and quadrilaterals are judged as equal in length; *jnd* refers to the just noticeable difference in the judgments of the length of the longer sides of tables and quadrilaterals—that is, the smallest difference that can be detected.
[a]Size-depth constancy occurs.
[b]Size-depth constancy does not occur.

of the first. Because the apparatus and procedures used in the two studies were identical, and the only difference was in the sizes of the comparison stimuli used, the two studies are reported in parallel.

Method

Participants

Two of the authors (C. B., R. D.) were participants in the first experiment. The remaining eight participants in the first experiment and the six participants in the second experiment were volunteers drawn from staff and students in the School of Psychology at Deakin University. All participants had normal or corrected-to-normal visual acuity, and all except the two authors were naive with respect to the hypotheses being investigated.

Apparatus, Stimuli, Methodology, and Design

Experiment 1. All stimuli were generated using a proprietary 3-D graphics engine (MindRender by ThemeKit Systems, Leicester, United Kingdom). Stimuli were drawn with a screen resolution of 1024 horizontal and 768 vertical pixels and were presented on a computer monitor (Acerview 761E; screen dimensions of 300 mm horizontal by 225 mm vertical; Acer, San Jose, California) that was driven by a Pentium-II-based PC running at 266 MHz. This PC was used to generate stimuli and to control stimulus presentation and collect data. All participants in the tables conditions of the first experiment viewed displays that consisted of a simulation of a 3-D view of a pair (a standard and a comparison) of gray-colored tables standing on a green, featureless ground plane (see Figure 9.4). The simulated surface on which the tables stood extended from the bottom of the computer screen to a horizon midway up the screen above which was a blue sky. The relative orientation-in-depth of the two tables (defined in terms of their *longer* sides) was varied systematically: (a) The *longer* sides could both be in a transverse plane (T-T displays, transverse standard, and transverse comparison; Figure 9.4A); or (b) the longer sides could both be in a medial plane (M-M displays; Figure 9.4B); (c) the *longer* side of the standard table could be in the medial plane, with the *longer* side of the comparison table in the transverse plane (M-T displays; Figure 9.4C); or (d) the *longer* side of the standard table could be in the transverse plane, with the *longer* side of the comparison table in the medial plane (T-M displays; Figure 9.4D). Participants in the quadrilaterals conditions viewed similar displays consisting only of the colored-colored quadrilateral segments of the ground surface. These were, in fact, the tabletops of the tables used in the tables conditions, which contained perspective depth information, but not shadow or occlusion depth information.

The tables and quadrilaterals were generated to appear centrally in the display as if they were viewed from an eye height of 1.8 m and from a viewing distance of 7.2 m to the nearer sides of the stimuli. These nearer sides were aligned parallel to the transverse plane of the simulated observer, and there was a horizontal separation of 1.2 m between the adjacent sides of the stimuli. The dimensions of the standard stimuli were 2.7 m long and 1.2 m wide; the legs of the tables were 0.6 m long. Note that these metric values refer to the dimensions of the simulated 3-D standard table that was being represented as a 2-D display, with the viewing conditions being simulated. To provide some idea of the actual dimensions of the stimuli on the computer screen, the nearer *longer* side of the transverse standard table had an extent of 92 mm on the screen (subtending a visual angle of approximately 13 deg at the participant's viewing distance of about 40 cm); when this *longer* side was presented in the medial plane, it had an extent of 22 mm (subtending a visual angle of approximately 3 deg). That is, when the 3-D-rendering software rotated the tables and quadrilaterals so that their *longer* sides lay in the medial plane of the simulated observer, the extent of the *longer* sides was foreshortened by approximately 75% of their extent when in the transverse plane. As indicated previously, the method of constant stimuli was used to collect data to derive estimates of PSEs and corresponding *jnds* of the *longer* sides of standard and comparison stimuli in four display conditions (i.e., T-T, M-M, M-T, and T-M). Three separate sets of nine comparison stimuli were generated; one set was used in T-T and M-M conditions, and the other two were used in M-T and T-M conditions, respectively.

The three sets of comparison stimuli were generated by taking the standard table or quadrilateral and using the MindRender software to scale up or scale down the standard stimulus according to the values shown in Table 9.2. The comparison stimuli in each set varied from one in which the *longer* side of the comparison stimulus appeared clearly longer than that of the standard stimulus, to one in which the *longer* sides of the comparison and standard stimuli appeared equal, to one in which the *longer* side of the comparison stimulus appeared clearly shorter than that of the standard stimulus. However, during pilot testing undertaken to determine appropriate stimulus values, it became clear that the assumption that Shepard's (1981) size-depth

Table 9.2.   Percentage Ranges of Sealed Sizes of Comparison Stimuli.

Comparison stimulus	Experiment 1				Experiment 2	
	T-T Condition	M-M Condition	M-T Condition	T-M Condition	M-T Condition	T-M Condition
CS1	85	85	69	101	51	111
CS2	93	93	77	109	61	121
CS3	97	97	81	113	67	127
CS4	99	99	83	115	69	129
CS5	100	100	84	116	70	130
CS6	101	101	85	117	71	131
CS7	103	103	87	119	73	133
CS8	107	107	91	123	79	139
CS9	115	115	99	131	89	149

Note. All measures of scaled size are given in percentages. In Experiment 1, the scale values were symmetrical about 100% (T-T; M-M), 84% (M-T), and 116% (T-M). In Experiment 2, the values were symmetrical about 70% (M-T), and 130% (T-M). The T-T and M-M conditions involved presentation of both tables and quadrilaterals making up displays with their longer axis in the transverse plane and medial plane respectively; the M-T and T-M conditions were as described in Table 1. In both experiments, the *longer* sides of all medial comparison stimuli in T-M conditions were "longer" than the transverse standard stimulus; the *longer* sides of all transverse comparison stimuli were "shorter" than the medial standard stimulus in M-T conditions. The shaded row in the table indicates the size of the longer side of the standard stimuli used in the six experimental conditions of Experiments 1 and 2; the values in this row are the median values of the comparison stimuli used in these six conditions.

constancy mechanism operates in the viewing of realistic rendering of 3-D objects did not seem to hold. When two identical tables were presented in the configurations represented in Figures 9.4C and 9.4D, the *longer* sides of the medial table appeared *shorter* (by about 25%) than the corresponding *longer* sides of the transverse table. For this reason it was necessary to use different ranges of comparison stimuli for displays in T-T/M-M and M-T/T-M conditions to allow the derivation of PSE and *jnd* data needed to evaluate the hypotheses being tested.

The range of scaled-size values used to generate comparison stimuli did not differ by equal intervals; small increases or decreases were used near the estimated PSE values between standard and comparison stimuli, and larger increases or decreases were used at the upper and lower limits of the range. During pilot testing, it was clear that observers showed variability in their ability to perform the judgment task. Rather than design separate stimulus sets for participants to "match" their individual PSEs, it was decided to use the extended range of comparison-stimulus values in Table 9.2. Participants were tested individually; they sat comfortably so that their eyes were at a distance of approximately 40 cm from the computer monitor and provided responses with viewing unrestrained by a chin or head rest. Prior to collection of data, participants were shown examples of the stimuli and were given practice at the task. Participants in the tables condition were told that the stimuli would be pairs of 2-D representations of tables with rectangular table-tops (i.e., having *longer* and *shorter* sides) in the combinations shown in Figure 9.4. They were told their task was to attend to and compare the *longer* sides and then to identify the table (forced choice; "left" table or "right" table) with the longer *longer* sides. Participants were told that the length of the *longer* sides of one table would vary across trials, as would the difficulty of the judgment. Instructions for the quadrilaterals condition were similar. All participants completed four blocks of 90 trials (10 presentations of each of the nine possible combinations of standard stimulus plus comparison stimulus); each block involved one of the four possible combinations of relative orientations of the *longer* sides of standard and comparison stimuli described previously (i.e., T-T, M-M, T-M, and M-T). In any block of trials, the pairing of the standard stimulus (which was presented on each trial) with the nine possible comparison stimuli was randomized across trials, as was the side of the screen on which the standard stimulus was presented. Each stimulus pair was presented for 2.5 s, with a 2.5-s interval between trials during which responses were given. Rest periods were provided between blocks of trials, and the order of testing of the four blocks was randomized. Six participants viewed the tables displays, and four viewed the quadrilateral displays.

Experiment 2. The apparatuses used to generate and present the stimuli and to collect data in the second study were identical to those used in the first study. The testing procedures were similar to those described for Experiment 1. The major difference in the second study was that each participant was shown, in separate blocks, both tables and quadrilaterals displays, and a larger range of scaled sizes of comparison stimuli was used. The range of scaled sizes of comparison tables and quadrilaterals used is shown in Table 9.2. Each participant completed four blocks of 90 trials made up of 10 presentations of each of the nine possible combinations of standard stimulus plus comparison stimulus, with each block consisting of either tables or quadrilaterals displays presented at one of the two orthogonal relative orientations of the *longer* sides of the standard and comparison stimuli described earlier (i.e., M-T, T-M). In any block of trials, the pairing of the standard stimulus (which was presented on each trial) with the nine possible comparison stimuli was randomized across trials, as was the side of the screen on which the standard stimulus was presented. Each stimulus pair was presented for 2.5 s, with a 2.5-s interval between trials during which responses were given. Rest periods were provided between blocks of trials, and the order of testing of the four blocks was randomized.

Results and Discussion

Experiment 1. For each participant, separate psychometric functions were generated for each of the four orientation-in-depth conditions. For T-T and M-M conditions, correct responses were defined in terms of whether participants correctly identified the stimulus (left or right table or quadrilateral) with the longer *longer* sides; the maximum possible score was 10. For M-T and T-M conditions, this scoring convention was not appropriate because in these conditions comparison stimuli were simulations of tables or quadrilaterals with *longer* sides that were either *always* shorter than those of the standard stimuli (M-T conditions) or *always* longer than those of the standard stimuli (T-M conditions); see Table 9.1 for the actual scaled sizes of comparison stimuli. In these conditions it was decided to score participants' responses in terms of the number of times they identified the transverse stimulus as having the longer *longer* sides. The maximum possible score was 10. The individual responses of the six participants who viewed the tables displays and the four who viewed the quadrilaterals displays are presented in Figure 9.A1 in the Appendix. Figure 9.5 shows group psychometric functions based on part of the data displayed in Figure 9.A1 averaged across participants for each of the four orientation-in-depth conditions as a function of the scale of comparison stimuli. Results provided by two participants who viewed the tables (T. D., K. C.; both in T-M condition) and two participants who viewed the quadrilaterals (S. W. in T-M and M-T conditions; C. C. in T-M condition) were not included in the averaged data. Their results did not conform to the standard psychometric function expected when using the method of constant stimuli. To aid visual comparisons, the psychometric functions in Figure 9.5 are repeated with and without standard deviation error bars in the left and right panels, respectively.

Inspection of the standard deviations in the upper right panel of Figure 9.5 shows that with tables displays, participants were generally more consistent in T-T and M-M conditions compared with M-T and T-M conditions. This was also the case with quadrilaterals (see lower right panel of Figure 9.5). Overall, participants were generally most variable when responding to quadrilaterals displays in M-T and T-M conditions, that is, when judgments involved standard and comparison stimuli with their *longer* sides at orthogonal orientations-in-depth. The dashed horizontal lines in the left panels of Figure 9.5 represent chance levels of responding. The values of the horizontal axis corresponding to the intersection of these dashed lines with each curve approximate the PSE value for the condition represented by the curve. From the left panels of Figure 9.5 it can be seen that the PSEs for both tables and quadrilaterals displays in T-T and M-M conditions are almost 100%. Because the standard stimuli were set at 100% (from which comparison stimuli were scaled up or down), this finding shows that participants were accurate in their judgments of extent when the *longer* sides of standard and comparison stimuli were parallel. However, performance in M-T and T-M conditions was consistent with that found with pilot testing. In M-T conditions (the left-most functions in Figure 9.5), the average PSEs were less than 100%; that is, the medial 100% standard was judged to be equal to a transverse comparison stimulus of about 80%: In T-M conditions (the right-most functions in Figure 9.5), the PSEs were more than 100%; that is, the transverse 100% standard was judged to be equal to a medial comparison of about 120%.

Curve-fitting software (Igor Pro; WaveMetrics, Lake Oswego, Oregon) was used to fit normalized cumulative Gaussian functions to each participant's data (except for those participants already identified as not providing appropriate data). This function was used following the recommendation of Harvey (1986) in relation to curve-fitting psychometric functions in forced-choice detection tasks. From these functions, PSEs were defined as the scaled-size value of the comparison stimulus that corresponded to 50% "accuracy" in

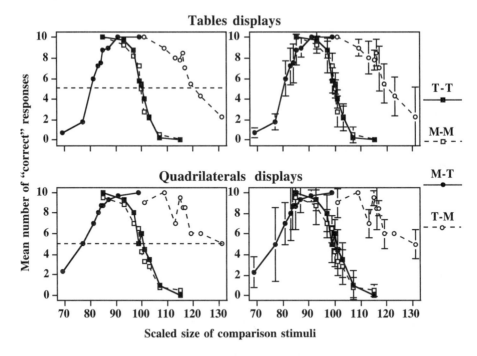

Figure 9.5. Psychometric functions (without standard deviation error bars on the left; with error bars on the right) for tables displays (upper panels) and quadrilaterals displays (lower panels) based on partial group data in Experiment 1. Curves are presented as a function of the scaled size of the comparison stimuli for the four conditions defined by the relative orientation-in-depth of standard and comparison stimuli. The separate definitions of "correct" responses for these conditions are given in the text. The dashed horizontal lines correspond to chance levels of responding.

responding (accuracy was defined differently in T-T/M-M and M-T/T-M conditions as described earlier); *jnd*s were defined as half the range on this dimension between the values corresponding to 17% to 83% "correct" responding. Table 9.3 shows the mean PSE and *jnd* values (together with standard deviations in parentheses and the number of participants whose scores were averaged) for the tables and quadrilaterals displays across the four orientation-in-depth conditions. As already indicated, participants were very accurate in identifying differences in the extent of the *longer* sides of standard and comparison stimuli in T-T and M-M conditions. Table 9.3 shows that differences of about 1% were identified in these conditions. Participants were also sensitive in detecting changes in stimulus length under these conditions with *jnd*s being about 3% for tables displays and slightly larger (about 5%) for quadrilaterals displays. These values are consistent with those reported by Norman, Todd, Perotti, and Tittle (1996) in a length discrimination task that involved different stimuli and methodology but that did not involve standard and comparison lines presented in parallel, as was the case in the present study.

Whereas performance in T-T/M-M conditions differed only slightly for tables and quadrilaterals displays, performance differences with these displays were more marked in M-T and T-M conditions. When participants

Table 9.3.   Mean PSE and *jnd* Scores for Displays in Experiment 1.

	Tables displays				Quadrilaterals displays			
	T-T $N = 6$	M-M $N = 6$	M-T $N = 6$	T-M $N = 4$	T-T $N = 4$	M-M $N = 4$	M-T $N = 3$	T-M $N = 2$
PSE	100.2	100.0	80.4	122.7	100.6	99.5	76.1	130.8
	(0.3)	(0.4)	(0.8)	(6.2)	(0.9)	(0.8)	(5.3)	(4.9)
jnd	3.3	3.3	4.5	8.6	4.9	5.9	5.4	19.6
	(1. 1)	(2.3)	(1.3)	(1.8)	(1.7)	(3.6)	(1.5)	(14.6)

Note. Scores are a function of the relative orientation-in-depth of standard and comparison stimuli. Standard deviations are given in parentheses. The numbers of participants (*N*) whose data allowed curve fitting are shown for each condition.

were shown medial standard stimuli, a transverse comparison tables scaled only to 80.4% and comparison quadrilaterals scaled to 76.1% were judged to have equal *longer* sides to the 100% standard. That is, medial extents were *underestimated* by about 20% for tables and 24% for quadrilaterals in M-T conditions. This pattern of responding is opposite to the predictions summarized in Table 9.2. Results opposite to predictions were also obtained when participants were shown transverse standard stimuli. In T-M conditions, medial comparison tables needed to be scaled to 122.7% and comparison quadrilaterals needed to be scaled to 130.8%, to be judged to have equal *longer* sides to the 100% standard. As in M-T conditions, medial extents were underestimated and had to be scaled up by about 23% (tables) and 31% (quadrilaterals) to appear equal to 100% transverse standards. This pattern of underestimation of medial extents relative to transverse extents was associated with a slight loss of sensitivity compared with judgments in T-T/M-M conditions. Average *jnd*s for M-T conditions were 4.5% and 5.4% for tables and quadrilaterals displays, respectively. Sensitivity was even more reduced in T-M conditions, with average *jnd*s being 8.6% and 19.6% for tables and quadrilaterals displays, respectively. These *jnd* data indicate that the extent-judgment task was more difficult when the standard stimuli were transverse and the comparison stimuli were medial; participants required a larger change in the comparison stimulus for a difference to be noticed. The task was most difficult with quadrilaterals displays in this condition (see Norman et al., 1996). This relative task difficulty is reflected also in the standard deviations shown in Figure 9.5, and in the numbers of participants who were unable to complete all conditions appropriately, despite practice.

Data from all participants could be used in deriving PSE and *jnd* scores in T-T and M-M conditions; data from all but one participant could be used in deriving these scores in M-T conditions; but data from four participants were unsuitable in T-M conditions. Inspection of the scatter plots in Figure 9.A1 in the Appendix shows that participants who did not complete the task appropriately in T-M and particularly M-T conditions did so because they tended to judge the transverse member of the stimulus pair as always having the longer *longer* sides. That is, the ranges of scaled sizes of comparison stimuli in Experiment 1 were such that for one participant in T-M conditions, a medial comparison quadrilateral scaled up to 131% was still judged to have shorter *longer* sides than the 100% transverse standard quadrilateral. For four participants in T-M conditions (two with tables, two with quadrilaterals), transverse comparison stimuli scaled down to 69% were still judged to have longer *longer* sides than the 100% medial standard stimuli. It was for this reason that we decided to use wider ranges of comparison stimuli in the critical M-T and T-M conditions in carrying out a partial replication and extension of Experiment 1 described earlier.

Experiment 2. As occurred in analyzing the results of Experiment 1, separate psychometric functions were generated for each of the six participants in the four orientation-in-depth conditions for both tables and quadrilaterals displays in Experiment 2; the same scoring convention used in the first experiment was used in the second. The individual responses of the six participants are presented in Figure 9.A2 in the Appendix. Figure 9.6 shows group psychometric functions based on part of the data displayed in Figure 9.A2. These are averaged across participants for each of the four orientation-in-depth conditions as a function of the scaled size of comparison stimuli. Despite the increased ranges of scaled sizes of comparison stimuli, results provided by two participants (P1 and P4) were not included in the averaged data because their results did not conform to the standard psychometric function expected when using the method of constant stimuli. Inspection of the standard deviations in the right panel of Figure 9.6 shows, for both tables and quadrilateral displays, a pattern of responding similar to that in Figure 9.5. That is, participants were generally more consistent in performing the task with tables displays than with quadrilaterals displays. Performance also tended to be more consistent in M-T conditions than in T-M conditions, although this was not as marked as in Experiment 1 (see Figure 9.5). From the left panel of Figure 9.6, it can be seen that the PSEs for both tables and quadrilaterals displays in M-T condition were both less than 100%, as occurred in Experiment 1. However, unlike the results of Experiment 1, the PSEs for table and quadrilaterals were similar. The left-most functions in Figure 9.6 show that the medial 100% standard was judged to be equal to a transverse comparison of about 70%. In T-M conditions (the right-most functions in Figure 9.6), the PSEs were more than 100%; that is, the transverse 100% standard was judged to be equal to a medial comparison of about 130%. As was the case in Experiment 1, there was a difference in PSEs for tables and quadrilaterals.

Table 9.4 shows mean PSE and *jnd* scores derived from participants' data in the second study by using the same curve-fitting procedures employed in the first study. In M-T conditions (in which participants were shown medial standard stimuli), transverse comparison tables scaled to 70.2%, and comparison quadrilaterals scaled to 68.1% were judged to have equal *longer* sides to the 100% standard. As was found in M-T conditions in Experiment 1, medial extents were underestimated in Experiment 2, but by about 30% for tables (compared with about 20% in Experiment 1) and 32% for quadrilaterals (compared with about 24% in Experiment 1). In T-M conditions in which participants were shown transverse standard stimuli, a medial comparison table needed to be scaled to 138.6% and a comparison quadrilateral needed to be scaled to 148.6% to be judged to have equal *longer* sides to the 100% standard.

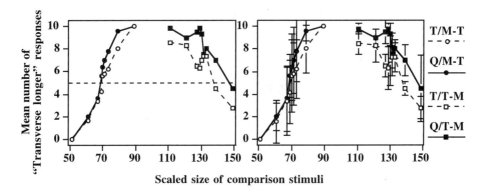

Figure 9.6. Psychometric functions (without standard deviation error bars on the left; with error bars on the right) based on partial group data in Experiment 2 (see text). Curves are presented as a function of the scaled size of the comparison stimuli for the four conditions defined by the relative orientation-in-depth of standard and comparison stimuli. The separate definitions of "correct" responses for these conditions are as for Experiment 1. The dashed horizontal line corresponds to chance levels of responding.

That is, in T-M conditions in Experiment 2, medial extents were underestimated by about 39% for tables (compared with about 23% in Experiment 1), and 49% for quadrilaterals (compared with about 31% in Experiment 1).

The *jnd* scores in the second study for M-T conditions were slightly larger than the corresponding *jnd* scores in the first study (6.7% and 5.5% vs. 4.5% and 5.4% for tables and quadrilaterals displays, respectively). As was the case in Experiment 1, sensitivity was markedly reduced in T-M conditions, with average *jnd*s being 22.6% and 15.7% for tables and quadrilaterals displays, respectively (compared with the corresponding *jnd*s in Experiment 1 of 8.6% and 19.6%). In summary, the data in Table 9.4 generally replicated those of the first study shown in Table 9.3. That is, with realistically simulated 3-D versions of Shepard's Tables illusion, medial extents were underestimated rather than overestimated, as predicted. Furthermore, this underestimation tended to be larger for quadrilaterals displays than for tables displays. As reflected in *jnd*s, participants found the comparison of extents in orthogonal

Table 9.4. Mean PSE and *jnd* Scores for Displays in Experiment 2.

	Tables displays		Quadrilaterals displays	
	M-T N = 5	T-M N = 4	M-T N = 5	T-M N = 4
PSE	70.2	138.6	68.1	148.6
	(5.4)	(2.9)	(3.9)	(8.1)
jnd	6.7	22.6	5.5	15.7
	(1.5)	(8.2)	(1.3)	(6.1)

Note. Scores are a function of the relative orientation-in-depth of standard and comparison stimuli. Standard deviations are given in parentheses. The number of participants (*N*) whose data allowed curve fitting is shown for each condition.

orientations-in-depth difficult, particularly when the standard stimulus was presented with its longer sides in the medial orientation and the stimuli were quadrilaterals.

General Discussion

Table 9.5 summarizes both the paradox that prompted our research and the results we obtained. Descriptions of five separate observation conditions are set out in terms of the visual angles subtended by medial and transverse extents and the appearance of these extents under the conditions. The five observation conditions are as follows:

1. *Normal viewing in full cue conditions.* The visual angle subtended by a medial extent is smaller than that subtended by an identical transverse extent. Because of the size-depth constancy "visual machinery" posited by Shepard (1981, 1990), the medial and transverse extents should appear the same length.

2. *Shepard's Tables illusion, for example, as shown in Figure 9.1.* The *longer* sides of the medial and transverse tables are drawn so they subtend visual angles of the same size. The size-depth constancy visual machinery is misapplied, and the *longer* sides of the medial table look longer than the corresponding sides of the transverse table.

3. *Road signs painted on road surfaces, for example, as represented in Figure 9.3.* Road signs are painted so that their medial extents are elongated relative to their corresponding transverse extents. This results in corresponding medial and transverse segments subtending visual angles of approximately the same size at viewing distances sufficient to allow appropriate response to the signs. However, making medial and transverse extents subtend equal visual angles as in the Shepard's Tables illusion does not produce a similar illusion with road signs; they appear uniform.

4. *Realistically rendered tables in Shepard's Tables illusion configuration.* The retinal images of medial extents were smaller than those of transverse extents (by about 80%, simulating what occurs during normal viewing). However, the *longer* sides of medial tables were not perceived as equivalent in length to those of transverse tables (see Condition 1), nor were they overestimated relative to corresponding sides (see Condition 2). Medial *longer* sides were underestimated by about 25% to 30% relative to transverse *longer* sides.

5. *Realistically rendered quadrilaterals in Shepard's Tables illusion configuration.* The relative sizes of medial and transverse retinal images were identical to those in the tables version. Greater underestimation of medial extents was found with quadrilaterals (about 30% to 40% underestimation) compared with tables (about 25% to 30%).

We suggested in the beginning of this chapter that the apparently contradictory pattern of relationships between visual angles and corresponding perceived extents reflected in the first three rows of Table 9.5 may be

Table 9.5. Relationships Between Medial (M) and Transverse (T) Extents.

Observation conditions	Relative visual angles subtended by M and T extents	Appearance of M and T extents
Normal viewing	Medial < Transverse	Medial should = Transverse
Shepard's Tables illusion (STI)	Medial = Transverse	Medial > Transverse
Road sign	Medial ≈ Transverse	Medial = Transverse
Simulated STI; M-T condition tables displays	Medial < Transverse (by about 80%)	Medial < Transverse (100% M ≈ 75% T)
Simulated STI; T-M condition tables displays		Medial < Transverse (130% M ≈ 100% T)
Simulated STI; M-T condition quadrilaterals displays	Medial < Transverse (by about 80%)	Medial << Transverse (100% M ≈ 70% T)
Simulated STI; T-M condition quadrilaterals displays		Medial << Transverse (140% M ≈ 100% T)

Note. Relationships between medial (M) and transverse (T) extents are defined in terms of the actual visual angles they subtend (and consequently their retinal images sizes) and their predicted or actual appearance, under five observation conditions.

explained by two factors. The first factor was the quality of the 3-D rendering of the tables in Figure 9.1. We hypothesized that the Shepard's Tables illusion may occur only with nonrealistic representations of the type shown in Figure 9.1, and not with more realistically rendered 2-D representations of 3-D objects. Initial consideration of the pattern of underestimations of medial extents found in the two experiments (summarized in Table 9.5) may seem to support our hypothesis. That is, the Shepard's Tables illusion did not occur with the realistically rendered 3-D tables we used. However, we want to suggest that our results are in fact consistent with Shepard's (1981, 1990) explanation of the Shepard's Tables illusion. The rationale for this suggestion is as follows. As we have indicated, the 3-D-rendering software reduced medial extents in our displays by almost 80% compared with their corresponding transverse extents. The PSE data we obtained indicated that medial extents were indeed underestimated, but the degree of underestimation was less than half that expected if perceived extents were determined by visual angle/retinal image sizes. This finding is consistent with the operation of a size-depth constancy mechanism that was only partially effective in "compensating" for the medial foreshortening produced by the software in the displays we used. Nevertheless, it did result in the medial extents being perceived as *more like* their corresponding transverse extents than would be expected if responses were based on visual angle/retinal image sizes. The second factor we considered involved possible differences in perception of objects and perception of segments of ground planes. We hypothesized that the illusion may occur only during processing extents of objects (e.g., tables) and not extents of ground planes (e.g., signs painted on the road surface). The PSE data we obtained are partially consistent with our hypothesis in that the perceived underestimation of medial extents was about 10%–15% greater when these extents were parts of segments of a ground plane than when they were parts of tables.

That is, the failure to "compensate" for the reduced visual angles/retinal image sizes of medial extents was more pronounced with displays that simulated segments of ground planes than with those simulating segments of objects.

In general, the results we obtained seem to support the proposition that 2-D representations of 3-D medial extents are processed differently from corresponding transverse extents. This different processing seems to have the function of compensating for the reduced visual angles/retinal image sizes of 3-D medial extents that follow as a consequence of the laws of projective geometry and optics. Shepard (1981) proposed that this compensatory visual machinery evolved within 3-D environments and had "been evolutionarily shaped to become so involuntary, automatic, and efficient" (p. 297) that observers are unaware of its operation. It can be concluded from this proposition that this size-depth visual machinery should operate best during perception within such 3-D environments. The pattern of results we obtained (i.e., more compensation with simulated tables; less compensation with simulated segments of ground planes) is consistent with this conclusion. Although the displays we used were designed to render 3-D scenes more realistic than in the standard Shepard's Tables display (see Figure 9.1), our displays were nevertheless minimalist in nature with respect to spatial-depth information. Moreover, the quadrilaterals displays contained less spatial-depth information than did the tables displays. The more spatial-depth information available in the displays we used, the less underestimation of medial extents was reported and the more did comparisons of medial and transverse extents reflect their relative visual angle and retinal images sizes. This dependence of size-depth constancy of the spatial depth information available is, of course, well known (e.g., see Holway & Boring's classic 1941 study). In these terms, it follows that if we had used actual tables presented in a 3-D layout, size-depth constancy would be complete; that is, little if any underestimation of medial extents should occur. But everyday experience (e.g., with the road signs depicted in Figure 9.3) indicates that significant underestimation of medial extents does, in fact, occur under conditions containing the maximum amount of spatial-depth information.

If the interpretation we have just provided of our results is accepted, we are left with the paradox that prompted our research: On the one hand, we have overestimation of medial extents reflected in the "distorted" appearance of the Shepard's Tables illusion; on the other hand, we have underestimation of the elongated medial extents of road signs resulting in their "normal" appearance at a distance on road surfaces. We conclude by offering a resolution to this paradox based on questioning the continuum we proposed in our interpretation. The continuum was one based on the amount of spatial-depth information available in various "displays." It was anchored at the low-information end by the "virtual" quadrilaterals displays we used and at the high-information end by "real-world" road signs of the type depicted in Figure 9.3. The Shepard's Tables display in Figure 9.1 and the tables displays we used were taken to form part of this continuum, the former lying toward the low-information end and the latter toward the high-information end. In proposing this continuum, we assumed an equivalence between perception of pictures such as the Shepard's Tables illusion and 2-D simulations of 3-D scenes, and perception of real-world environments such as signs painted on road surfaces. The paradox prompting our research ceases to be a paradox if we accept Gibson's (1979) distinction between seeing the natural environment and seeing pictures.

Gibson's (1979) treatment of perception of pictures in the context of his treatment of ecological perception is instructive, in particular for his clear statement of the complexity and difficulty of perception of pictures. "The kind of vision we get from pictures is harder to understand than the kind we get from ambient light, not easier. It should be considered at the end of a treatise on perception, not at the beginning" (p. 267). He argues that pictures should not be thought of as copies or representations of real scenes:

> We have been misled for too long by the fallacy that a picture is *similar* to what it depicts, a *likeness*, or an *imitation* of it. A picture supplies some of the information for what it depicts, but that does not imply that it is in projective correspondence with what it depicts. . . . There is no such thing as a literal re-presentation of an earlier optic array. The scene cannot be re-established; the array cannot be reconstituted. Some of its invariants can be preserved, but that is all. (p. 279)

Gibson makes even more explicit the distinction between seeing pictures and seeing natural scenes by describing objects in pictures as "*virtual objects*" (p. 283) and discusses the different invariants that can be specified (in part at least) in pictures of these virtual objects. He concludes by stating

> A picture requires two kinds of apprehension, a direct perceiving of the picture surface along with an indirect awareness of what it depicts. This dual apprehension is inescapable under normal conditions of observation. The "fooling of the eye," the illusion of reality, does not occur. (p. 291)

In these terms, overestimating medial extents in pictures (like the different version of the Shepard's Tables illusion in Figures 9.1 and 9.3), and underestimating medial extents of signs on road surfaces do not constitute a paradox. This difference is evidence for Gibson's distinction.

An alternative analysis of the Shepard's Tables illusion summarized in Figure 9.7 provides further support for the proposition that different processes are involved in the Shepard's Tables illusion and in looking at signs painted on road surfaces. Figure 9.7A shows a version of the horizontal-vertical illusion (Avery & Day, 1969; Künnapas, 1955, 1957) in which lines have been replaced by identical rectangles with their *longer* sides in the vertical (medial rectangle) and horizontal (transverse rectangle) axes. Inspection of Figure 9.7A shows that in the absence of the depth cues presented in Figure 9.1, the *longer* sides of the medial rectangle look longer than the corresponding sides of the transverse rectangle. This finding is consistent with the horizontal-vertical illusion. Figure 9.7B shows the rectangles in Figure 9.7A with the addition of segments corresponding to the ends of the tabletops in Figure 9.1. Inspection of Figure 9.7B indicates to us that these segments do not add to the perception of depth in Figure 9.7B, but do increase the relative misperception that occurs when looking at Figure 9.7A. For example, overestimation of the longer sides of the medial rectangle above the added segment in Figure 9.7B compared with the *longer* sides of the transverse rectangle in Figure 9.7B is greater than the overestimation of corresponding *longer* sides in Figure 9.7A.

A

B

C

D

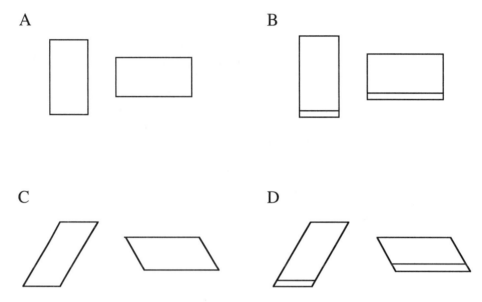

Figure 9.7. Analysis of Shepard's Table illusion in terms of the horizontal-vertical and Delboeuf illusions. (A) Horizontal-vertical illusion in the form of rectangles. The two rectangles are identical, but the one on the left (medial rectangle) appears longer and narrower than the one on the right (transverse rectangle). (B) Delboeuf illusion-type segments are added to the lower sides of both rectangles, and these increase the apparent differences between the medial and transverse rectangles. (C) and (D) These correspond to A and B, respectively, except that the longer sides of the medial rectangles have been tilted 30 deg to the right, and the shorter sides of the transverse rectangles 30 deg to the left. The parallelograms in C and D increase the apparent differences between the medial and transverse components compared with A and B, respectively.

We suggest that this apparent increase in the length of the longer sides of the medial rectangle and the shorter sides of the transverse rectangle in Figure 9.7B is a variation of the misperception of length that occurs in the Delboeuf illusion (see Coren & Girgus, 1978; Robinson, 1972). Figures 9.7C and 9.7D are versions of Figures 9.7A and 9.7B, respectively, in which the *longer* sides of the rectangles have been tilted away from the major axes by 30 deg, forming parallelograms similar to the quadrilaterals in Figure 9.1. The effect of the tilt is also to enhance the relative misperception of the *longer* sides of the parallelograms. It may be the case that by tilting the *longer* sides as we have done in Figures 9.7C and 9.7D, we are introducing a spatial-depth cue, namely, a weak form of perspective. Any enhanced overestimation of medial extents relative to transverse extents may therefore be explained by misapplied size-depth constancy. However, the enhanced misperception brought about by the addition of the Delboeuf-type components in Figures 9.7B and 9.7D cannot be explained in this way. Rather, this seems to represent a process whereby the smaller parts of a coherent figure (a virtual object in Gibson's terms) assimilate to the larger parts.

In summary, our results only partially helped us to resolve the paradox that prompted our experiments. In this sense our research passes Leibowitz's test: Good research should answer some questions and raise other questions. Our results do raise questions—in particular, whether it is justifiable to assume that looking at pictures and looking at objects in real-world environments involve identical processes. In terms of function (an approach in psychology to which Hersh Leibowitz has been committed throughout his career; see Leibowitz, 1992) these two types of looking clearly are different: Looking at Shepard's Table illusion is undertaken for amusement; looking at road signs is undertaken for guidance during driving. As Gibson (1979) said

> Vision is simplest when it fulfills its function, not when it meets the criterion of one-to-one projective correspondence in geometry. Its function is to help the observer cope with the environment. (p. 269)

Appendix 9.1

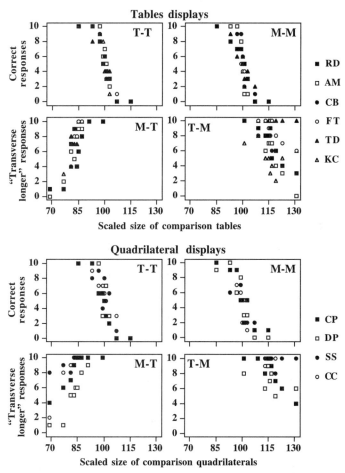

Figure 1.   Individual responses (maximum score possible is 10) of the six participants who viewed the tables displays (upper four panels) and the four participants who viewed the quadrilaterals displays (lower four panels) in Experiment 1. Results are presented as a function of the size of the comparison stimuli for each of the four conditions defined by the relative orientation of the *longer* sides of the standard and comparison stimuli. The separate definitions of "correct" responses for these conditions are given in the Results and Discussion section.

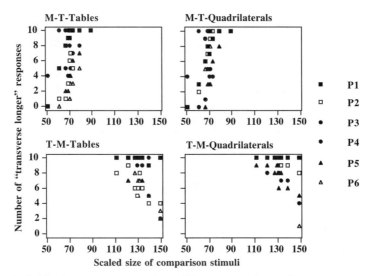

Figure 2.   Individual responses (number of "transverse longer" responses; maximum score possible is 10) of the six participants who viewed tables and quadrilaterals in Experiment 2. Results are presented as a function of the scaled size of the comparison stimuli for each of the four conditions defined by the relative orientation of the *longer* sides of the standard and comparison stimuli.

References

Avery, G. C., & Day, R. H. (1969). Basis of the horizontal-vertical illusion. *Journal of Experimental Psychology, 81,* 376–380.

Baird, J. C., & Wagner, M. (1991). Transformation theory of size judgment. *Journal of Experimental Psychology: Human Perception and Performance, 17,* 852–864.

Coren, S., & Girgus, J. S. (1978). *Seeing is deceiving: The psychology of visual illusions.* Hillsdale, NJ: Erlbaum.

Gibson, J. J. (1979). *The ecological approach to visual perception.* Boston: Houghton Mifflin.

Gregory, R. L. (1990). *Eye and brain. The psychology of seeing* (4th ed.). Oxford, England: Oxford University Press.

Harvey, L. O., Jr. (1986). Efficient estimation of sensory thresholds. *Behavior Research Methods, Instruments and Computers, 18,* 623–632.

Hennessy, R. T., & Leibowitz, H. W. (1973). Perceived vs. retinal relationships in the Ponzo illusion. *Bulletin of the Psychonomic Society, 28,* 111–112.

Holway, A. H., & Boring, E. G. (1941). Determinants of apparent visual size with distance invariant. *American Journal of Psychology, 54,* 21–37.

Künnapas, T. M. (1955). An analysis of the vertical-horizontal illusion. *Journal of Experimental Psychology, 49,* 134–140.

Künnapas, T. M. (1957). Vertical-horizontal illusion and surrounding field. *Acta Psychologica, 13,* 35–42.

Leibowitz, H. W. (1985). Grade crossing accidents and human factors engineering. *American Scientist, 73,* 558–562.

Leibowitz, H. W. (1992). Functional psychology and its societal contributions. In D. A. Owens & M. Wagner (Eds.), *Progress in contemporary psychology: The legacy of American functionalism* (pp. 17–29). Westport, CT: Praeger.

Leibowitz, H. W. (1996). The symbiosis between basic and applied research. *American psychologist, 51,* 366–370.

Leibowitz, H. W., & Pick, H. A. (1972). Cross-cultural and educational aspects of the Ponzo perspective illusion. *Perception and Psychophysics, 12,* 430–432.

Leibowitz, H. W., Wilcox, S. B., & Post, R. B. (1978). The effect of refractive error on size constancy and shape constancy. *Perception, 7,* 557–562.

Loomis, J. M., & Philbeck, J. W. (1999). Is the anisotropy of perceived 3-D shape invariant across scale? *Perception and Psychophysics, 61,* 397–402.

Macdonald, W. A., & Hoffmann, E. R. (1973). The recognition of road pavement messages. *Journal of Applied Psychology, 57,* 314–319.

Norman, J. F., Todd, J. T., Perotti, V. J., & Tittle, J. S. (1996). The visual perception of three-dimensional length. *Journal of Experimental Psychology: Human Perception and Performance, 27,* 173–186.

Robinson, J. O. (1972). *The psychology of visual illusion.* London: Hutchinson.

Shepard, R. N. (1981). Psychophysical complementary. In M. Kubovy & J. Pomerantz (Eds.), *Perceptual organization* (pp. 279–341). Hillsdale, NJ: Erlbaum.

Shepard, R. N. (1990). *Mind sights.* New York: W. H. Freeman.

Walsh, V., & Kulikowski, J. (Eds.). (1998). *Perceptual constancy. Why things look as they do.* Cambridge, England: Cambridge University Press.

10

Field Dependence With Pitched, Rolled, and Yawed Visual Frame Effects

Lawrence T. Guzy, Malcolm M. Cohen, and Sheldon M. Ebenholtz

The Festschrift for Herschel W. Leibowitz (Hersh), Evan Pugh Professor at The Pennsylvania State University, honors a truly remarkable individual. Hersh's scientific contributions to basic and applied visual perception, transportation safety, and so on are impressive. However, it is his role as mentor, collaborator, and friend that places him with the truly exceptional. He is responsible for shaping the research careers of many students and colleagues. His special style of support using unconditional positive regard enabled both budding researchers and established scientists to reach new heights. He often suggested ideas or potential studies during a lab meeting, while he trained for the next 10-km or marathon run, or during a casual conversation. He would then step back. He planted the seeds and patiently waited for them to germinate. Days, weeks, and even months would pass, and then someone would say to him, "Hersh, I was wondering whether . . ." and there was one of those ideas ready to bloom. Hersh would smile. I asked him if this was a risky approach. Hersh's response was "that's the chance you have to take." Hersh was reluctant to assign research topics, for it was telling someone "what to do." He believed that such efforts are rarely effective, as the person never really "owns the study." Hersh is enthusiastically receptive when approached by researchers wishing to be involved with his research or when he is asked to share his expertise. He is a master at putting everyone at ease with his humor and smile. Collaborating with Hersh was a peak experience. He embodied the Sigma Xi motto of being a "zealous companion in research."

Correspondence can be addressed to Lawrence T. Guzy, Department of Psychology, SUNY College at Oneonta, Oneonta, New York 13820 (e-mail: guzylt@oneonta.edu); Malcolm M. Cohen, NASA Ames Research Center, Mail Stop 239-11, Moffett Field, California 94035-1000 (e-mail: mmcohen@mail.arc.nasa.gov); or Sheldon M. Ebenholtz (e-mail: jme-sme@msn.com)

We sincerely appreciate and thank our fellow laboratory researchers, Jeannine Mealey, Jason Rogers, and Charles Deroshia for their efforts in various phases of these experiments; Jon Griffith, Dan Gundo, and Tony Purcell, who willingly offered suggestions and assisted with construction of various parts of the apparatus; the National Research Council for supporting L.T.G as a Senior Fellow at the NASA Ames Research Center; our participants, who willingly volunteered their time and efforts; and Jeff Andre, D. Alfred Owens, and the Leibowitz family for making the Festschrift a truly festive occasion.

The research was conducted in the Gravitational Science Branch of the NASA Ames Research Center, Moffett Field, California, while L.T.G. was on leave as a National Research Council Senior Fellow.

The present research reflects some of Hersh's influence. In the mid 1980s, Hersh, Mal Cohen, and Len Matin met at the "Mystery Spot" in Santa Cruz, California. Within this area gravity is apparently defied—for instance, a ball rolls uphill, a pendulum hangs at an oblique angle, and peoples' apparent heights change just by switching locations (see Banta, 1995, for a pictorial presentation of this and other mysterious sites; Shimamura & Prinzmetal; 1999). However, Figure 10.1 shows that it is strictly a perceptual effect as the house and other related structures are rolled, pitched, and yawed. In 1992, Hersh and Rick Tyrrell had just returned from a visit to Len Matin's lab to view his research version of a mystery spot, and they shared their enthusiasm and Matin's methodology with L.T.G.

The purpose of the present research was to examine the relationship among the perceptual effects associated with rolled, pitched, and yawed visual frames. Figure 10.2 depicts selected orientations of a visual array and the perceptual effects associated with each. The following research represents our efforts to honor Hersh on his Festschrift.

Rod-and-frame task. Using the classic rod-and-frame apparatus, numerous investigators have shown that a visual array that is not aligned with gravity, but rolled clockwise (CW) or counterclockwise (CCW), can alter the perception of the upright for most observers (e.g., Ebenholtz, 1977, 1985; Ebenholtz & Glaser, 1982; Witkin & Asch, 1948; Zoccolotti, Antonucci, & Spinelli, 1993). In this task, a rod that is upright and located in the center of the rolled frame may appear rolled in the direction opposite to that of the frame (see Figure 10.2). Observers who misalign the rod away from the upright and in the direction of the frame's roll are identified as field dependent. Observers who are not influenced by the rolled frame and align the rod to the upright are referred to as field independent (e.g., Witkin & Asch, 1948). If a rolled frame spatially disorients field-dependent persons, then pitched or yawed frames may similarly disorient them.

Pitched visual array task. Figure 10.3 shows that when a target is placed at the actual eye level and viewed against a vertically oriented visual array, it appears to be just slightly above its true physical position (e.g., Stoper & Cohen, 1986). When the array is pitched in the median plane with the top away from the observer (a negative pitch), or with the top toward the observer (a positive pitch), eye level may be biased in the direction of the pitch of the array. Several techniques have been used to measure Visually Perceived Eye Level (VPEL), the most common being a small circular target from either a laser light or an incandescent bulb contained within the optical array (e.g., Kleinhans, 1970; Li & Matin, 1995; MacDougall, 1903; Matin & Fox, 1989; Matin & Li, 1992, 1994, 1995, 1999; Stoper & Cohen, 1989, 1991; Welch & Post, 1996). Cohen, Ebenholtz, and Linder (1995) incorporated a second technique along with a small target. They recorded gaze elevation using a small infrared camera system and found that gaze

Figure 10.1.   The "Mystery Spot" in Santa Cruz, California, where a ball apparently rolls uphill and a person stands at an off-upright orientation. The insert identifies the actual state of affairs. Personal photo: L.T.G. Reprinted with permission.

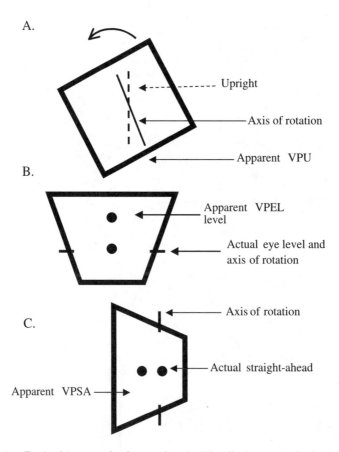

Figure 10.2.   Retinal image of a frame that is (A) rolled counterclockwise, (B) pitched to a positive orientation (top closer to observer), and (C) yawed left (left side closer to observer) and the respective effects on Visually Perceived Upright (VPU), Visually Perceived Eye Level (VPEL), and Visually Perceived Straight Ahead VPSA).

elevation and target placement were essentially identical. Poquin, Ohlmann, and Barraud (1997) deviated from the customary circular target and used a short stripe (1 cm).

Yawed frame task. An observer is relatively accurate when locating the straight-ahead. When the frame is yawed to the left (left side is closer to the observer; see Figure 10.2) or the right (right side is closer), perception of the straight-ahead as measured by a circular target may be displaced in the direction of the yawed frame's orientation (Kleinhans, 1970).

Three experiments were conducted to examine the relationship between field dependence and field independence as determined by the classic rod-and-frame task on the settings of targets to VPEL with a pitched frame and the Visually Perceived Straight Ahead (VPSA) with a yawed frame.

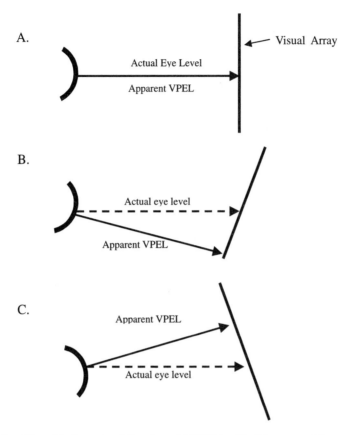

Figure 10.3. Visually Perceived Eye Level (VPEL) with (A) an erect frame, (B) a negatively pitched frame (top farther away from observer), and (C) a positively pitched frame (top closer to observer).

Experiment 1

Method

Participants. Thirty-two men and 21 women volunteered to participate. They ranged in age from 18 to 59 years ($M = 24.9$ years). All reported normal eyesight, hearing, and vestibular functioning. The NASA Ames Human Institutional Review Board approved all of the following procedures.

Apparatus. A rectangular frame containing 1.27-cm-wide electroluminescent lines, 97 cm high x 86 cm wide, was capable of being rolled, pitched, and yawed. In the yaw orientation, the longer sides of the frame were on the top and bottom. For the roll orientation, an electroluminescent rod (24 x 1.27 cm) located in the middle of the frame was capable of being rotated CW and CCW from the vertical position. For the pitch and yaw orientations of the frame, a 2 mm in diameter target was positioned by the participant to the VPEL and VPSA, respectively.

These targets were produced by two small laser light sources. For identifying VPEL, the laser was located immediately to the left and level with the outer canthus of the left eye. Using a toggle switch, the participant controlled the target's upward and downward movement. For identifying VPSA, a second laser was positioned in the median plane just above the head. Using the same toggle switch, the participant controlled the target's left-right movement. As measured from the nasion, participants were seated at a distance of 1.4 m from the frame. From this distance, the frame diagonal subtended a visual angle of 43 deg.

Procedure. Participants' head movements were reduced with a chin and forehead rest. Their eyes were aligned with respect to the center of the frame, which also coincided with actual eye level and the straight-ahead.

For the pitch, roll, and yaw orientations, the frame was positioned at zero and at 30-deg deviations in each direction from zero, that is, pitched with the top toward or away from the participant, rolled CW or CCW, and yawed with the right side closer to the participant or the left side closer, respectively. Negative values were assigned to a frame when it was pitched with the top away from the participant, rotated in a CCW direction, and yawed to the left, with the left side of the frame closer to the observer. The order of presentation of the three frame orientations was counterbalanced, and for each frame orientation, the three angles of frame rotation also were counterbalanced. Four trials were presented for each frame position. Quasi-randomly determined, the target's starting position for the pitch task approached the inside top or bottom edge of the frame and for the yaw task approached the left and right inside edge of the sides of the frame; presentation order was either top-bottom-bottom-top or bottom-top-top-bottom and left-right-right-left or right-left-left-right, respectively. For roll, the rod was rotated at least 23–27 deg beyond the vertical position. Its starting position followed a presentation order of CW-CCW-CCW-CW or CCW-CW-CW-CCW.

The instructions for each task were presented just prior to performing that task. For roll, the participants were instructed to place the rod so that it was upright or vertical with respect to gravity and the long axis of their body (postural vertical). They were shown a drawing of how the rod would look if it were placed upright with respect to their bodies and to gravity. They were presented with a rod and shown how the rod should be placed so that it would not fall to the left or right if properly aligned. A minimum of two practice trials were given in which the experimenter rotated a rod and the participant indicated when the rod appeared upright. For pitch, participants were instructed to align the small target to eye level. Eye level was defined as that position where gaze elevation was parallel with the ground, which also corresponds to gravity-referenced eye level. They were shown a drawing of an eye looking to eye level at a far wall. The experimenter explained that if measurements were taken of the distances from where the eyes were looking on the far wall to the floor and then from the participant's eyes to the floor, the two measures would be identical. A minimum of two practice trials were given in which the starting position on a spot was above and below actual eye level and the participant identified when it was at eye level. For yaw, participants were instructed to place the target to the point that was straight-ahead. Straight-ahead was

defined as that point where the eyes converged and an imaginary line extending from the nose would contact that spot. The participant was shown a
drawing of two eyes converging on a point directly straight-ahead. A minimum
of two practice trials were given in which a spot was moved from left to right
and the participant identified when it reached the straight-ahead. When the
experimenter was assured that the participant understood the task, the room
lights were extinguished. After 1 min elapsed, an opaque screen, blocking the
view of the apparatus, was removed. Prior to each trial, participants were
requested to close his or her eyes. Frame orientation, rotation, or initial target
placement, or a combination of the three was accomplished with all lights
extinguished. At the start of each trial, the frame and the appropriate target
stimulus were illuminated, and the experimenter instructed the participant to
open his or her eyes, and set the rod or target to upright, eye level, or straight-
ahead. The method of adjustment with bracketing was used for the three tasks.
Participants were given as much time as they needed to position the target
stimulus and to signal when they were satisfied with the setting. A posttest
interview was conducted immediately after completion of the data collection.
Participants were asked to describe their strategy for placing the target
stimulus to the upright, to eye level, and to the straight-ahead. One participant's data were omitted. The participant indicated that the rolled frame was
confusing and affected the setting of the rod to the upright. To reduce the confusion, the participant squinted until the frame could no longer be perceived.

Results and Discussion

The performance across the four trials was highly reliable. To allow a more
direct comparison with Experiments 2 and 3, only the first two trials for each
stimulus orientation were analyzed.

Figure 10.4 presents the results of the within-subjects analysis of
variance (ANOVA) interaction between Visually Perceived Upright (VPU)/roll,
VPEL/pitch, and VPSA/yaw and each frame's negative, zero, and positive rotations, $F(4, 204) = 9.23$, $p < .0001$. According to the figure, changes in the
frame's orientation and rotation produced systematic linear changes in the
perception of the VPU/rolled frame, VPEL/pitched frame, and VPSA/yawed
frame. The yaw frame's effects on the straight-ahead were very small. Main
effects for frame orientation and rotation were significant: $F(2, 102) = 9.94$, $p
< .0001$, and $F(2, 102) = 64.03$, $p < .0001$, respectively. A post hoc test showed
that the perceptual effects on the VPU/rolled frame and VPEL/pitched frame
were not significantly different from each other, but both were significantly
different from the VPSA/yawed frame, Tukey Honestly Significant Difference
test, $p < .002$.

Slope functions were computed and yielded mean values of 0.15 for VPU/
roll, 0.13 for VPEL/pitch, and 0.035 for VPSA/yaw effects. A within-participants
ANOVA showed a significant effect, $F(2, 102) = 9.23$, $p < .001$. A Pearson correlation test showed no relationship in perceptual effects with rolled, pitched,
and yawed frame slopes. Poquin et al. (1997) compared VPEL using a short rod
and the VPU orientation with the standard-sized rod and reported a significant

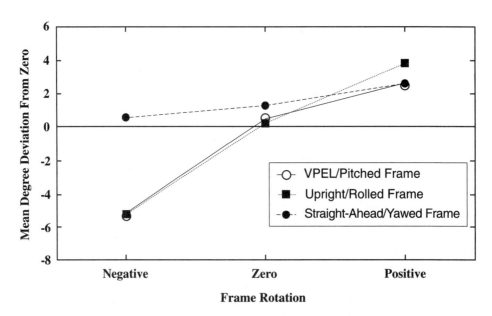

Figure 10.4.   Mean degree deviation from zero in the perception of upright, eye level, and straight-ahead as a function of frame orientation and rotation in Experiment 1, which used dissimilar stimuli and binocular viewing.

relationship.[1] Possibly, this short line for VPEL settings was a more appropriate target stimulus than a circular target used in our study.

Field dependence. Participants were categorized as either field dependent or field independent based on their slope scores in setting a rod to the upright. The mean slope for the field dependent group was 0.29 ($N = 26$, $SD = 0.27$, range = 0.063–0.96). For the field independent group, the mean slope was 0.02 ($N = 26$, $SD = 0.03$, range = –0.036–0.057). These two groups were significantly different, $F(1, 50) = 25.25$, $p < .0001$.

Two one-way ANOVAs were separately conducted on the slope values of the pitch and yaw frame effects for field-dependent and field-independent observers. Field-dependent observers showed a larger shift in VPEL than did the independent observers, $F(1, 50) = 9.05$, $p < .01$. Although a pitched frame affected the perception of eye level for both field-dependent and field-independent individuals, field-dependent observers showed an effect almost double that of their Independent counterparts ($M = 0.17$ vs. 0.09). No difference for yawed frame effects was found between field-dependent and field-independent individuals.

The limitation of a VPSA was its small slope effect ($M = 0.04$) and high variability ($SD = 0.07$), a problem also noted by Kleinhans (1970; see also Li & Matin 1995). Neither Kleinhans' study nor our research was able to identify

---

[1]We reanalyzed our slope results using the Spearman nonparametric correlation coefficient test as reported by Poquin et al. (1997). In Experiment 1, VPEL and VPU were related, $rs = 0.33$. For Experiments 2 and 3, all intercorrelations were significant and ranged from 0.41 to 0.59 and 0.34 to 0.39, respectively.

whether the performance with a yawed frame was an independent process or simply resulted from a small slope value and high variability, which masked any possible relationship. We modified the apparatus and target stimulus to be more comparable in Experiments 2 and 3, which may increase the systematic effects and precision of the VPSA.

In Experiment 1, we used target stimuli that were commonly associated with each of the tasks, that is, an illuminated rod for determining upright with a rolled frame and a small circular target for determining the VPEL/pitched frame and the VPSA/yawed frame. Possibly, circular targets are not appropriate when comparing frame effects, especially with a rolled frame in which a rod is used. A similarly dimensioned target stimulus may be more appropriate for comparing frame effects, as shown in Figure 10.5.

Experiment 2

The apparatus was modified to ensure that the frame and rod produced the same retinal image when they were placed in the null positions. The frame's dimensions were modified to form a square and not a rectangle as found in Experiment 1. The resulting diagonal visual angle of the frame was reduced from 43 to 40 deg. An electroluminescent target rod, 60 cm x 2.5 cm, was used for determining all adjustments.

Method

Participants. Twenty-eight men and 21 women volunteered to participate. They ranged in age from 18 to 60 years, with a mean age of 34.8 years. By self-report, all were healthy and without visual or vestibular impairment.

Procedure. We used identical manipulanda for adjustments to the VPU, VPEL, and VPSA with rolled, pitched, and yawed frames, respectively. We reduced the number of trials from four to two for each of the three tasks, and the frame was positioned 22 deg instead of 30 deg, considered to be an optimum orientation for the rolled frame. Except for these changes, the procedure was essentially the same as that of Experiment 1.

Results and Discussion

Figure 10.6 contains the within-subjects ANOVA's significant interaction of frame orientation plotted as a function of frame rotation, $F(4, 192) = 23.28$, $p < .0001$. According to the figure, frame rotation resulted in a linear change in the apparent perception of upright, VPEL, and the straight-ahead. Results were similar to those of Experiment 1. Main effects for frame orientation and rotation were significant: $F(2, 96) = 7.87$, $p < .001$; and $F(2, 96) = 83.27$, $p < .0001$, respectively.

Mean slope values of 0.21 for VPU/rolled, 0.19 for VPEL/pitched, and 0.05 for VPSA/yawed frame effects were computed. A within-participants ANOVA showed a significant difference, $F(2, 96) = 27.5$, $p < .0001$. As in Experiment 1,

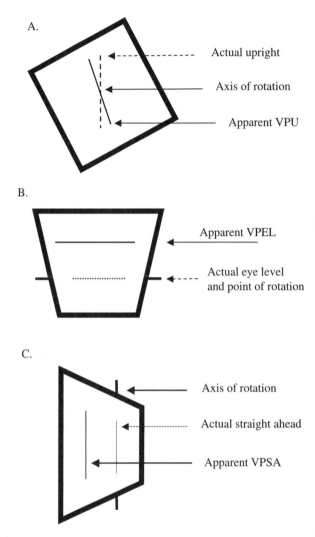

Figure 10.5.   Retinal image of (A) rolled, (B) pitched, and (C) yawed frame orientations and the common stimulus rods used for identifying Visually Perceived Upright (VPU), Visually Perceived Eye Level (VPEL), and Visually Perceived Straight Ahead (VPSA) in Experiments 2 and 3.

a Tukey Honestly Significant Difference test showed that pitch and roll slopes did not differ from each other but were significantly different from yaw, $p <$ .001. An intercorrelational analysis showed that perception of the VPU/rolled frame and VPEL/pitched frame were related, r (47) = 0.38, $p <$ .01, and VPEL and the VPSA/yawed frame were related r (47) = 0.34, $p <$ .02. However, perception of the upright and the straight-ahead were not related.

Field dependence. Observers were categorized as field dependent (N = 31, M = 0.26, SD = 0.20, range = 0.093–0.91) or field independent (N = 18, M = 0.06, SD = 0.12, range = –0.052–0.07) based on their rolled frame effect slope

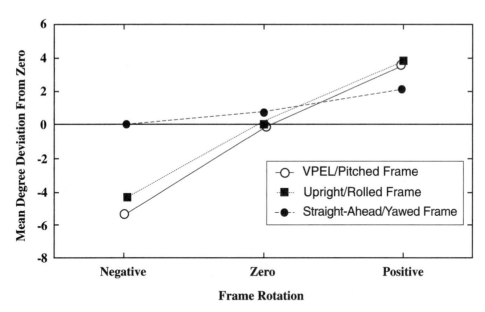

Figure 10.6.   Mean degree deviation from zero of the perception of upright, eye level, and straight ahead as a function frame orientation and rotation in Experiment 2, which used identical stimuli and binocular viewing.

values. The groups were significantly different from each other, $F(1, 47) = 16.1$, $p < .001$.

Two one-way ANOVAs were conducted on the slope values of the pitched and yawed frames for field-dependent and field-independent observers. VPEL for both field-dependent and field-independent observers was affected by the frame's pitch. Field-dependent observers showed a larger shift in perceived VPEL ($M = 0.23$) than did the field-independent observers ($M = 0.16$), $F(1, 47) = 4.20$, $p < . 05$. No difference for the effects of yawed frame slopes was found between field-dependent and field-independent individuals. A test–retest correlation analysis of the two trials showed that unlike roll ($r = 0.96$, $p < .001$) and pitch ($r = 0.89$, $p < .001$), the correlation of the two trials for the perception of the straight-ahead was significant but not as stable, $r (47) = 0.78$, $p < .001$.

Results from Experiments 1 and 2 showed that regardless of the rotation of the yawed frame, the mean VPSA was biased to the right of the actual straight-ahead, an effect found in Kleinhans' (1970) results as well. This bias may reflect the dominance of the right eye when the straight-ahead was aligned with that eye or the difficulty in attempting to converge on an ambiguous point under impoverished viewing conditions.

Experiment 3

We reasoned that requiring the use of monocular vision might capitalize on the tendency to align the rod with one and not both eyes and thereby increase the effects of a yawed frame (e.g., Porac & Coren, 1986). In our experiments the surrounding frame subtended an angle of at least 40 deg. A large visual frame stimulates the ambient visual system (Leibowitz & Post, 1982; Post & Welch, 1996). This phenomenon is mediated by peripheral retinal processing, functions automatically, and contributes to spatial orientation. Ebenholtz (1985) compared coplanar (monocular) and binocular viewing with a depth separation between the rod and frame. No difference was found between the two viewing conditions. Ebenholtz assumed that the rod-and-frame effect was primarily due to retinal stimulation and ambient-system processing. However, distance is invariant for the traditional rod-and-frame task, but not for pitch and yaw. Nevertheless, research indicates that binocular and monocular vision with a pitched array produced no appreciable difference between them (e.g., Li & Matin, 1995; Matin & Li, 1999; Stoper & Cohen, 1989). Further, tilting two vertically placed lines on a flat surface with their tops closer together and bottoms farther apart produces the equivalent of a negatively pitched frame on the retina. These line rotations eliminate the influence of perceived depth and have been found to produce changes in VPEL effects similar to those of a pitched visual array (Matin & Li, 1992, 1999; Post & Welch, 1996). Because a yawed frame is a 90-deg rotation of the pitched frame, it may be the case that yawed frame effects are subserved by ambient-system processing as well.

Method

Participants. Thirty-one men and 26 women volunteered to participate. They ranged in age from 18 to 65 years, with a mean of 36.7 years. By self-report, all were healthy and without visual or vestibular impairment.

Procedure. With the left eye occluded (monocular vision) , the participants' right eye was aligned with the center of the frame regardless of eye dominance.[2] The apparatus and procedure were identical to those of Experiment 2.

Results and Discussion

A one-way between subjects meta-analysis was conducted on the yawed slope scores across the three experiments. Slope values were significantly different: $F (2, 155) = 7.75$, $p < .001$. A Tukey Honestly Significant Difference test showed that VPSA in Experiment 3 produced systematically larger effects than did Experiments 1 and 2. A Pearson correlation coefficient showed that performance between Trials 1 and 2 in Experiment 3 was increased and very reliable, $r (55) = 0.87$, $p < .001$.

Figure 10.7 shows the interaction of the three-by-three within-subjects ANOVA (pitch-roll-yaw orientation $\times$ rotations within each orientation). Results were similar to those of Experiments 1 & 2, in which the main effects

---

[2]Eye dominance was assessed by two different tasks. In one, participants were asked to pick up a small magnifying glass placed on the table in their median plane and examine their fingertip. The eye that looked through the lens was identified as the dominant eye. In the other task, they were requested to point at a distant target with both eyes opened and then selectively close and open each eye and identify which finger was still pointing to the target.

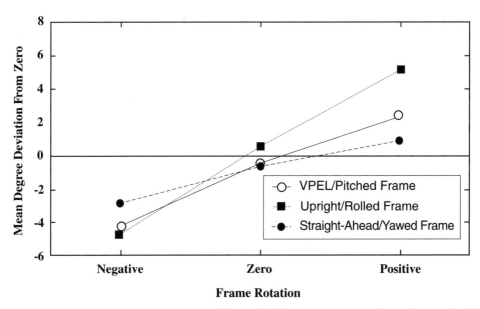

Figure 10.7.   Mean degree deviation from zero of the perception of upright, eye level, and straight-ahead as a function frame orientation and rotation in Experiment 3, which used identical stimuli and monocular viewing.

for frame orientation, rotation, and their interaction were significant: $F(2, 112) = 4.42$, $p < 0.02$; $F(2, 112) = 135.91$, $p < 0.0001$; and $F(4, 224) = 14.15$, $p < 0.0001$, respectively.

Mean slope values of 0.22 for the perception of VPU/rolled frame, 0.15 for perception of VPEL/pitched frame, and 0.08 for perception of straight-ahead with a yawed frame were computed. Pearson correlation coefficient values for rod settings to VPU, VPEL and VPSA were significant: roll and pitch r (55) = 0.29, $p < .01$, and roll and yaw r (55) = 0.28, $p < .02$.

Field dependence. The participants were assigned to field-dependent ($M = 0.29$, $N = 42$, $SD = 0.19$, range 0.07–0.79) and field-independent groups ($M = 0.03$, N = 15, SD = 0.02, range = -.004–0.066) groups, $F(1, 55) = 27.4$, $p < .001$.

Figure 10.8 contains the interaction between field-dependent and field-independent observers as a function of the rotation of the yawed frame, $F(2, 110) = 4.28$, $p < 0.02$. Field-dependent observers showed a systematic linear increase, whereas field-independent observers showed a smaller and less systematic effect. With the use of slope values, separate ANOVAS were conducted for VPEL and straight-ahead for field-dependent and field-independent observers. Field-dependent observers showed a significantly larger shift in VPEL than did field-independent observers, $F(1, 55) = 7.22$, $p < 0.01$. The mean slope value for field-dependent observers was 0.17 and for field-independent observers was 0.09. Yawed frame slopes differed significantly between the field-dependent ($M = 0.09$) and the field-independent ($M = 0.05$) groups, $F(1, 55) = 5.44$, $p < .05$.

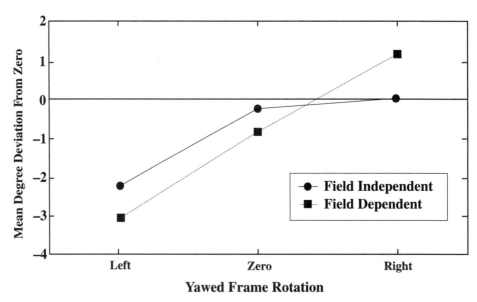

Figure 10.8. Mean degree deviation from zero for field-dependent and field-independent observers with a yawed frame's negative (left), zero, and positive (right) rotations in Experiment 3.

General Discussion

The procedural changes in Experiment 3 systematically increased the linear effects of the yawed frame over those found in Experiments 1 and 2. These larger effects permitted a comparison with setting the rod to the VPU orientation/rolled frame and VPEL/pitched frame. According to the results, observers who were affected by a rolled frame in locating VPU were similarly influenced by pitch and yaw in setting the target rod to VPEL and VPSA, respectively. These findings suggest a commonality in perceptual effects among the three frame orientations. Field dependence may be a valid construct for describing the perceptual influence of any off-axis orientation of a visual array; however, field dependence accounted for only a modest portion of the variance (maximum $r^2 = 0.14$) (see Shimamura & Prinzmetal, 1999, for a discussion of an orientation framing theory and tilt-induced effects).

However, the relationship of yawed frame effects to that of pitch and roll is problematic. Poquin et al. (1997) found that VPU and VPEL were related, as both effects are the result of the sum of the influence of gravity-related cues and visual cues. On the other hand, gravity-related cues are absent with a yawed frame, and target placement would be based solely on the influence of the visual cues associated with the frame's left-right orientation (see also Li & Matin, 1995). Li and Matin examined the relationship between VPSA and VPEL. They reported that the mean slope for the VPSA was zero, and hence no relationship was found with VPEL. They suggested three alternative explanations for the failure of their horizontally placed lines to produce systematic effects: (a) the insufficiency of the visual stimulus, by its nature, to produce systematic effects, (b) problems with extraretinal eye position information, and (c) the lack of gravity-based information (Li & Matin, 1995, p. 80). Both research by Kleinhans (1970) and our present research did reveal a small systematic effect with a closed visual array. Possibly, such a figure with defined left-right limits contains sufficient aspects of visual stimulation to produce a small systematic influence for the VPSA/yawed frame; see (a) above. The lack of a stronger effect associated with the VPSA/yawed frame may be due primarily to extraretinal eye position information without any gravity-based information. Placing a rod to the VPSA with a yawed frame may rely on binocular vision, as was the case in Experiments 1 and 2. In this situation, vergence cues were sufficient to reduce the yawed frame's effects. In Experiment 3, which used monocular vision, these cues were absent and the VPSA was affected by the yawed frame.

Another problematic issue occurred with the visual effects of the pitched and yawed frames for field-independent and field-dependent observers. Both groups were influenced by these off-axis orientations of the frames, more so for field-dependent observers. This was not the case for the rolled frame. The rolled frame detrimentally affected field-dependent observers, whereas the field-independent observers continued to identify the upright correctly.

In summary, each of the three frame orientations has its own unique function in the terrestrial environment. These different cues—roll, pitch, and yaw—provide two kinds of information, direction and elevation, and different processes encode them. All three cues play a role in locomotor activity. Roll and pitch cues have the added dimension of maintaining postural stability. Isableu, Ohlmann, Cremieux, and Amblard (1997) reported that field-dependent observers showed greater instability on the sharpened-Romberg task, that is, placing one foot directly in front of the other and crossing arms across the chest, than did field-independent observers, regardless of the orientation of the frame (upright or rolled). This lateral swaying affects postural stability. Pitched cues may pose a similar risk, but to median plane postural stability. For example, MacDougall (1903) cited an observation made by Munsterberg in the course of traveling in hill country. Munsterberg reported "that a curious negative displacement of the subjective horizon took place when one looked across a downward slope to a distant cliff, the attitude (in relation to the observer's own standpoint) of specific points on a wall of rock being largely overestimated" (MacDougall, 1903, p. 161).

We now end by returning to Hersh's influence. A number of years ago, a budding researcher came up with a research problem and asked Hersh for his advice on its merits. Without hesitation, Hersh replied, "You have a right to be wrong." Hersh indicated that the only way to discover whether a problem merits further investigation is to pursue it and not seek advice from an expert. He then cited the unfortunate case of Edwin B. Twitmeyer (ca. 1900), who was investigating whether the patellar tendon reflex was affected by the emotional or motivational state of his subjects. After hundreds of trials in which a warning light alerted the subject that a small hammer was about to hit the patellar tendon, Twitmeyer accidentally triggered the light without dropping the hammer. To his surprise, the classic knee jerk response still occurred without patellar tendon stimulation. At about the same time but unknown to

Western psychologists, Pavlov was examining a similar phenomenon, which he called a psychic reflex. Twitmeyer presented his research at a meeting of the American Psychological Association (1904), where he received a silent reception from "experts" including the chair of his session, William James. Twitmeyer dropped this line of research (Miseo & Samelson, 1983).

This anecdote reflects two key features about Hersh: He knows the inside story of the history of psychological research, and he immediately encourages a research idea enthusiastically and unequivocally so as not to repeat those past mistakes. Hersh is aware that even a moment of silence can be misinterpreted.

From his Festschrift, Hersh can rest assured that his fondest expectations have been exceeded in that his unique style is embodied in so many of us.

References

Banta, C. (1995). *Seeing is believing? Haunted shacks, mystery spots, and other delightful phenomena*. Agoura Hills, CA: Funhouse Press.

Cohen, M. M., Ebenholtz, S. M., & Linder, B. J. (1995). Effects of optical pitch on oculomotor control and the perception of target elevation. *Perception and Psychophysics, 57*, 433–440.

Ebenholtz, S. M. (1977). Determinants of the rod and frame effect: The role of retinal size. *Perception and Psychophysics, 22*, 531–538.

Ebenholtz, S. M. (1985). Depth separation fails to modulate the orientation inhibition effect. *Perception and Psychophysics, 37*, 533–535.

Ebenholtz, S. M., & Glaser, G. W. (1982). Absence of depth processing in the large-frame rod-and-frame effect. *Perception and Psychophysics, 32*, 134–140.

Isableu, B., Ohlmann, T., Cremieux, J., & Amblard, B. (1997). Selection of spatial frame of reference and postural control variability. *Experimental Brain Research, 114*, 584–589.

Kleinhans, J. L. (1970). *Perception of spatial orientation in sloped, slanted, and tilted visual field*. Unpublished doctoral dissertation, Rutgers University, Rutgers, New Jersey.

Leibowitz, H. W., & Post, R. B. (1982). The two modes of processing concept and some implications. In J. J. Beck (Ed.), *Organization and representation in perception* (pp. 343–363). New York: Erlbaum.

Li, W., & Matin, L. (1995). Differences in influence between pitched-from-vertical and slanted-from-frontal horizontal lines on egocentric localization. *Perception and Psychophysics, 57*, 71–83.

MacDougall, R. (1903). The subjective horizon. *Psychological Review Monograph, 4*, 145–166.

Matin, L., & Fox, C. R. (1989). Visually perceived eye level and perceived elevation of objects: Linearly additive influences from visual field pitch and from gravity. *Vision Research, 29*, 315–324.

Matin, L., & Li, W. (1992). Visually perceived eye level: Changes induced by a pitched-from-vertical 2-line visual field. *Journal of Experimental Psychology: Human Perception Performance, 18*, 257–289.

Matin, L., & Li, W. (1994). The influence of a stationary single line in darkness on the visual perception of eye level. *Vision Research, 34*, 311–330.

Matin, L., & Li, W. (1995). Multimodal basis for egocentric spatial localization and orientation. *Journal of Vestibular Research, 6*, 499–518.

Matin, L., & Li, W. (1999). Combining influences from lines of different orientation on visually perceived eye level: I. Averaging and summation between two long lines differing in pitch or roll-tilt. *Vision Research, 39*, 307–329.

Miseo, G., & Samelson, F. (1983). History of Psychology: XXXIII. On textbook lessons from history, or how the conditioned reflex discovered Twitmeyer. *Psychological Reports, 52*, 447–454.

Poquin, D., Ohlmann, T., & Barraud, P. A. (1997). Isotropic visual field effects on spatial orientation and egocentric localization. *Spatial Vision, 1*, 261–278.

Porac, C., & Coren, S. (1986). Sighting dominance and egocentric localization. *Vision Research, 26*, 1709–1713.

Post, R. B., & Welch, R. B. (1996). The role of retinal versus perceived size in the effects of pitched displays on visually perceived eye level. *Perception, 25,* 853–859.

Shimamura, A. P., & Prinzmetal, W. (1999). The Mystery Spot illusion and its relation to other visual illusions. *Psychological Science, 10,* 501–507.

Stoper, A. E., & Cohen, M. M. (1986). Judgments of eye level in light and in darkness. *Perception and Psychophysics, 40,* 311–316.

Stoper, A. E., & Cohen, M. M. (1989). Effect of structured visual environments on apparent eye level. *Perception and Psychophysics, 46,* 469–475.

Stoper, A. E., & Cohen, M. M. (1991). Optical, gravitational, and kinesthetic determinants of judged eye level. In S. R. Ellis, M. K. Kaiser, & A. C. Grunwald (Eds.), *Pictorial communication in virtual and real environments* (pp. 390–403). New York: Taylor & Francis.

Welch, R. B., & Post, R. B. (1996). Accuracy and adaptation of reaching and pointing in pitched visual environments. *Perception and Psychophysics, 58,* 383–389.

Witkin, H. A., & Asch, S. (1948). Studies in space orientation: IV. Further experiments on perception of the upright with displaced visual fields. *Journal of Experimental Psychology, 38,* 762–782.

Zoccolotti, P., Antonucci, G., & Spinelli, D. (1993). The gap between rod and frame influences the rod-and-frame effect with small and large inducing displays. *Perception and Psychophysics, 54,* 14–19.

11

Perception and Action

Two Modes of Processing Visual Information

Robert B. Post, Robert B. Welch, and Bruce Bridgeman

Visual perception and action have traditionally been assumed to involve a sequential relationship in which one first visually perceives an object and then responds (e.g., reaches, grasps) with respect to it on the basis of this perceptual representation. This relationship between perception and action is straight-forward and appears consistent with everyday experience and introspection. However, a different view has recently been proposed and developed. In this alternate view, early vision is the source of *parallel* inputs to both visual perception (and therefore cognition and memory) and motor behavior. Thus, the relationship between these two systems, termed the *perceptual-cognitive* and *sensorimotor* systems, respectively, is one of common input rather than identity. These two views of the relationship between perception and action are outlined in Figure 11.1.

Background

An early demonstration of the existence of separate neurological processing for different visual functions was provided by Schneider (1967, 1969), who studied the deficits resulting from lesions of the visual cortex and superior colliculus of the hamster. Specifically, animals with lesions of the visual cortex suffered impairments of form perception but were able to localize objects, whereas those with damage to the superior colliculus experienced the opposite effects. Trevarthen (1968) reported a similar example of dissociation of form and location processing via selective lesion in the monkey and proposed the terms *focal* and *ambient* for the systems mediating object perception and visual orienting, respectively. Both Schneider and Trevarthen (1968) described their findings at a symposium titled "Two Modes of Visual Processing" at the 1967 Eastern Psychological Association meetings. As part of the same symposium, Ingle (1967) reported differences in the role of vision for object perception and spatial orientation in fish, and Held (1968, 1970) applied the distinction between focal and ambient vision to humans. Held's argument was that the responses of the two systems to exposure to optical rearrangement (e.g., prismatic displacement) were different, the ambient system being capable of adaptation and the focal system not being capable of it.

Traditional View

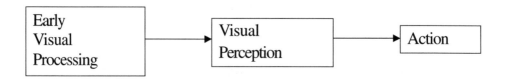

Alternate View

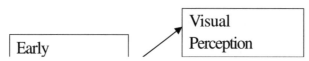

Figure 11.1   Traditional and alternate views of the relationship between perception and action.

Soon after this concept of two visual systems was proposed, evidence emerged suggesting that the systems could be dissociated in humans as the result of central nervous system damage. Specifically, it was found that despite the fact that patients with scotomata from focused damage to the visual cortex failed to report the presence of stimuli located in the "blind" areas of their visual fields, they were able to point at or direct their eyes to them with little or no error (e.g., Poppel, Held, & Frost, 1973; Sanders, Warrington, Marshall, & Weiskrantz, 1974). This phenomenon was termed *blindsight* and received considerable further attention (e.g., Bridgeman & Staggs, 1982; Weiskrantz, 1996; Weiskrantz, Warrington, Sanders, & Marshall, 1974). It should be noted, however, that blindsight is not universally obtained in cases of cortical damage, and methodological concerns have been raised about some of the findings and their interpretations (Campion, Latto, & Smith, 1983; Fendrich, Wessinger, & Gazzaniga, 1992). More recently, a form of blindsight was obtained for human observers whose visual cortexes were intact. Kolb and Braun (1995) showed that normal observers are able to localize targets that are defined by texture contrast with their backgrounds but that are not consciously experienced, as indicated by only chance levels of detection.

Another concept to emerge from the two visual systems hypothesis is that substantial functional differences exist between the focal and ambient visual systems. The proposal by Held (1968, 1970) that these systems are differentially influenced by exposure to optical rearrangement was mentioned previously. A number of additional functional differences were suggested by Leibowitz and his colleagues (e.g., Leibowitz & Post, 1981; Leibowitz, Shupert-Rodemer, & Dichgans, 1979), as seen in Table 11.1. Leibowitz and colleagues argued further that the functional distinctions between the two systems were likely to have important implications for performance of tasks such as driving (e.g., Leibowitz and Owens, 1977, 1986). For example, night-time conditions are likely to impair focal function but leave the ambient functions unaffected. This in turn could give rise to an unwarranted degree of confidence in drivers at night.

Although the two visual systems hypothesis emerged from work demonstrating a role of the cortex in focal vision and the midbrain structures in ambient vision, Mishkin, Ungerleider, and Macko (1983) subsequently proposed two *cortical* visual processing streams with a functional dichotomy analogous to the two visual systems hypothesis. According to them, the ventral stream in the inferotemporal cortex subserves the *what* system (analogous to focal vision), whereas the dorsal stream in the posterior parietal cortex subserves the *where* system (analogous to ambient vision). Bridgeman (1991) revised the dichotomy again, noting that meaningful *what* questions can be asked of *both* branches—one merely receives different answers from the two systems, at least under certain circumstances. Paillard (1987) described a precursor of this distinction, as have Milner and Goodale (1995). According to the latter authors, the real distinction between ventral and dorsal cortical streams is that the former is the channel for visual perception (the *what*), whereas the latter subserves visually guided behavior (the *how*). The presumed evolutionary advantage of this arrangement is that it allows spatially directed behavior to be very rapid and efficient because it is being implemented by a dedicated processor that operates solely upon the here-and-now goal of the motor action. The perceptual-cognitive system, in contrast, specializes in recognizing the identities of objects based on comparisons with prior knowledge, as well as their spatial interrelationships (i.e., allocentric location).

The existence of parallel processing streams suggests the possibility that they compute and use different spatial values and are dissociable (i.e., perception-action dissociation). Because under most circumstances the sensorimotor and perceptual–cognitive systems lead to perceptual experiences and motor actions that are consistent with one another, evidence for their dissociability is most likely to come from studies in which this congruence is disrupted. Such perturbations can occur as a result of either experimental intervention in normal participants or certain

Table 11.1. Functional Differences Between the Two Visual Systems

	Visual field location	Refractive error	Awareness	Luminance sensitivity	Resolution
Focal	Greatest in central vision	Blur-sensitive	Aware	Sensitive	Fine
Ambient	Uniform	Insensitive	Unaware	Insensitive	Coarse

types of brain injury in clinical patients. For example, Goodale, Milner, Jakobson, and Carey (1991) described a carbon monoxide-poisoned patient, D. F., who was unable to identify the orientation of a slot perceptually but who could nevertheless correctly place objects in it. Many other instances of behavior in the absence of perception, as well as perception in the absence of behavioral capability (i.e., double dissociation), have been reviewed by Milner and Goodale (1995). For example, some neurologically impaired patients reveal symptoms of visual apraxia—the inability to reach for and grasp objects appropriately despite being able to identify them. This deficit is not the result of general motor damage, because grasping responses that are not guided by vision remain normal. In this pathologic condition, information in the perceptual pathway needed to control accurate grasping and reaching is unavailable. Conversely, Rossetti, Rode, and Boisson (1995) describe neurologically impaired patients who could grasp objects appropriately but, like D. F., were unable to describe them.

However, neither the possession of two anatomically distinct visual systems nor evidence of perception-action dissociation in brain-damaged patients guarantees that such dissociation obtains for the intact brain. Rather, there is the possibility that a system that is unified and coordinated in normal individuals becomes fragmented in brain-damaged patients. Thus, it should be clear that incontrovertible evidence that perception-action dissociation occurs for normal (i.e., brain-intact) human beings can only be obtained from studies that use them as participants. Perceptual-motor dissociation (or possible dissociation) has been reported in normal humans for a variety of situations. These include

- size-contrast illusions (Aglioti, DeSouza, & Goodale, 1995; Haffenden & Goodale, 1998),
- the Mueller-Lyer illusion; (Creem, Wraga, & Proffitt, 1998; Gentilucci, Chieffi, Daprati, Saetti, & Toni, 1996),
- misperception of depth intervals (Loomis, Da Silva, Fujita, & Fukusima, 1992),
- induced motion (Bridgeman, Kirch, & Sperling, 1981),
- saccadic eye movements (Bridgeman, Lewis, Heit, & Nagle, 1979),
- estimates of hill pitch (Creem & Proffitt, 1998),
- the Roelofs effect (Bridgeman, Peery, & Anand, 1997), and
- judging eye level in pitched visual environments (Welch & Post, 1996).

Testing the perception-action dissociation hypothesis in normal observers requires psychophysical methods capable of isolating the sensorimotor and perceptual-cognitive systems and obtaining separate measures of the spatial information used by each. Two specific criteria that must be met for a valid test of dissociation are as follows:

- The motor response is *visually open-loop* (i.e., no error-corrective visual feedback is provided).
- The perceptual-cognitive and motor responses refer to the *same physical parameter* of the environment (e.g., egocentric location or perceived direction, linear extent, motion).

Problems With Previous Research

Most of the research with normal human participants cited earlier can be criticized for failing to meet one or both of the criteria for a valid test of dissociation. In the following section, each of the instances listed in the preceding section will be evaluated in the context of these criteria.

Size-contrast illusions. The best known size illusion is the Ebbinghaus illusion, in which a circle surrounded by an array of larger circles is perceived as smaller than the same-sized circle surrounded by smaller circles (see Figure 11.2). In an oft-cited study by Aglioti, DeSouza, and Goodale (1995), participants viewed an Ebbinghaus illusion made of *solid* (and therefore graspable) objects. The investigators reported that grasping responses directed at the surrounded object conformed to its true size despite the illusion—apparent evidence of dissociation. However, this study appears to fail on the basis of both of the research criteria. Specifically, (a) the grasping responses were visually monitored by the participant (i.e., closed-loop, rather than open-loop) and (b) perceived size and egocentric localization of the edges of the target object were confounded. The latter confounding represents a potential problem because it is possible that the Ebbinghaus illusion is limited to perceived size and has no effect on egocentric localization. If this is the case, any disparity between perceived object size and grasping behavior would be evidence not of

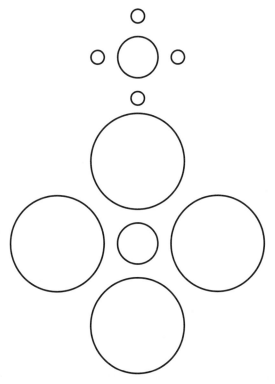

Figure 11.2.   The Ebbinghaus illusion. The circle surrounded by smaller circles (top) appears larger than the same size circle surrounded by larger circles (bottom).

perception-action dissociation but of a compromise between changed apparent size and unchanged localization. In any event, subsequent attempted replications of this study have met with failure (Franz, Gegenfurtner, Bultkoff, & Fahle, 2000) or only qualified success (Haffenden & Goodale, 1998).

The Mueller-Lyer illusion. Gentilucci et al. (1996) have reported that open-loop pointing at the endpoints of Mueller-Lyer figures is accurate despite the presence of a size illusion, a result that some have interpreted as dissociation. An alternative explanation, however, is that the two measures are assessing distinctly different perceptions—linear extent for the perceptual measure and egocentric location for the motor response—and thus that the second research criterion has been violated. According to this account, the fact that visual perception and hand–eye coordination produced contrary results is not evidence of dissociation but rather of the fact that this illusion influences perceived extent, but not location (Gillam & Chambers, 1985; Mack, Heuer, Villardi, & Chambers, 1985; Post & Welch, 1996). In another study, Creem et al. (1998) had participants walk, with eyes shut, along the length of large Mueller-Lyer figures placed on the floor and found in some conditions that the "blind walking" responses were accurate despite the illusion. The investigators concluded that they had thus demonstrated dissociation of the sensorimotor and perceptual-cognitive systems. However, as argued here, it is more parsimonious to interpret this result as merely revealing the independence of perceived extent and perceived egocentric location.

The misperception of depth intervals. Loomis, Da Silva, Fujita, and Fukusima (1992) showed that, despite the fact that observers greatly underestimate the size of intervals presented in the distance dimension, they are able to walk and point accurately at targets presented in that dimension. This result suggests dissociation between the perceptual-cognitive and sensorimotor systems. However, as with the Ebbinghaus and Mueller-Lyer illusion studies described previously, it is possible that the observed discrepancy between perceptual and behavioral measures was actually due to the confounding of two independent perceptual capacities—length (for the interval estimation measure) and egocentric location (for the walking response measure).

Induced motion. An early report of perception-action dissociation was provided by Bridgeman et al. (1981), who found that participants were able to point surprisingly accurately at a target that was physically stationary but appeared to be in motion because the surrounding frame stimulus was moving (induced motion). Similarly, pointing responses directed at targets that were physically moving but apparently stationary because of a frame that was moving in the same direction were found to represent a compromise between the perceived (stationary) and actual target motion. In both cases it is possible to interpret the finding that pointing responses were only partially influenced by induced motion as evidence for (imperfect) vision-action dissociation. However, a nondissociation interpretation of these results is that the motor measures are of perceived target location, whereas the perceptual measures are of perceived target velocity (Abrams & Landgraf, 1990; Smeets & Brenner, 1995).

Saccadic eye movements. Festinger and Canon (1965) and Honda (1985) demonstrated that hand-eye coordination is fairly accurate immediately after saccadic eye movements, despite the visual suppression that occurs during these movements. Similarly, Bridgeman et al. (1979) showed that on trials on which participants failed to perceive a target shift that occurred during a saccade they still pointed accurately (open-loop) at the new target location. In a subsequent experiment, Bridgeman and Stark (1979) refuted the possibility that this result was caused by participants' use of differing *response criteria* (higher for verbal detection than for pointing) by showing that the apparent dissociation between (failed) perception and correct action occurred even when a criterion-free forced-choice measure was used. However, these studies of perception and hand-eye coordination during saccadic eye movements suffer from the fact that the perceptual-cognitive and motor responses do not refer to the same environmental attribute. Specifically, whereas the perceptual-cognitive measure was of perceived motion, the motor measure was of egocentric location.

Instances of Perception-Action Dissociation That Meet the Research Criteria

The Roelofs effect. Bridgeman and colleagues (Bridgeman & Huemer, 1998; Bridgeman et al., 1997) have attempted to avoid the pitfalls present in dissociation research by means of a pictorial illusion known as the Dietzel-Roelofs effect. Dietzel (1924) and Roelofs (1935) independently discovered that if a rectangular frame is presented to the observer such that more of it is to one side of the observer's midline than the other, it appears to be displaced in the direction of the observer's midline. For example, if the right vertical edge of the pattern is in the observer's midline, that edge will appear to be somewhat to the right of straight-ahead. Similarly, if a dot is placed inside the asymmetrically presented figure, it will appear displaced as well (see Figure 11.3). Using this so-called "induced Roelofs effect," Bridgeman et al. (1997) showed that although all of their participants experienced an illusory shift in the dot's egocentric location, half of them nevertheless pointed (open-loop) accurately at it (i.e., dissociation). This was true, however, only when the pointing response was made immediately after the visual stimulus had been removed; with delays of as little as 4 s, all participants pointed in the direction of the illusion. Bridgeman et al. (1997) interpreted the effect of response delay as a consequence of the loss of veridical information available only in the sensorimotor pathway. According to these investigators, having lost the accurate representation in this system shortly after stimulus offset, participants were forced to "import" remembered spatial information (and thus the illusion) from the perceptual-cognitive system. The fact that pointing responses for half of their participants were influenced by the illusion (i.e., association rather than dissociation) was explained by arguing that for these individuals the sensorimotor memory decayed so rapidly that it had disappeared completely even in

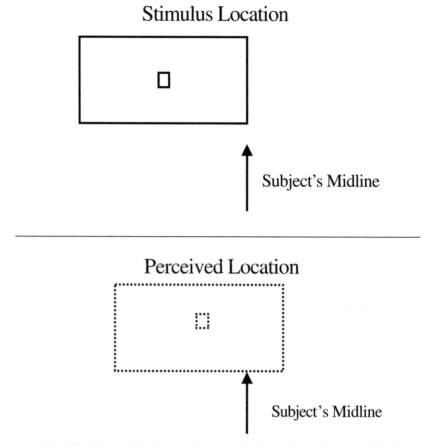

Figure 11.3. The Dietzel-Roelofs effect. Physical location of rectangular frame and spot stimulus is placed asymmetrically with respect to the subject's midline (top). Perceived location is shifted in the direction of the subject's midline (bottom).

the "no-delay" condition that actually occurred about a second after stimulus offset. In a recent study, Bridgeman and Huemer (1998) showed that when the goal of participants' motor responses was to make a specific impact on the environment (i.e., jab at a target), the "no-delay" condition resulted in accurate pointing at the Roelofs effect target by nearly all participants, as compared with only half of the participants in the study by Bridgeman et al. (1997). This finding suggests that an instrumental response goal is more conducive to dissociation than is the goal of communicating a perceptual experience.

In contrast to most or all of the previous research with normal participants, use of the Roelofs effect by Bridgeman et al. (1997) to examine the perception-action dissociation hypothesis appears to meet both of the critical research criteria. That is, (a) the motor responses were visually open-loop, and (b) they and the perceptual-cognitive measure referred to the same physical characteristic (egocentric location).

Judging eye level in pitched visual environments. A number of studies (e.g., Matin & Fox, 1989; Stoper & Cohen, 1989) have revealed that judgments of apparent eye level (i.e., the visual horizon) in the presence of a pitched visual display are strongly biased in the direction of its pitch. For example, an observer who is in a room that has been pitched forward or backward by 20 deg will judge apparent eye level to be in a location displaced from true eye level by approximately 10 deg in the direction of the room pitch. Despite this very substantial misperception, open-loop pointing at objects on the back wall of the pitchroom located at apparent eye level or at other locations above or below eye level are only slightly inaccurate (Cohen & Ballinger, 1989; Welch & Post, 1996). One interpretation of this pattern of results is that it signifies perception-action dissociation. As was the case with the Dietzel-Roelofs effect, the two research criteria appear to be satisfied.

It is perhaps meaningful that in both the Dietzel-Roelofs effect and the pitchroom situation observers view a visual framework that has been displaced or rotated. Thus, with the Dietzel-Roelofs effect, the visual framework is either horizontally translated or rotated in the yaw axis, whereas in the pitchroom, the framework is rotated in the pitch dimension. This pattern of results suggests that evidence for dissociation may be found in *any* situation that entails rotations or displacements of the visual surround. It is well known that a visual framework tilted from vertical in the roll dimension causes objects within it to appear tilted in the opposite direction (e.g., Witkin & Asch, 1948). We have recently found that open-loop pointing with respect to the endpoints of a stimulus that appears tilted as a result of a tilted surround reveals a compromise between veridical and illusory locations (Post & Welch, 1999). Thus, as predicted, this result appears to be evidence of a certain amount of perception-action dissociation. Whether perception-action dissociation is *limited* to situations involving rotation or displacement of the visual context remains to be seen. It may be important to note in this regard that perception-action dissociation does not appear to occur with the Judd illusion, which is similar to the Mueller-Lyer illusion with the exception that the chevron at one end of the shaft is rotated to point in the same direction as the chevron at the opposite end (see Figure 11.4). The Judd illusion affects perceived egocentric localization but does not involve surround rotation or displacement (Post & Welch, 1996). That is, subjects pointing open-loop at a concurrently viewed Judd illusion figure make the errors predicted by their mislocalization of its endpoints (i.e., association rather than dissociation). This fact is consistent with the hypothesis that dissociation does not occur for all figural illusions but rather is limited to those involving rotations or displacements of the visual array.

Summary and Implications

The review of apparent dissociation in normal observers has yielded three instances in which the evidence of perceptual-motor dissociation meets the specified criteria for the valid study of this phenomenon. In each instance, observers are presented with a visual framework that has been displaced or rotated in one of the three principal axes of rotation. Whether this pattern is meaningful or merely coincidental remains to be determined by future research. It is also the case that each of the instances of apparent dissociation

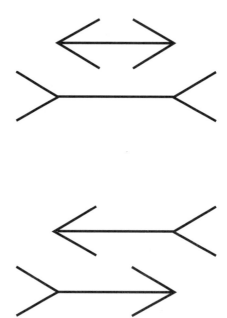

Figure 11.4.   (Top) Mueller-Lyer figures. The two horizontal lines are equal in length. (Bottom) The Judd illusion. The upper horizontal line is directly above the bottom one.

that satisfies the criteria involves perceptual and motor measure of apparent *location*. These instances therefore appear to be evidence consistent with the *what* versus *where* system distinction more than with the *what* versus *how* system distinction.

References

Abrams, R. A., & Landgraf, J. Z. (1990). Differential use of distance and location information for spatial localization. *Perception and Psychophysics, 47,* 349–359.

Aglioti, S., DeSouza, J. F. X., & Goodale, M. A. (1995). Size-contrast illusions deceive the eye but not the hand. *Current Biology, 5,* 679–685.

Bridgeman, B. (1991). Complementary cognitive and motor image processing. In G. Obrecht & L. W. Stark (Eds.), *Presbyopia research: From molecular biology to visual adaptation* (pp. 189–198). New York: Plenum.

Bridgeman, B., & Huemer, V. (1998). A spatially oriented decision does not induce consciousness in a motor task. *Consciousness and Cognition: An International Journal, 7,* 454–464.

Bridgeman, B., Kirch, M., & Sperling, A. (1981). Segregation of cognitive and motor aspects of visual function using induced motion. *Perception and Psychophysics, 29,* 336–342.

Bridgeman, B., Lewis, S., Heit, G., & Nagle, M. (1979). Relation between cognitive and motor-oriented systems of visual position perception. *Journal of Experimental Psychology: Human Perception and Performance, 5,* 692–700.

Bridgeman, B., Peery, S., & Anand, S. (1997). Interaction of cognitive and sensorimotor maps of visual space. *Perception and Psychophysics, 59,* 456–469.

Bridgeman, B., & Staggs, D. (1982). Plasticity in human blindsight. *Vision Research, 22,* 1199–1203.

Bridgeman, B., & Stark, L. (1979). Omnidirectional increase in threshold for image shifts during saccadic eye movements. *Perception and Psychophysics, 25,* 241–243.

Campion, J., Latto, R., & Smith, Y. M. (1983). Is blindsight an effect of scattered light, spared cortex and near-threshold vision? *Behavioral and Brain Sciences, 6,* 423–486.

Cohen, M. M., & Ballinger, C. J. (1989). Hand-eye coordination is altered by viewing a target in a pitched visual frame [Abstract]. *Aviation, Space and Environmental Medicine, 60,* 477.

Creem, S., & Proffitt, D. (1998). Two memories for geographical slant: Separation and interdependence of action and awareness. *Psychonomic Bulletin and Review, 5,* 22–36.

Creem, S. H., Wraga, M., & Proffitt, D. R. (1998). Perception-action dissociation in a large-scale Mueller-Lyer figure. Paper presented at the Association for Research in Vision and Ophthamology, Fort Lauderdale, FL.

Dietzel, H. (1924). Untersuchungen uber die optische Lokalisation der Mediane [Studies of the visual straight-ahead]. *Zeitschrift für Biologie, 80,* 289–316.

Fendrich, R., Wessinger, C. M., & Gazzaniga, M. S. (1992). Residual vision in a scotoma: Implications for blindsight. *Science, 258,* 1489–1491.

Festinger, L., & Canon, L. (1965). Information about spatial location based on knowledge about efference. *Psychological Review, 72,* 373–384.

Franz, V. H., Gegenfurtner, K. R., Bultkoff, H. H., & Fahle, M. (2000). Grasping visual illusions: No evidence for a dissociation between perception and action. *Psychological Science, 11,* 20–25.

Gentilucci, M., Chieffi, S., Daprati, E., Saetti, M. C., & Toni, I. (1996). Visual illusion and action. *Neuropsychologia, 34,* 369–376.

Gillam, B., & Chambers, D. (1985). Size and position are incongruous: Measurements on the Mueller-Lyer figure. *Perception and Psychophysics, 37,* 549–556.

Goodale, M. A., & Milner, A. D. (1995). Separate visual pathways for perception and action. *Trends in Neuroscience, 15,* 20–25.

Goodale, M. A., Milner, A. D., Jakobson, L. S., & Carey, D. P. (1991). A neurological dissociation between perceiving objects and grasping them. *Nature, 349,* 154–156.

Haffenden, A. M., & Goodale, M. A. (1998). The effect of pictorial illusion on prehension and perception. *Journal of Cognitive Neuroscience, 10,* 122–136.

Held, R. (1968). Dissociation of visual functions by deprivation and rearrangement. *Psychologische Forschung, 31,* 338–348.

Held, R. (1970). Two modes of processing spatially distributed visual stimulatio. In F. O. Schmidt (Ed.), *The neurosciences: Second study program* (pp. 317–324). New York: Rockefeller University Press.

Honda, H. (1985). Spatial localization in saccade and pursuit-eye-movement conditions: A comparison of perceptual and motor measures. *Perception and Psychophysics, 38,* 41–46.

Ingle, D. (1967). Two visual mechanisms underlying the behavior of fish. *Psychologische Forschung, 31,* 44–51.

Kolb, F. C., & Braun, J. (1995). Blindsight in normal observers. *Nature, 377,* 336–338.

Leibowitz, H. W., & Owens, D. A. (1977). Nighttime driving accidents and selective visual degradation. *Science, 197,* 422–423.

Leibowitz, H. W., & Owens, D. A. (1986). We drive by night. *Psychology Today, 20,* 54–58.

Leibowitz, H. W., & Post, R. B. (1982). The two modes of processing concept and some implications. In J. Beck (Ed.), *Organization and representation in perception* (pp. 343–363). Hillsdale, NJ: Erlbaum.

Leibowitz, H. W., Shupert-Rodemer, C., & Dichgans, J. (1979). The independence of dynamic spatial orientation from luminance and refractive error. *Perception and Psychophysics, 25,* 75–79.

Loomis, J. M., Da Silva, J. A., Fujita, N., & Fukusima, S. S. (1992). Visual space perception and visually directed action. *Journal of Experimental Psychology: Human Perception and Performance, 18,* 906–921.

Mack, A., Heuer, F., Villardi, K., & Chambers, D. (1985). The dissociation of position and extent in Mueller-Lyer figures. *Perception and Psychophysics, 37,* 335–344.

Matin, L., & Fox, C. R. (1989). Visually perceived eye level and perceived elevation of objects: Linearly additive influences from visual field pitch and from gravity. *Vision Research, 29,* 315–324.

Milner, D., & Goodale, M. (1995). *The visual brain in action.* Oxford, England: Oxford University Press.

Mishkin, M., Ungerleider, L. G., & Macko, K. A. (1983). Object vision and spatial vision: Two cortical pathways. *Trends in Neurosciences, 6,* 414–417.

Paillard, J. (1987). Cognitive versus sensorimotor encoding of spatial information. In P. Ellen & C. Thinus-blanc (Eds.), *Cognitive processes and spatial orientation in animal and man* (pp. 43–77). Dordrecht, Netherlands: Martinus Nijhoff.

Poppel, E., Held, R., & Frost, D. (1973). Residual visual function after brain wounds involving the central visual pathways in man. *Nature, 243,* 295–296.

Post, R. B., & Welch, R. B. (1996). Is there dissociation of perceptual and motor responses to figural illusions? *Perception, 25,* 569–581.

Post, R. B., & Welch, R. B. (1999). [Open-loop pointing, with roll-induced tilt]. Unpublished data.

Roelofs, C. (1935). Optische Localisation. *Archives für Augenheilkunde, 109,* 395–415.

Rossetti, Y., Rode, G., & Boisson, D. (1995). Implicit processing of somaesthetic information: A dissociation between where and how. *Neuroreport, 6,* 506–510.

Sanders, M. D., Warrington, E. K., Marshall, J., & Weiskrantz, L. (1974). "Blindsight": Vision in a field defect. *The Lancet, 20,* 707–708.

Schneider, G. E. (1967). Contrasting visuomotor functions of tectum and cortex in the golden hamster. *Psychologische Forschung, 31,* 52–62.

Schneider, G. E. (1969). Two visual systems. *Science, 163,* 895–902.

Smeets, J. B. J., & Brenner, E. (1995). Perception and action are based on the same visual information: Distinction between position and velocity. *Journal of Experimental Psychology: Human Perception and Performance, 21,* 19–31.

Stoper, A. E., & Cohen, M. M. (1989). Effect of structured visual environments on apparent eye level. *Perception and Psychophysics, 46,* 469–475.

Trevarthen, C. (1968). Two mechanisms of vision in primates. *Psychologische Forschung, 31,* 229–237.

Weiskrantz, L. (1996). Blindsight revisited. *Current Opinion in Neurobiology, 6,* 215–220.

Weiskrantz, L., Warrington, E. K., Sanders, M. D., & Marshall, J. (1974). Visual capacity in the hemianopic field following a restricted occipital ablation. *Brain, 97,* 709–728.

Welch, R. B., & Post, R. B. (1996). Accuracy and adaptation of pointing responses in pitched visual environments. *Perception and Psychophysics, 58,* 383–389.

Witkin, H. A., & Asch, S. E. (1948). Studies in space orientation. IV. Further experiments on perception of the upright with displaced visual fields. *Journal of Experimental Psychology, 38,* 762–782.

Part VI _____

Traffic Safety

12

Twilight Vision and Road Safety

Seeing More Than We Notice but Less Than We Think

D. Alfred Owens

A Perspective in Retrospect

Herschel Leibowitz's students enjoy reminiscing about the good-humored lessons learned at Penn State. The most famous lesson, which appears recurrently in this volume, was Leibowitz's first law: You can't see a damn thing in the dark. Other lessons were more subtle, yet they expanded on a theme embodied in the first law. Professor Leibowitz taught us to appreciate the value of knowledge on practical as well as intellectual grounds. He urged us to consider "first things first," to respect simple facts as much as complex abstractions, and to examine the historical along with the most recent research and ideas. Leibowitz championed the view that persistent practical problems are interesting because they expose gaps in understanding. Thus, practical matters can serve as a useful guide for devising more fruitful experiments. From his perspective, no model or theory—no matter how clever—was self-justified, for it had to face Leibowitz's simple question, "Why is that important?" (See chapter 2, "Why Is That Important? Hersh Leibowitz as a Model for Mentors," by Sharon Toffey Shepela). An acceptable answer needed to include implications beyond the science. When we students were stumped, he was reluctant to offer an answer but would just say, "I don't understand," and leave it at that. Professor Leibowitz was strangely unwilling to assign problems or design our research projects, although he was always attentive to our laboratory activities. He maintained that a graduate student must become an independent investigator to merit the PhD degree. He never shared authorship of a student's dissertation.

After some initial adjustment ("Why won't he just tell me what to do?!"), we found Hersh Leibowitz's mentorship to be great fun. His jokes set the tone of our situation: simply funny, frequently redundant, and oddly central to Hersh's modest and boyish character. His love of history taught us to look into the classic literature for insight. His wide-ranging collaborations taught us also to seek learning from other disciplines. Hersh's students remember

This chapter is based on a presentation at the APA Symposium honoring the career contributions and inspiration of Herschel W. Leibowitz, Penn State University, June 1999.

This research was supported by grants from the National Eye Institute, Franklin & Marshall College, the University of Michigan Industry Affiliation Program for Human Factors in Transportation Safety, and the Queensland University of Technology. I am grateful to Anthony Chemero, Lewis Harvey, Deborah Owens, Justin Owens, Robert Owens, and Mary-Lynne Weber for helpful comments on previous drafts of this chapter.

working in other disciplines at Penn State—athletics, engineering, human development, computer science, and medicine—and we recall collaborating with visitors from Australia, Canada, China, Germany, Israel, Japan, and the Netherlands, not to mention California, Florida, Massachusetts, New York, Texas, and others I cannot remember. Hersh connected his students to anthropology, biomechanics, clinical psychology, jurisprudence, military science, neurology, optometry, and transportation. He took us along to sit with advisory panels of the National Research Council, to see a pilot's view of landing at night, and even to conduct experiments in psychiatric wards. He showed us that serious science does not need to be narrowly specialized or highly abstract. On the contrary, our science thrives from multiple points of view, from a friendly attitude toward colleagues in all corners, and, perhaps most important, from a healthy respect for problems that are larger than theories. As seen in this volume, Hersh Leibowitz's students carried these lessons in many directions.

I thank Hersh Leibowitz for showing me how to build a career in science that has room for hobbies, curiosity, public service, and the joy of learning. From early childhood, I was intrigued by the devices of transportation—trains, planes, and automobiles—and by the peculiar phenomena of visual perception, a faculty that my wise old Grandpa Owens had somehow lost.

My contribution to this festschrift begins with investigations of vision under difficult conditions. The experiments lead unexpectedly to a public health problem: The fact that transportation accidents, especially road fatalities, are greatly overrepresented under conditions of poor visibility. This connection turned us back toward psychological questions regarding the performance of skilled tasks and particularly the role of conscious deliberation in the conduct of risky activities. If we gain any new insight on these matters, it will, I suppose, feed back to problems of public health and safety.

Early Research on Twilight Vision

Leibowitz's first law describes an absolute limit of vision: We need light to see. It leaves open the question, however, of how much light is needed to see well enough. Many tasks are routinely performed in low illumination, some with difficulty and some with ease, and when the situation is difficult, some individuals are consistently more capable than others. Chuck Yeager's (1985) autobiography provides an exciting example of extraordinary sight in difficult conditions. Why could General Yeager recognize a distant aircraft in an empty sky sooner than his adversary could? Was it just a matter of better acuity? Why can my wife, Deborah, read street signs at night sooner than I can? My acuity is as fine as hers, at least in daylight. Why do some students and office workers experience discomfort, eyestrain, and headaches after a brief period of work at a computer terminal, whereas others can go on for hours with no apparent problem? I had the good fortune to study with Hersh when a new device, the laser optometer, gave promising answers to all of these questions.

Our discovery with the laser optometer was simple and unexpected (see Figure 7.1, p. 70). We found that the eyes adjust to an intermediate "resting point" when visibility is degraded and that this resting state, or *dark focus*, varies widely from one person to another (Figure 12.1). Jeff Andre gives a fuller version of this story in his contribution to this volume (chapter 7, "Controversies Concerning the Resting State of Accommodation: Focusing on Leibowitz"). For the present purpose, the key finding can be summarized as a basic quirk in the focusing behavior of the eyes: Whenever visibility is poor (as it is at night or in bad weather) or when ocular focus is supplemented by external devices (as with optical instruments) or when one just does not care to see (as in a boring lecture), the eyes passively return to a characteristic resting focus. For many young adults (especially college students) the resting focus corresponds to a relatively near "myopic" focus, although for a small percentage, like my wife, the eyes relax at optical infinity.

Hersh's keen attention to the historical literature revealed that our "discovery" of the intermediate resting focus of the eyes had been anticipated by several earlier researchers (Cogan, 1937; Weber, 1855, cited in Cornelius, 1861; Morgan, 1946; Schober, 1954), but their evidence had been generally dismissed as an artifact of optical aberrations. I suspect this erroneous dismissal of good data reflected the towering influence of Helmholtz and Donders, eminent 19th-century scientists who had concluded that the human eye relaxes at optical infinity.[1] In any case, Hersh recognized that we would have to "overprove" the intermediate resting state hypothesis. So we ran a series of experiments designed as converging operations (Garner, Hake, & Eriksen, 1956), which aimed to explore the relation of the dark focus to multiple behavioral consequences. Our results showed that the eyes adopt the same intermediate focus in darkness, in a bright empty *Ganzfeld* (like an empty sky), in a dissecting microscope, when viewing laser interference patterns or sinusoidal gratings of very low or high spatial frequency, when viewing through pinhole pupils, and when consciously "spacing out." It was an instructive and enjoyable series of collaborations bridging from the years of Bob Hennessy and Charles Abernethy through those of Chris Johnson, Bob Miller, Bob Post, Bob Owens, and myself, to the later work of Bai-Chuan Jiang, Rick Tyrrell, Ellie Francis, and Hersh's last student, Jeff Andre.

From the start, the experiments on ocular accommodation and binocular vergence were aimed at solving practical problems such as visual fatigue and anomalous refractive errors like "night myopia." Experiments in this direction were successful, so we were eager to apply the dark focus in real-world situations. In one study, we found that special night glasses, prescribed on the basis of the individual's dark focus, enhanced acuity under simulated night driving conditions. A field test showed that drivers consistently chose our dark-focus correction as superior to their normal daytime glasses and a third stronger correction (Owens & Leibowitz, 1976a). Our subjects were eager to purchase dark-focus glasses for added comfort and safety in night driving, although we were not prepared (or qualified) to dispense eyewear. Furthermore, the research attracted some attention from the media, so it seemed that the problem of night

---

[1]Prior to the laser optometer, methods for measuring accommodation included stimuli that triggered an automatic focusing response, so it was difficult (if not impossible) to measure the actual *resting* state of the eye. Therefore, early investigators relied on measures of cadavers, whose eyes had reached their final resting place.

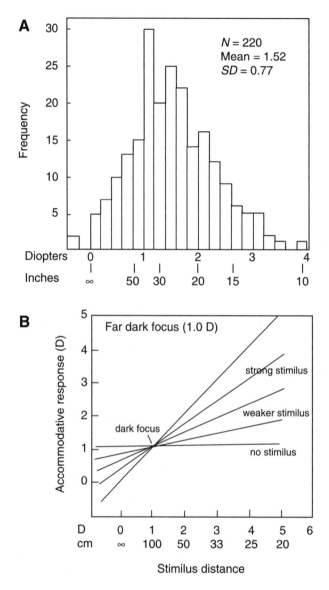

Figure 12.1. (A) Distribution of dark-focus values for 220 college students. Individual dark-focus values varied widely around a sample mean distance of 70 cm or 1.5 diopters. (B) Accommodative response functions for stimuli of variable quality. The most accurate responses (higher slope) is obtained for bright, high-contrast targets. Accommodation is progressively biased toward the individual's dark focus as stimulus quality is degraded. Panel A from "New Evidence for the Intermediate Position of Relaxed Accommodation," by H. W. Leibowitz and D. A. Owens, 1978, *Documenta Ophthalmologica*, *46*(1), p. 136. Copyright 1996 by Kluwer Academic Publishers. Reprinted with permission. Panel B from "Oculomotor Information and Perception of Three-Dimensional Space" by D. A. Owens, 1987, in H. Heuer and A. F. Sanders (Eds.), *Perspectives on Perception and Action*, p. 224. Copyright 1987 by Lawrence Erlbaum Associates. Reprinted with permission.

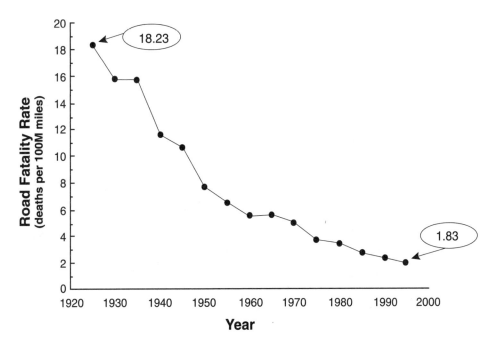

Figure 12.2   Annual U.S. road fatality rates per mileage traveled declined by a factor of 10 from 1925 to 1995 (based on data derived from publications of the National Safety Council).

myopia was solved, and as a result our public roads would soon become safer at night (Owens & Leibowitz, 1976b).

Problems of Night Driving Involve More Than Blurry Vision

The fact is that traffic safety has improved dramatically over the past century (Figure 12.2). Data from the National Safety Council show that the death rate in the early 1920s was approximately 20 per 100 million miles. By the end of the 20th century, the fatality rate had fallen by more than a factor of 10. Crash statistics also show, however, that driving is most dangerous in low light, with the majority of road fatalities in the United States occurring at night. Corrected for mileage, this finding translates into a death rate that runs three to four times higher at night than in daylight (Figure 12.3; National Safety Council, 1925–1998). The overall improvement in road safety is probably attributable to vast improvements in the design and engineering of motor vehicles, highways, and traffic control systems, coupled with the advent of rapid emergency medical services. But the persistent problem of night crashes is more likely due to human than to technological limitations. No doubt multiple factors, including alcohol and fatigue, contribute to this problem, but we now know that impaired visibility is a key contributor, particularly for classes of accidents overrepresented at night, like those involving pedestrians (Owens &

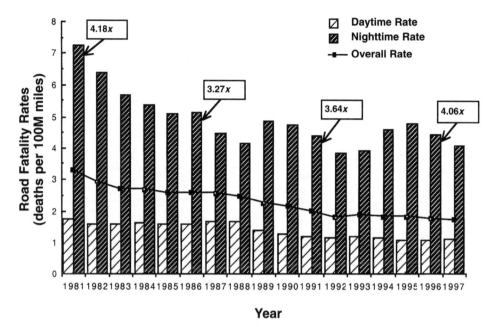

Figure 12.3. Comparison of road fatality rates in the United States under day and night conditions; overall fatality rates are given by the continuous line. Nighttime fatality rates are consistently three to four times higher than daytime rates (based on data derived from publications of the National Safety Council). From "The Place of Ambient Vision in Understanding the Problems of Mobility and Aging" by D. A. Owens, 2000, in K. W. Schaie and M. Pietrucha (Eds.), *Mobility and Transportation in the Elderly*, p. 51. Copyright 2000 by Springer Publishing Company, Inc. Adapted with permission.

Sivak, 1996). It seemed reasonable that correction of night myopia could improve the vision of many drivers and thereby reduce the death toll.

Eventually, though, we realized that few individuals are troubled by night myopia—which is not to say that few suffer the problem. The evidence shows that many drivers do have night myopia, and when it is corrected, they appreciate the benefit (Owens & Leibowitz, 1976a). But apparently drivers with night myopia hardly noticed the problem until they happened to participate in our experiments. This was puzzling because comparable refractive errors in daylight would surely raise concerns and, indeed, result in failure of the vision test for a driver's license. Many research participants exhibited night myopia of greater than −0.5 diopters (D) and some as much as 1.5 D.[2] Such myopia blurs vision, resulting in serious losses of acuity in bright light. But it seemed that night drivers had no idea their night vision was poor or that it could be better, perhaps because they had never experienced optimal vision at night.

More interesting from a psychological standpoint, we realized that drivers do not compensate behaviorally for the visual degradation that inevitably occurs at night. Casual observations revealed no decrease in traffic speeds at

---

[2]In bright light, a myopic refractive error of 1 D will degrade visual acuity to about 20/100. The cutoff for an unrestricted driver's license in most jurisdictions is 20/40.

night, and this was confirmed by published traffic studies (Herd, Agent, & Rizenbergs, 1980). Despite reduced visibility (which could only be partially corrected by dark-focus glasses), drivers commonly travel as fast or faster at night compared with daylight. To a practical psychophysicist, this fact raised an interesting question: Why do drivers act as though they have no visual problem at night? A possible answer was suggested by concepts from neurophysiology and astronomy.

The Two Modes of Vision Concept

I cannot remember exactly how the next piece of our puzzle fell into place: Hersh has credited me with the insight (he would!), but more likely he stumbled across the idea while jogging around State College. We called it the *selective degradation hypothesis*. The central idea is that some visual abilities remain highly efficient in low light, whereas others are severely impaired. Vehicle control—steering and speed, in particular—remains relatively easy in dim conditions despite losses of visual acuity and color vision.

The scientific basis for the selective degradation hypothesis rests on a study of parallel visual processes in the golden hamster done by Gerald Schneider (1967, 1969) when he was a graduate student at the Massachusetts Institute of Technology (MIT). Consistent with much earlier research, he had shown that lesions of the visual cortex rendered animals incapable of discriminating visual patterns. Surprisingly, however, Schneider's study also showed that these "blind" animals were still able to orient visually toward an approaching sunflower seed and to other salient visual events. The reverse deficit was found following lesions to a structure in the midbrain, called the superior colliculus, which rendered animals unable to orient or to guide locomotion visually, although they were still able to discriminate patterns.

In a symposium entitled "Two Modes of Visual Processing" at the 1967 meeting of the Eastern Psychological Association, Schneider's findings were reinforced by evidence from fish and primates (Ingle, 1967; Held, 1968; Trevarthen, 1968). Taking an evolutionary perspective on visual-motor coordination, Colwin Trevarthen coined the terms *focal* and *ambient* as labels for "anatomically distinct brain mechanisms" that serve parallel functions of visual recognition and guidance of action, respectively. Anticipating greater neurological complexity, Richard Held recommended distinguishing between "modes" rather than "mechanisms" of vision. True to Held's expectations, later work has shown the visual brain to be far more complicated than two distinct mechanisms (Zeki, 1993), but the functional distinction between recognition and guidance processes remains heuristic. Weiskrantz, Warrington, Sanders, and Marshall (1974) highlighted the strange phenomenon of "blindsight" in patients who have suffered damage to the visual cortex and, much like Schneider's hamsters, are still capable of localizing visual events that they absolutely cannot *see* (see also Kolb & Braun, 1995; Payne, Lomber, MacNeil, & Cornwell, 1996). Other research has revealed parallel (but interacting) cortical pathways in primates: (a) one that mediates visual perception of object properties via the *ventral stream* from occipital to frontal cortex and (b) another that mediates visual control of action via a *dorsal stream* from occipital through parietal to motor cortex (e.g., Boussaoud, di Pellegrino, & Wise, 1996; Goodale, 1983; Goodale & Milner, 1992; Humphrey, 1974; Mishkin, Ungerleider, & Macko, 1983; Norman, 2001; Stoerig, 1996). A similar functional separation has been found in visual areas of the frontal cortex (Boussaoud et al., 1996) and, more recently, in central pathways of the auditory system (Kaas & Hacket, 1999; Romanski, Tian, Mishkin, Goldman-Rakic, & Rauschecker, 1999).

The concept of two modes of processing posed a radical reconception of how vision works. Instead of a unified system that funnels sensory information to a central unconscious interpreter, which informs consciousness about the world (e.g., Boring, 1942; Gregory, 1997; Rock, 1983, 1997), we now understand that many important visual functions happen automatically outside of conscious awareness and without "unconscious inference." This viewpoint sees visual *awareness* as being closely associated with *focal vision,* which includes such abilities as pattern discrimination, color, and object recognition, which are all vastly superior in the center of our visual field (the *fovea*) under daylight (photopic*)* conditions. But vision also operates over a much wider field of view, and for many creatures, indeed the majority of species with eyes, it serves well under dim nocturnal conditions (Walls, 1942). This kind of visual ability probably emerged in the earliest stages of evolution (Dawkins, 1996). Similar to the concept of ambient vision, peripheral and nocturnal visual functions are coarse and weakly represented in conscious awareness, but they are essential for normal control of posture and guidance of action. From this perspective, it seemed obvious that both modes of vision, both recognition and guidance, must participate in driving.

Examining the relative effect of low light on the two modes of vision revealed an important functional dissociation, as illustrated in Figure 12.4. Virtually all aspects of focal vision—here represented by acuity, peak contrast sensitivity, and accommodation—deteriorate rapidly when light falls from day to night. Ambient vision, however—here represented by vection, or visually induced self-motion—maintains high efficiency in very low luminances, even near the absolute scotopic threshold (Brooks & Owens, 2001; Leibowitz, Shupert-Rodemer, & Dichgans, 1979).

The Astronomers' Definition of Twilight

Scientists began to study vision in low light long before the advent of experimental psychology and psychophysics. Tests of visual acuity were devised by early astronomers who aimed to determine how well one can discern weak celestial stimuli (Leibowitz, personal communication, early 1990s). Closer to Earth, the astronomers delineated the daily transitions between day and night as three phases of twilight, which were defined on the basis of visual capabilities (Leibowitz, 1987). They observed that vision is unimpaired at sunset and sunrise, when the upper limb of the sun is tangent to the horizon, and it remains adequate for "normal" outdoor activities until the sun falls more than 6 deg below the horizon. This period, called *civil twilight,* lasts for about 30 min before sunrise and following sunset at the latitude of State College, Pennsylvania. During civil twilight, illumination from the sky varies from ~300 to ~3 lux (Figure 12.5). At the dim limit of civil twilight, visual abilities are impaired, but not lost completely. It is still possible, for example, to

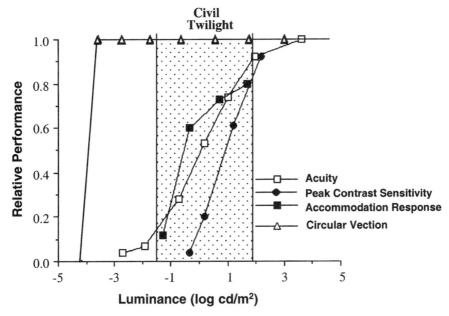

Figure 12.4. Relative visual performance as a function of luminance for three types of "recognition (focal) vision" and one type of "guidance (ambient) vision." Dotted area identifies the range of luminances commonly encountered in civil twilight. From "Effects of Luminance, Blur, and Age on Nighttime Visual Guidance: A Test of the Selective Degradation Hypothesis," by D. A. Owens and R. A. Tyrrell, 1999, *Journal of Experimental Psychology: Applied,* 5(2), p. 116. Copyright 1999 by the American Psychological Association. Reprinted with permission.

visualize the horizon at sea—an asset to navigation with a sextant—when the sun is 6–12 deg below the horizon. The astronomers named this period, when illumination varies from 3 to 0.03 lux, *nautical twilight.* Very little terrestrial illuminance is present when the sun is more than 12 deg below the horizon, although there is still enough sky light to interfere with celestial observations. Thus, the period when the sun is between 12 and 18 deg below the horizon was designated as *astronomical twilight.* After that comes night, with light from only the stars and moon. Even in starlight (< 0.003 lux), some visual abilities remain, but these are limited to ambient vision.

From our viewpoint, the astronomers' definition of twilight was interesting for three reasons. First, it called attention to the fact that natural illumination varies systematically as a function of solar position when the sun is between 0 and 18 deg below the horizon; illumination is otherwise practically independent of solar position. Second, it acknowledged that in lower illumination some visual processes operate better than others. Third, it provided us with some benchmarks for predicting visual performance in low light. Most interesting is the definition of civil twilight, which stated that normal outdoor activities are possible with illumination as low as 3 lux.

We thought it would be interesting to compare the astronomers' analysis with data from later studies of vision (Owens, Francis, & Leibowitz, 1989). Many experiments have quantified changes in vision as a function of light conditions (Graham, 1965*).* How do the changes of visual performance, measured

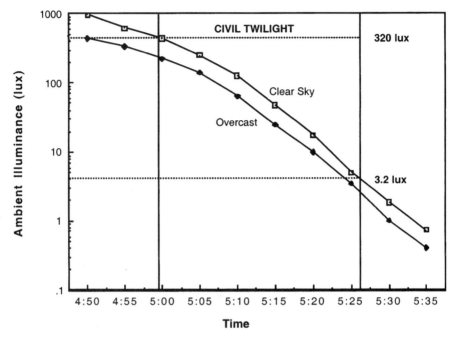

Figure 12.5.   Mean ambient illuminance during evening twilight on clear and over-cast days in November in Lancaster, Pennsylvania.

under carefully controlled laboratory conditions, compare with the astronomers' qualitative observations? To answer this question, we needed to compute the range of object brightness, or luminances, commonly encountered in civil twilight. The luminance of a surface depends on two physical variables: (a) First is the intensity of light falling on the surface—this is called *illuminance* and is measured in lux units; (b) Second is the proportion of incident light that is reflected from the surface to enter the observer's eyes—this is called *reflectance* and is expressed as a proportion of 0 to 1. A snow-white surface has a reflectance of about 0.8; new denim blue jeans have a reflectance of about 0.03. A white surface at sunset (the bright limit of civil twilight) can represent bright limit of civil twilight, whereas blue jeans seen 30 min later can represent the dim limit of civil twilight. Using a standard formula,[3] we calculated the dim and bright luminance boundaries of civil twilight to be 0.03 and 76 cd/m^2, respectively. (In Figure 12.4, these values are expressed on a logarithmic scale, as -1.5 and 1.88 log cd/m^2, because the activation of sensory systems is generally proportional to the log of stimulus energy.) As seen in Figure 12.4, the range of civil twilight corresponds nicely to the selective degradation of focal abilities, which occurs when the eyes shift from cone-mediated *photopic* to rod-mediated *scotopic* vision.

Thus the astronomers' definition of civil twilight proved to be a valid benchmark for predicting limits of recognition vision. We questioned, however, whether the astronomers' claim that normal outdoor activities can be con-

[3]Luminance (candelas/m^2) = Illuminance (lux) × Reflectance / π

ducted throughout civil twilight is still appropriate in the modern world. It seems unlikely that common tasks like mowing grass and driving cars can be conducted safely near the dimmest part of civil twilight (Leibowitz & Owens, 1991). Nevertheless, traffic flows as rapidly in darkness as in daylight, and our mobility at night comes at the cost of increased road fatalities.

To what extent is the higher death rate at night a consequence of impaired vision, as opposed to other factors like alcohol intoxication and drowsiness? Michael Sivak and I analyzed data from all fatal crashes in the United States over a period of 11 years ($N = 439,860$; National Highway Traffic Safety Administration, Fatality Analysis Reporting System). The evidence indicated that night road fatalities can be clustered into two categories: (a) single-vehicle and multi-vehicle collisions, in which alcohol is a major factor, and (b) crashes with low-contrast obstacles like pedestrians and cyclists, in which reduced visibility is a leading contributor (Owens & Sivak, 1996).

This finding brings us back to the question of why the hazards of night vision are not a matter of greater public concern. Traffic accidents are the leading cause of accidental death for Americans between the ages of 1 and 25 years; in this age group, road fatalities outnumber total deaths from all other causes combined (National Safety Council, 1925–1998). We estimate that more than 17,000 (mostly young) lives would be saved each year, if the night fatality rate were reduced to match the daytime rate (Owens, Helmers, & Sivak, 1993). Yet neither driving behavior nor regulatory practices (e.g., speed limits) gives any indication that a special problem exists at night. In contrast with public concerns over crash protection (from air bags to sport utility vehicles), alcohol, and "road rage," it seems puzzling that so few worry about the thousands of sober, alert drivers who can't see very well when driving at night.

On the basis of the selective degradation hypothesis, we proposed that, for the most part, night drivers are simply not aware that their vision is impaired. We reasoned that driving, like many complex tasks, involves both the recognition and the guidance modes of vision. Because steering is of constant importance, driving success and confidence probably depend heavily on guidance vision, which still operates quite effectively at night. Of course, tasks that require visual recognition are also important at night. But thanks to good engineering, these focal abilities are partially enhanced by lighting and reflectorization. Consequently, drivers are not likely to recognize that their ability to see dim, low-contrast objects is drastically degraded in the night road environment. So they tend to be overconfident at night, driving as though they can see as well as in daylight (Leibowitz & Owens, 1977, 1991; Leibowitz, Owens, & Post, 1982). Unfortunately, one's actual limitations are not likely to be discovered until one encounters a low-contrast obstacle—perhaps a pedestrian—on the roadway.

Testing the Selective Degradation Hypothesis

The selective degradation hypothesis was attractive because it drew a connection from research on perception and neurophysiology to an important problem of public safety, but it was clearly speculative, and for several years it seemed difficult to test empirically. Ethical considerations weighed against

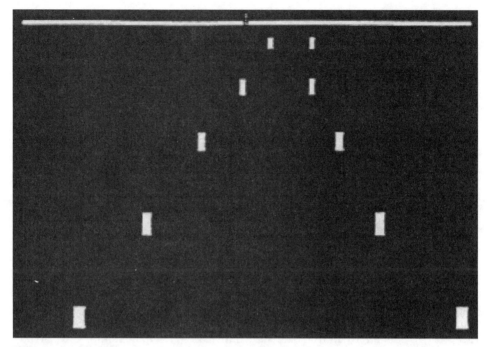

Figure 12.6. Video display of the night driving simulator at the University of Michigan Transportation Research Institute. Lane delineators flowed toward the foreground from the horizon, sweeping smoothly from side to side as an unpredictable (sum of sines) path. From "Effects of Luminance, Blur, and Age on Nighttime Visual Guidance: A Test of the Selective Degradation Hypothesis," by D. A. Owens and R. A. Tyrrell, 1999, *Journal of Experimental Psychology: Applied, 5*(2), p. 117. Copyright 1999 by the American Psychological Association. Reprinted with permission.

experiments on the effects of visual impairment on actual driving behavior. This difficulty was resolved several years later when Rick Tyrrell and I had an opportunity to use a night driving simulator at the University of Michigan Transportation Research Institute (UMTRI; Figure 12.6).

Following the example of Schneider's study with hamsters, we investigated the effects of (noninvasive!) conditions that were designed to interfere selectively with either focal or ambient vision. In our first experiment, focal vision was degraded in two ways: (a) with ophthalmic lenses that created artificial myopia of 2 to 10 D, and (b) with neutral-density filters that reduced luminance from photopic (30 cd/m^2) through twilight to low scotopic (0.003 cd/m^2) levels. A third condition was designed to degrade ambient vision by simulating "tunnel vision" by viewing through plastic drinking straws that had been trimmed and mounted in spectacle frames to limit binocular vision to a central region less than 2 deg in diameter. Dependent measures included visual acuity (the focal task) and steering accuracy (the ambient task). The simulator projected a simple roadway on a large screen at a 6-m distance. Curves varied unpredictably from side to side as the road markers flowed in perspective from a virtual horizon toward the foreground (Green & Olson, 1989). The participants' task was to adjust the steering input in order to remain centered in the lane.

Consistent with the selective degradation hypothesis, the results showed that tunnel vision severely impaired steering performance, whereas it had no effect on visual acuity. Conversely, myopic blur severely degraded visual acuity and had no effect on steering accuracy. Reduced luminance had a similar, though not so clear cut, effect. At the lowest scotopic level, which was much dimmer than values encountered in night driving, we found significant degradation of *both* acuity and steering accuracy, although the effect on steering accuracy was relatively small compared with that for acuity. The advantage of ambient vision was clearly evident at less extreme reductions of luminance, however. At the dark limit of civil twilight (0.03 cd/m^2), acuity had deteriorated from better than 20/20 to 20/100, whereas steering accuracy showed no significant change from photopic conditions. Thus, our results confirmed the functional dissociation predicted by two modes of vision. Tunnel vision impaired steering abilities while having no effect on acuity, whereas blur and reduced luminance degraded acuity while having little or no effect on steering (Owens & Tyrrell, 1999).

In a second experiment, we examined the effects of advancing age, which appeared as a somewhat ironic exception to the night driving problem. Unlike younger adults, older drivers are reluctant or unwilling to drive at night because they lack confidence in their visual abilities (Kosnik, Sekuler, & Kline, 1990). The older drivers' greater caution at night is prudent, and it stands in contrast to the overconfidence of younger drivers. It is well known that normal age-related changes of vision, such as reduced pupillary dilation and clouding of the crystalline lens, progressively impair night vision (Loewenfeld, 1979; Owsley & Sloane, 1990; Pitts, 1982; Schieber, 1994; Weale, 1963), and these difficulties may well contribute to the older drivers' unease at night. But the fact remains that no one, not even young, healthy drivers, can see very well at night. Why are older drivers more conscious of their visual limitations? We hypothesized the difference might be associated with age-related impairment of ambient vision.

Our second experiment used the UMTRI simulator to test steering performance of younger and older drivers under luminances ranging across civil twilight to scotopic levels. The younger participants were mostly graduate students (mean age, 24 years), and older participants were active, independent residents of the surrounding community, reportedly in good health and still driving at night (mean age, 72 years). It is interesting to compare the data of these groups with those from the first experiment, which tested a convenient sample of middle-aged participants (mean age, 38 years).

As shown in Figure 12.7, steering errors generally increased with age. More interesting, the deleterious effects of luminance also increased with advancing age. Steering errors for the youngest group were virtually unaffected in the dimmest conditions, whereas errors for the oldest group increased even at intermediate twilight levels, and those for middle-aged participants fell between the younger and older groups.[4]

---

[4]Analyses of effect sizes (Winer, Brown, & Michaels, 1991), which estimated the proportion of variance in steering accuracy that can be attributed to light condition, yielded ω^2 values of 0.178, 0.289, and 0.592 for the youngest, middle, and oldest age groups, respectively.

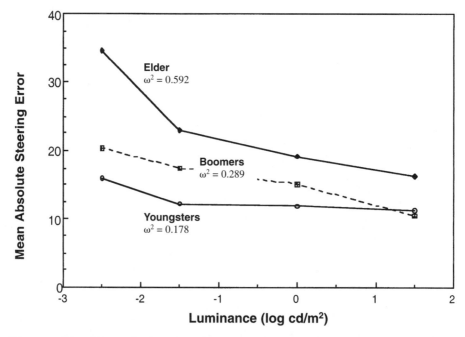

Figure 12.7.   Mean absolute steering errors as a function of luminance for drivers in three age groups. Mean ages were 72 years for "Elders," 38 years for "Boomers," and 24 years for "Youngsters." Omega (ω^2) values indicate the magnitude of effects of luminance on steering accuracy for each age. From "Effects of Luminance, Blur, and Age on Nighttime Visual Guidance: A Test of the Selective Degradation Hypothesis," by D. A. Owens and R. A. Tyrrell, 1999, *Journal of Experimental Psychology: Applied,* 5(2), p. 122. Copyright 1999 by the American Psychological Association. Reprinted with permission.

Our experiments with the UMTRI night driving simulator provided some empirical support for the selective degradation hypothesis. Participants' ability to steer the simulator, considered an ambient task, was clearly unrelated to visual acuity and as predicted from the two modes of vision, it was resistant to blur and reduced luminance, which both cause severe impairment of focal vision. Further, the second experiment indicated that steering performance, and its resistance to reduced luminance decline with age. This finding suggested that difficulties with night driving experienced by aging drivers may result from age-related changes of ambient as well as focal vision (Owens & Andre, 1996). Consistent with this interpretation, Warren, Blackwell, and Morris (1989) found that the ability to perceive the direction of self-motion from visual information (optical flow) also declines with age.

Although our experiments were encouraging, one must be cautious about generalizing results from a limited number of individuals tested in a simulator. It is not clear whether the small samples of participants, particularly for the elder group, are representative of the general population. The elder participants led active lives, they may have been healthier than average, and their responses to a questionnaire suggested they had less difficulty with night driving than others of their cohorts. Moreover, the simulator was much simpler than actual night driving situations. Steering performance on the road might be affected by numerous variables that were not included in our study. Driving might be influenced, for example, by transient variations in lighting and visual adaptation or by competing demands on attention or by the participants' opportunity to control speed as well as heading.

Experiments on the Road

A search of the literature turned up surprisingly little empirical evidence on driving behavior and its variation with conditions in the actual road environment. Consider the following basic question: *To what extent do drivers actually adjust their speed in response to reduced visibility?* As noted earlier, some data indicate that drivers do not reduce their speed when visibility is degraded. For example, one traffic study, conducted in the 1970s, found no difference between day and night speeds (53.1 vs. 53.4 mph) on rural roads (Herd, Agent, & Rizenbergs, 1980). This finding is difficult to interpret, however, because of possible changes in traffic density and driving population. At night, roads are usually less congested, and the mix of drivers has shifted to a younger population. Other studies have used simulators to investigate the effects of vision on speed control (Gray & Regan, 2000; Snowden, Stimpson, & Ruddle, 1998), but these data also are open to various interpretations because most simulators lack realistic inertial motion, and none involves the actual risks associated with speed on the road.

A more realistic approach has been taken by Joanne Wood and her colleagues in studies of visual impairment and driving on a closed road course in Queensland, Australia (Wood, 1998; Wood & Troutbeck, 1994). One study by Higgins, Wood, and Tait (1998) found that severe blur degraded some aspects of the driving task, including sign recognition and avoidance of low-contrast hazards, but it had little effect on other aspects of driving, like judgment of gap clearance between roadway barriers and steering through a slalom of high-contrast traffic cones. Their methodology presented a potentially valuable approach to investigating the effects of lighting on driving behavior. In 1998, a sabbatical leave and generous support from the Queensland University of Technology provided an exciting opportunity for me to collaborate with Professor Wood and her graduate students in an experiment on the effects of age and light conditions on actual driving.

As with the simulator study at UMTRI, our experiment in Queensland tested the driving behavior of participants in three age groups (mean ages: 22, 47, and 72 years) under light conditions ranging from full daylight to near-darkness. All participants were currently active drivers with normal vision (20/40 or better) and at least 3 years of driving experience. Each participant drove a 1.8-km closed road course twice under five different lighting conditions. Each was instructed to proceed normally as she or he would on ordinary rural roads, to maintain a comfortable speed, and to be alert for unpredictable hazards (like wild animals). For half of the trials, referred to as *commentary runs*, the participants were required to report aloud all objects and events relevant to the drive. These targets included 28 road signs; four low-contrast speed bumps positioned at variable locations along the circuit, two pedestrians walking on the opposite shoulder of the road, again at unpredictable locations, and an occasional toad, rabbit, snake, or wallaby. A few participants suspected that the wildlife was under the experimenters' control (no way!).

The pedestrians were included in order to examine potential benefits of retroreflective markings. Both wore dark sweat suits, which were fitted with equivalent areas of special retroreflective material. One, called "Slash," was marked with a single retroreflective stripe (2.5 cm wide) that extended diagonally from the right shoulder to the left hip. The other, called "BioMotion," was marked with narrower (0.75 cm) stripes at the waist and major limb joints to produce the powerful perceptual effect called *biological motion*, which was discovered by Gunnar Johansson in the 1960s (Johansson, 1973; see chapter 13, "Educating Pedestrians About Their Own Nighttime Visibility: An Application of Leibowitzian Principles," by Richard A. Tyrrell and Chad W. Patton).

The test circuit was part of the Mt. Cotton Training Facility of the Queensland Department of Transportation. Situated in a rural "bush" setting, the two- and three-lane asphalt road was virtually identical to public byways, traversing multiple hills, curves, and straight sections, complete with intersections and standard road signs. At night, glare was created by automotive headlights in the oncoming lane at two locations, which were activated by remote sensors as the test vehicle approached. Our test vehicle was a 1997 Holden Commodore station wagon, equipped with automatic transmission and a digital video system to measure lane position. View of the speedometer was occluded by translucent vellum paper. High-beam headlights were active during all night tests to maintain a consistent beam pattern. In addition to normal high beam, lower headlight intensities were obtained by surreptitiously attaching filters, which attenuated intensity by -75%, -87.5%, and -97%. Light with the densest filter was so weak that several participants complained they would never own a car with such poor headlights.[5]

The question we were interested in, of course, was how their *driving behavior* would change with such wide variations in lighting. Our dependent measures included clinical tests of vision in bright and dim light, various measures of driving behavior, and responses to an extensive questionnaire. For the present story, I will focus on behavioral data that aimed to assess the roles of focal and ambient vision, that is, recognition of signs, speed bumps, and pedestrians for the former, and measures of average speed of travel for the latter.

Recognition performance was defined as the mean percentage of signs and speed bumps reported on commentary runs under each light condition. As shown in Figure 12.8, recognition decreased as a function of both age and light condition. There was no significant interaction of age and lighting. Not sur-

---

[5]Participants included four women and four men in each age group. Orders of test conditions were counterbalanced within all age groups. Equal numbers of subjects were first tested under day and night conditions. For night tests, half of the subjects were tested first with the brightest headlights, followed by successively lower levels, and half were tested in the opposite order of intensities. For all subjects, normal (N) and commentary (C) tasks were alternated every two laps. Half of the subjects began with the normal task, and the other half began with the commentary task condition. For daytime tests, all subjects drove the circuit four times, alternating between normal and commentary tasks, with equal numbers in each group following the NCCN or CNNC orders.

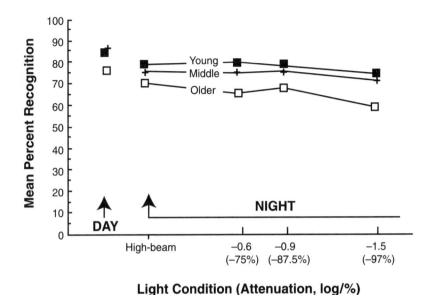

Figure 12.8. Mean percent recognition of signs and speed bumps as a function of light condition for drivers in three age groups. Data were collected on a closed road course in daylight and at night with variable headlight intensity.

prisingly, recognition was significantly better in daylight (81.9%) than in night conditions. Among the night lighting conditions, recognition with the lowest intensity (67.8%) was significantly worse than with the other headlight intensities (74.4%, 72.7%, and 73.2%), which did not differ significantly.

Ambient vision was assessed on the basis of average speed for completing the circuit. As shown in Figure 12.9, the younger drivers were consistently faster (45.6 km/hr) than the middle-aged drivers, who were faster (41.8 km/hr) than the older drivers (39.6 km/hr). Statistical tests showed a significant difference between younger and older groups ($p = .008$), with no difference in other comparisons. Light condition also had a significant effect on speed. The mean speed in daylight was significantly higher than that with full high beams (45.96 vs. 42.78 km/hr), and speed with high beams was significantly higher than that with −87.5% filters (41.05 km/hr) and −97% filters (40.20 km/hr). Also, speed was significantly higher during normal than during commentary trials (44.5 vs. 40.1 km/hr). Although light condition had a significant effect, it is interesting that the reduction of speed from daylight to night with high-beam headlights was only 3.2 km/hr (2.0 mph), and the reduction from full high beams to −97% attenuation was 2.6 km/hr (1.6 mph). This amounts to an overall reduction in speed of only 12.5% from daylight to near-darkness.

Unlike the data from traffic surveys, therefore, these data revealed that drivers actually do slow down under low-light conditions, but they do not slow down very much. The recognition data (see Figure 12.8) show that target recognition declined in low light. This happened despite the facts that (a) 28 of the 32 targets were highly reflective road signs and (b) participants had the option of slowing down enough to achieve 100% recognition. (In fact, one middle-aged driver did this.)

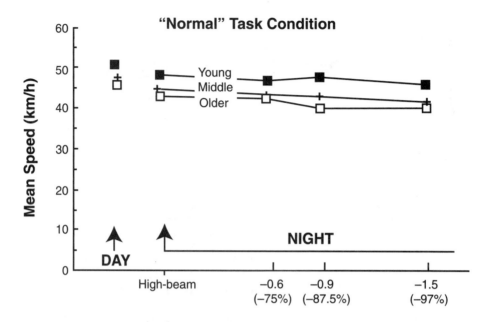

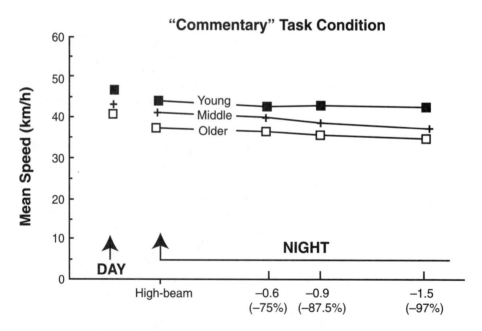

Figure 12.9. Mean speed as a function of light condition for drivers in three age groups under both "normal" and "commentary" task conditions. Drivers were required to report aloud all important objects on or beside the road as they drove; the speedometer was occluded to avoid cognitive bias of selected speed.

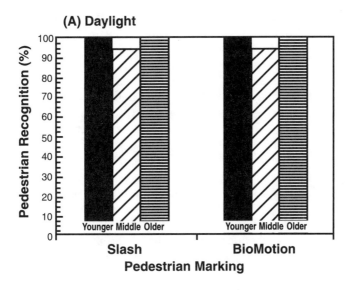

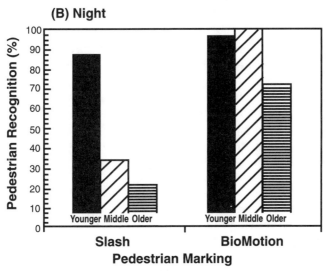

Figure 12.10. Mean pedestrian recognition of three age groups under both day (A) and night (B) conditions. Pedestrians were walking on the shoulder of the opposite side of the road, facing the oncoming test vehicle. The "Slash" marking was a diagonal retrore-flective strip extending from the right shoulder to the left hip; the "BioMotion" markings were narrower stripes around the waist and major limb joints.

The data for pedestrian recognition, treated separately from those for signs and speed bumps, confirmed the value of biological motion as an excellent nighttime marking configuration. As shown in Figure 12.10, pedestrian recognition was nearly perfect in daylight (97.9%), which is not surprising, as the dark sweat suits appeared in high contrast with the rural surroundings. More interesting, pedestrian recognition at night was much better for BioMotion than for Slash (93.8 vs. 72.9%, overall), and the advantage of biological motion increased with drivers' age. Participants in all age groups recognized pedestrians equally well in daylight, regardless of markings. At night, however, the perceptual advantage of BioMotion over Slash (torso) markings increased from ~10% for the younger drivers to ~66% for the middle-aged to ~50% for the older drivers. I want to emphasize that this advantage is one of *perceptual recognition, not detection*. Both marking configurations had equivalent retroreflective material, and because of its greater angular size, the Slash configuration would be detected at a greater distance than the BioMotion stripes under adverse conditions like fog. The important difference, however, is perceptual. Although it may be seen sooner, the larger stripe of the Slash marking does not look like a person, whereas biological motion is recognized instantly as a person. This difference has striking implications for optimizing pedestrian safety (Owens, Antonoff, & Francis, 1994). Along this line, I urge interested readers to see Rick Tyrrell's ingenious study of pedestrians' misconceptions about their own visibility and the prospects of education to promote appropriate precautionary measures (chapter 13).

Summary

Diagnosis and correction of night myopia are surely worthwhile, but they are not likely to solve the larger problem of hazardous driving at night. This problem requires a fuller understanding of driving behavior and especially its relationship to basic perceptual and cognitive processes. The two modes of vision concept has started us moving in the right direction.

Our first simulator experiment indicated that steering performance, at least for young adults, is strongly resistant to impairment by blur and reduced luminance. Indeed, for guidance of locomotion, nocturnal vision may be as good as high-resolution diurnal vision. Though unexpected from the viewpoint of traditional psychophysics, this finding seems natural from an evolutionary perspective. The second simulator experiment showed that the quality of guidance vision may diminish progressively over the adult lifespan (see Figure 12.4). This sort of age-related change in ambient vision may contribute to the uneasiness of older motorists at night, and as shown by recent work by Peter Cavanagh and Jill Higginson (see chapter 15, "What Is the Role of Vision During Stair Descent?") impaired ambient vision may also be associated with increased risk of falls when negotiating stairs.

The closed road experiment with Joanne Wood provided new evidence that drivers of all ages do, in fact, travel more slowly under low-light conditions (Figure 12.9). But reductions of speed were small in magnitude (from 46 km/hr in daylight to 40 km/hr in the dimmest condition), and they were not sufficient to maintain stable levels of recognition performance (Figures 12.8 and 12.10). Earlier studies had estimated the maximum safe speed at night with normal low-beam headlights, which are roughly comparable to the -75% condition of our study, to be 25–50 km/hr (Johansson & Rumar, 1968; Leibowitz, Owens, & Tyrrell, 1998). Although the average speed of our closed road measures falls within the upper portion of that range, maximum speeds were surely higher-than-average values, which include travel through curved segments of the circuit.

These findings are consistent with previous evidence that drivers are often unaware of degraded visibility with dirty headlights (Rumar, 1968). They are also consistent with the theory that drivers' speed control neglects impairment of their visual recognition and relies more on visual guidance capabilities that are highly efficient in low light (Kallberg, 1993; Owens & Tyrrell, 1999). All of these findings suggest that driving involves a variety of psychological processes that are not wholly conscious or deliberate. Planning one's route surely involves conscious cognition; controlling one's vehicle does not. The question of how volitional cognitive processes interact with automatic, real-time control of action is a fascinating problem for further research (Rasmussen, 1983).

Conclusion

Thanks to the unique mentorship and friendly encouragement of Herschel Leibowitz, we have been able to learn a bit about the nature of driving and to find some useful leads for enhancing public safety. For me, this work has been an enormously entertaining exploration guided by Leibowitz's dictum that much can be gained by crossing the usual boundaries between basic and applied science. This lesson seems especially important for psychological science (Leibowitz, 1992, 1996). Hersh takes delight in pointing to unexpected practical benefits of fundamental research. I see the path from Schneider's physiological studies of the golden hamster to the Mt. Cotton road circuit in Queensland as a nice example. Hersh also taught us that serious attention to practical problems can inspire valuable basic research.

In my view, driving represents one of countless everyday activities that can guide science toward new insight. Ironically, it is worth noting that contrary to emphasis on traffic accidents, humans are incredibly safe vehicle operators. We have estimated that if crashes were random events, one could expect to travel safely for more than 100 years before suffering an injury and for more than 4,000 years before encountering a fatal collision (Owens, Helmers, & Sivak, 1993). We are just beginning to understand how ordinary human beings, without much special training, are capable of safely maneuvering vehicles that weigh 10–40 times our body weight at speeds 5–10 times the maximum velocity of natural locomotion. Many questions remain. In 1938, Gibson and Crooks observed that "The relative importance of effortful attention and of habit in safe driving needs to be worked out" (p. 458). This is still true. We can expect that further investigation of driving will yield new insights into the interplay of perceptual, cognitive, and social processes in naturalistic circumstances, as well as the means to develop safer, more efficient transportation.

References

Boring, E. G. (1942). *Sensation and perception in the history of experimental psychology.* New York: D. Appleton-Century.

Boussaoud, D., di Pellegrino, G., & Wise, S. P. (1996). Frontal lobe mechanisms subserving vision-for-action versus vision-for-perception. *Behavioural Brain Research, 72,* 1–15.

Brooks, J. C, & Owens, D. A. (2001). *Effects of luminance, blur, and tunnel vision on postural stability.* Paper presented at the First Meeting of the Visual Sciences Society, Sarasota, FL, May 2001.

Cogan, D. G. (1937). Accommodation and the autonomic nervous system. *Archives of Ophthalmology, 18,* 739–766.

Cornelius, C. S. (1861). *Die theorie des sehens und raümlichen vorstellens* [A theory of vision and three-dimensional representation]. Halle, Germany: H. W. Schmidt.

Dawkins, R. (1996). *Climbing mount improbable.* New York: Norton.

Garner, W. R., Hake, H. W., & Eriksen, C. W. (1956). Operationism and the concept of perception. *Psychological Review, 63,* 149–159.

Gibson, J. J., & Crooks, L. E. (1938). A theoretical field-analysis of automobile-driving. *American Journal of Psychology, 51*(3), 453–471.

Goodale, M. A. (1983). Vision as a sensorimotor system. In T. E. Robinson (Ed.), *Behavioral approaches to brain research* (pp. 41–61). New York: Oxford University Press.

Goodale, M. A., & Milner, A. D. (1992). Separate visual pathways for perception and action. *Trends in Neuroscience, 15,* 20–25.

Graham, C. H. (1965). Some fundamental data. In C. H. Graham (Ed.), *Vision and visual perception* (pp. 68–80). New York: Wiley.

Gray, R., & Regan, D. (2000). Risky driving behavior: A consequence of motion adaptation for visually guided motor action. *Journal of Experimental Psychology: Human Perception and Performance, 26*(6), 1721–1732.

Green, P., & Olson, A. (1989). *The development and use of the UMTRI driving simulator* (Report No. UMTRI-89-25). Ann Arbor, MI: University of Michigan Transportation Research Institute.

Gregory, R. L. (1997). *Eye and brain: The psychology of seeing* (5th ed.). Princeton, NJ: Princeton University Press.

Held, R. (1968). Dissociation of visual function by deprivation and rearrangement. *Psychologische Forschung,* 31, 338–348.

Herd, D. R., Agent, K. R., & Rizenbergs, R. L. (1980). Traffic accidents: Day versus night. In *Traffic accident analysis and application of system safety* (pp. 25–30). Washington, DC: National Academy of Sciences.

Higgins, K., Wood, J., & Tait, A. (1998). Vision and driving: Selective effect of optical blur on different driving tasks. *Human Factors, 41*(2), 224–232.

Humphrey, N. K. (1974). Vision in a monkey without striate cortex: A case study. *Perception, 3,* 241–255.

Ingle, D. (1967). Two visual mechanisms underlying the behavior of fish. *Psychologische Forschung, 31,* 44–51.

Johansson, G. (1973). Visual perception of biological motion and a model for its analysis. *Perception and Psychophysics, 14*(2), 201–211.

Johansson, G., & Rumar, K. (1968). Visible distances and safe approach speeds for night driving. *Ergonomics, 11*(3), 275–282.

Kaas, J. H., & Hackett, T. A. (1999). 'What' and 'where' processing in auditory cortex. *Nature Neuroscience, 2*(12), 1045–1047.

Kallberg, V-P. (1993). Reflector posts—Signs of danger? *Transportation Research Record, 1403,* 57–66. Washington, DC: National Academy Press.

Kolb, F. C., & Braun, J. (1995). Blindsight in normal observers. *Nature, 377,* 336–338.

Kosnik, W. D., Sekuler, R., & Kline, D. W. (1990). Self-reported visual problems of older drivers. *Human Factors, 32*(5), 597–608.

Leibowitz, H. W. (1987). Ambient illuminance during twilight and from the full moon. In Committee on Vision, Working Group on Night Vision (Eds.), *Night vision: Current research and future directions* (pp. 19–22). Washington, DC: National Academy Press.

Leibowitz, H. W. (1992). The role of the functionalist school in the growth of psychology. In D. A. Owens & M. Wagner (Eds.), *Progress in modern psychology: The legacy of American functinoalism* (pp. 17–29). Westport, CT: Praeger Publishers.

Leibowitz, H. W. (1996). The symbiosis between basic and applied research. *American Psychologist, 51*(4), 366–370.

Leibowitz, H. W., & Owens, D. A. (1977). Nighttime driving accidents and selective visual degradation. *Science, 197,* 422–423.

Leibowitz, H. W., & Owens, D. A. (1978). New evidence for the intermediate position of relaxed accommodation. *Documenta Ophthalmologica, 46,* 133–147.

Leibowitz, H. W., & Owens, D. A. (1991). Can normal outdoor activities be carried out in civil twilight? *Applied Optics, 30*, 3501–3503.

Leibowitz, H. W., Owens, D. A., & Post, R. B. (1982). *Nighttime driving and visual degradation* (SAE Technical Paper Series, No. 820414). Warrendale, PA: Society of Automotive Engineers.

Leibowitz, H. W., Owens, D. A., & Tyrrell, R. A. (1998). The Assured Clear Distance Ahead Rule: Implications for nighttime traffic safety and the law. *Accident Analysis and Prevention, 30*, 93–99.

Leibowitz, H. W., Shupert-Rodemer, C., & Dichgans, J. (1979). The independence of dynamic spatial orientation from luminance and refractive error. *Perception and Psychophysics, 25*, 75–79.

Loewenfeld, I. E. (1979). Pupillary changes related to age. In H. S. Thompson, R. Daroff, L. Frisén, J. S. Glaser, & M. D. Sanders (Eds.), *Topics in neuro-ophthalmology* (pp. 124–150). Baltimore: Williams & Wilkins.

Mishkin, M., Ungerleider, L. G., & Macko, K. A. (1983). Object vision and spatial vision: two cortical pathways. *Trends in Neuroscience, 6*, 414–417.

Morgan, M. W. (1946). A new theory for the control of accommodation. *American Journal of Optometry and Archives of the American Academy of Optometry, 23*, 99–110.

National Safety Council (1925–1998). *Accident facts*. Chicago: National Safety Council.

Norman, J. (in press). Two visual systems and two theories of perception: An attempt to reconcile the constructivist and ecological approaches. *Behavioral and Brain Sciences*.

Owens, D. A. (1987). Oculomotor information and perception of three-dimensional space. In H. Heuer & A. F. Sanders (Eds.), *Perspectives on perception and action* (pp. 215–248). Hillsdale, NJ: Erlbaum.

Owens, D. A. (2000). The place of ambient vision in understanding problems of mobility and aging. In W. Schaie & M. Petrucha (Eds.), *Mobility and transportation in the elderly* (pp. 45–61). New York: Springer.

Owens, D. A., & Andre, J. T. (1996). Selective visual degradation and the older driver. *International Association of Traffic and Safety Sciences Research, 20*(1), 57–66.

Owens, D. A., Antonoff, R., & Francis, E. L. (1994). Biological motion and nighttime pedestrian conspicuity. *Human Factors, 36*(4), 718–732.

Owens, D. A., Francis, E. L., & Leibowitz, H. W. (1989). *Visibility distance with headlights: A functional approach* (SAE Technical Paper Series, No. 890684). Warrendale, PA: Society of Automotive Engineers.

Owens, D. A., Helmers, G., & Sivak, M. (1993) Intelligent vehicle highway systems: A call for user-centered design. *Ergonomics, 36*, 363–369.

Owens, D. A., & Leibowitz, H. W. (1976a). Night myopia: Cause and a possible basis for amelioration. *American Journal of Optometry and Physiological Optics, 53*, 709–717.

Owens, D. A., & Leibowitz, H. W. (1976b). The intermediate resting position of accommodation and its implications for night driving. In *Editions la prevention routiere internationale* (pp. 147–152). Paris: Linas-Monttheiry.

Owens, D. A., & Sivak, M. (1996). Differentiation of visibility and alcohol as contributors to twilight road fatalities. *Human Factors, 38*(4), 680–689.

Owens, D. A., & Tyrrell, R. A. (1999). Effects of luminance, blur, and age on nighttime visual guidance: A test of the selective degradation hypothesis. *Journal of Experimental Psychology: Applied, 5*(2), 115–128.

Owsley, C., & Sloane, M. E. (1990). Vision and aging. In F. Boller and J. Grafman (Eds.), *Handbook of neuropsychology* (Vol. 4, pp. 229–249). New York: Elsevier Science Publications.

Payne, B. R., Lomber, S. G., MacNeil, M. A., & Cornwell, P. (1996). Evidence for greater sight in blindsight following damage of primary visual cortex early in life. *Neuropsychologia, 34*, 741–774.

Pitts, D. G. (1982). The effects of aging on selected visual functions: Dark adaptation, visual acuity, stereopsis, and brightness contrast. In R. Sekuler, D. Kline, & K. Dismukes (Eds.), *Aging and human visual function* (pp. 131–159). New York: Alan R. Liss.

Rasmussen, J. (1983). Skills, rules, and knowledge; Signals, signs, and symbols, and other distinctions in human performance models. *IEEE Transactions on Systems, Man, and Cybernetics, SMC-13* (3), 257–266.

Rock, I. (1983). *The logic of perception*. Cambridge, MA: MIT Press.

Rock, I. (1997). *Indirect perception*. Cambridge, MA: MIT Press.

Romanski, L. M., Tian, B., Mishkin, M., Goldman-Rakic, P. S., & Rauschecken, J. P. (1999). Dual streams of auditory afferents target multiple domains in the primate prefrontal cortex. *Nature Neuroscience, 2*(12), 1131–1136.

Rumar, K. (1968). Dirty headlights — Frequency and visibility effects. *Ergonomics, 17*(4), 529–533.

Schieber, F. (1994). *Recent developments in vision, aging, and driving: 1988–1994* (Report No. UMTRI-94-26). Ann Arbor, MI: University of Michigan Transportation Research Institute.

Schneider, G. E. (1967). Contrasting visuomotor functions of tectum and cortex in the golden hamster. *Psychologische Forschung, 31*, 52–62.

Schneider, G. E. (1969). Two visual systems: Brain mechanisms for localization and discrimination are dissociated by tectal and cortical lesions. *Science, 163*, 895–902.

Schober, H. (1954). Über die Akkommodationsruhelage [About the resting position of accommodation]. *Optik, 6*, 282–290.

Snowden, R. J., Stimpson, N., & Ruddle, R. A. (1998, April 2). Speed perception fogs up as visibility drops. *Nature, 392*, 450.

Stoerig, P. (1996). Varieties of vision: From blind responses to conscious recognition. *Trends in Neuroscience, 19*, 401–406.

Trevarthen, C. (1968). Two mechanisms of vision in primates. *Psychologische Forschung, 31*, 229–337.

Walls, G. L. (1942). *The vertebrate eye and its adaptive radiation.* Bloomfield Hills, MI: The Cranbrook Press.

Warren, W. H., Jr., Blackwell, A. W., & Morris, M. W. (1989). Age differences in perceiving the direction of self-motion from optical flow. *Journal of Gerontology: Psychological Sciences, 44*(5), 147–153.

Weale, R. A. (1963). *The aging eye.* New York: Harper & Row.

Weiskrantz, L., Warrington, E. K., Sanders, M. D., & Marshall, J. (1974). Visual capacity in the hemianopic field following a restricted occipital ablation. *Brain, 97*, 709–728.

Winer, B. J., Brown, D. R., & Michaels, K. M. (1991). *Statistical principles in experimental design* (3rd ed., pp. 411–413). New York: McGraw-Hill.

Wood, J. (1998). Vision research, driving and the elderly. *Ophthalmic and Physiological Optics, 18* (6), 469–470.

Wood, J. M., & Troutbeck, R. (1994). Effect of visual impairment on driving. *Human Factors, 36*, 476–487.

Yeager, C., & Janos, L. (1985). *Yeager: An autobiography.* New York: Bantam.

Zeki, S. (1993). *A vision of the brain.* Boston: Blackwell Scientific Publications.

13

Educating Pedestrians About Their Own Nighttime Visibility

An Application of Leibowitzian Principles

Richard A. Tyrrell and Chad W. Patton

It would be difficult to summarize Herschel Leibowitz's approach to psychology without starting with a statement of his passionate belief in the *usefulness* of psychology. As is no doubt clear from even a quick skim through this volume, one of Leibowitz's most important contributions is to remind psychologists that psychology can and should be directed toward understanding and relieving societal problems. And Leibowitz is quick to point out that the beneficial relationship between psychology and concern for societal problems is bidirectional: Consideration of real-world problems can help reveal the limitations of current psychological theories and thereby accelerate the development of theories. These ideas are documented, exemplified, and extended throughout this volume and elsewhere (e.g., Leibowitz, 1996) and have no doubt contributed to the position of Leibowitz as one of the most cited authors in the field of perception (White, 1987). However, another of Leibowitz's beliefs—that a synergistic relationship should exist among an academic psychologist's teaching, research, and service efforts—has received less attention. This chapter describes an experiment in which both of these beliefs are taken to heart. The experiment demonstrates empirically that one of Leibowitz's theoretical contributions is sufficiently powerful and understandable that exposure to the theory can result in lasting and beneficial behavioral consequences.

Leibowitz has asserted that most modern societal problems have a strong behavioral component and that psychology is therefore well positioned to make important contributions to society. Epidemiological evidence seems to support the assertion. We are at a time in our history in which infectious diseases have largely come under control (and many of those that are not yet under control are known to be transmitted behaviorally). Meanwhile, the rate of suffering and premature death due to injuries (i.e., "accidents") has become paramount. This is particularly true of the youngest members of our society, for whom injury is the leading cause of both disabilities and deaths. In the United States, injuries cause almost half of the deaths of children between the ages of 1 and 4, more than half the deaths between ages 5 and 14, and nearly 80% of the deaths between ages 15 and 24 (National Research Council, 1985). Indeed, injuries are responsible for more prematurely lost years of life than any major disease group.

Although psychology may indeed be well positioned to make important contributions to understanding and reducing many behavioral problems, for the contributions to be realized requires significant investment. Unfortunately, although the costs associated with injuries are as staggering as their frequency, understanding and preventing injuries do not appear to be a national research priority. In fact, one 1985 analysis indicated that the federal nonmilitary budget allocated to research on injuries was less than 7% of the total allocated to cardiovascular disease and cancer, despite the fact that injuries are responsible for more years of lost work life than all forms of cancer and cardiovascular disease combined (National Research Council, 1985). In his testimony before the defense subcommittee of the Senate Appropriations Committee, Leibowitz emphasized the need for human factors research in the military domain and noted that despite the fact that human error is often given as the causal or contributing factor in military aviation accidents, the U.S. military spends less on human factors research than that which is lost in a single aircraft accident (Leibowitz, 1990).

Pedestrian Injuries and Fatalities

Traffic crashes, the most common source of injury, are responsible each year for roughly 40,000 fatalities in the United States and 500,000 fatalities worldwide each year (Evans, 1991). This chapter focuses on just one type of crash: collisions between vehicles and pedestrians. These incidents are both common and devastating. In 2000, 78,000 pedestrians were injured (2.4% of all traffic injuries) and 4,739 pedestrians were killed (11.3% of all traffic fatalities) in the United States alone (National Highway Traffic Safety Administration, 2002). Pedestrian–vehicle collisions often occur in situations in which the demands on the driver exceed the capacities of human perception and performance. Indeed, despite the presumed decrease in pedestrian exposure at night, more than 60% of all fatal pedestrian collisions occur at night (National Highway Traffic Safety Administration, 2002). Although this might be partially explained by factors such as alcohol consumption and fatigue, systematic analyses of the U.S. Fatal Accident Reporting System database indicate that when other factors are held constant, pedestrian collisions increase as illumination decreases (Owens & Sivak, 1993, 1996). Thus a key issue in nighttime pedestrian accidents is that of visibility. A fundamental problem is that even at the relatively low speed of 25 mph the total distance required to stop an automobile can be 1.2 to 3 times greater than the distance at which a dark-clad pedestrian can be seen under low-beam illumination (e.g., Leibowitz, Owens, & Tyrrell, 1998). This problem represents a substantial and multifaceted challenge to researchers. The experiment described later in this chapter is an empirical exploration of a relatively simple, low-tech, and potentially cost-effective approach to reducing the problem.

The fact that it can be difficult for drivers to see pedestrians at night has been documented for at least 3 decades. Allen, Hazlett, Tacker, & Graham (1968) had participants ride in the passenger seat of a car traveling at 30 mph. Pedestrians standing on the right side of the road wore either dark clothing, white clothing, or retroreflective strips around the collar and sleeves. The car passenger started a stopwatch when he or she was first able to see the pedestrians and stopped it when the pedestrian was reached. Even though their participants knew they would encounter pedestrians and could therefore react relatively quickly, the authors calculated that drivers would have to travel below 40 mph to ensure that they would be able to avoid a dark-clad pedestrian. Even shorter visibility estimates were obtained by Johansson and Rumar (1968), who asked 1,387 participants to drive their own cars under realistic driving conditions and brake as soon as they saw a dark-clad dummy. Even though the drivers were expecting to encounter the dummy, the 50th and 10th percentiles for the braking distance were only 75 and 49 ft, respectively, which led the authors to conclude that the maximum safe speed at night is 15.5–31 mph. Olson and Sivak (1983) also determined that the illumination provided by low-beam headlights is insufficient to support speeds greater than 30 mph.

Because contrast is the key factor that limits the visibility of a pedestrian, an obvious way to increase visibility is by increasing the pedestrian's contrast. Many researchers have documented that when pedestrians' clothing includes retroreflective materials the probability of their being detected at a safe distance is dramatically increased (e.g., Allen et al., 1968; Blomberg, Hale, & Preusser, 1986; Shinar, 1984). Still others have documented that pedestrians can be recognized even earlier when their conspicuity is enhanced by configuring the retroreflective material in such as way as to depict "biological motion" (Luoma, Schumann, & Traube, 1996; Owens & Antonoff, 1994). Despite the fact that these strategies can dramatically increase safety with little cost, however, their use remains relatively infrequent and a key problem remains: Until *all* pedestrians wear carefully configured retroreflective material at night, some pedestrians will be difficult to see and drivers must assume that they will occasionally encounter inconspicuous pedestrians.

Compounding the visibility problem is the fact that pedestrians overestimate their own visibility. It is understandable why this is the case. A pedestrian walking along an unlit roadway is likely to be adapted to a relatively low ambient illumination level, and when suddenly illuminated by an approaching vehicle's headlights, he or she is faced with an intense stimulus that has both high luminance and high contrast. Facing the glare of the oncoming headlights, the pedestrian may be unable to appreciate the difficulty of the driver's detection task and, convinced that he or she is visible, is more likely to assume that the driver will take responsibility for avoiding a collision. To our knowledge, only two studies have measured pedestrians' estimates of their own visibility. Allen et al. (1968) asked participants to stand on the side of the road and start a stopwatch when they were certain they were visible to a driver who approached at a constant speed. The participants stopped the stopwatch when the car passed. Using this approach, Allen et al. found that more than 95% of their participants overestimated their visibility. Estimated visibility distances were up to three times greater than actual visibility distances, with the mean estimated visibility distance being 343 ft. Using a similar methodology, Shinar (1984) also found pedestrians' estimates of their own visibility to be significantly greater than their actual visibility in all but one condition (low-beam headlights plus glare).

Pedestrians who overestimate their own visibility are more likely to behave in ways that increase their risk. Therefore, one potential solution is somehow to convince pedestrians that they are not as visible as they once thought. Indeed, calls for public education campaigns are often heard in traffic safety research. In discussing the fact that the typical pedestrian overestimates his or her visibility, Allen et al. (1968) emphasized "the need to educate him [sic] or to make him in fact more visible or both" (p. 298). Similarly, Leibowitz and his colleagues have argued that public education is of critical importance in reducing night driving problems (e.g., Leibowitz & Owens, 1977, 1984; Leibowitz et al., 1998). Unfortunately, few, if any, data exist to support the assertion that education is useful in this domain. Although several studies have explored the efficacy of educational approaches to increase pedestrian safety, the research has centered on the behavior of children in daylight conditions (e.g., Gregersen & Nolen, 1994; Yeaton & Bailey, 1978) and has been criticized as being relatively unproductive (Ampofo-Boateng & Thomson, 1989; Sandels, 1975). As a first step in addressing these questions, we conducted an experiment to determine whether adult pedestrians' estimates of their own nighttime visibility are malleable. That is, is it possible to convince pedestrians that their visibility is not what they think it is? A secondary goal was to determine whether pedestrians appreciate the extent to which their visibility is influenced by headlight beam setting (low beam vs. high beam) and by the reflectivity of their clothing.

The Experiment

The idea for this experiment was born from hearing the reactions of students who had heard the "selective degradation theory" described in class. This theory, which has been advanced by Leibowitz and his colleagues (Leibowitz & Owens, 1977, 1984; Leibowitz, Owens, & Post, 1982; Owens & Tyrrell, 1999) and which is described in more detail elsewhere in this volume (see chapter 12, "Twilight Vision and Road Safety: Seeing More Than We Notice but Less Than We Think," by D. Alfred Owens), asserts that one reason we tend not to drive slower at night is that we are not aware of the degree to which our vision is impaired. The feedback we get while driving is often misleading and is generally consistent with the impression that driving at night is an easy task (e.g., it is generally not challenging to maintain our position in our lane) and that we are still able to see well (e.g., road signs have been carefully designed to be readable at night from a substantial distance). Upon hearing these issues explained in depth, students often seem surprised to learn how challenging it can be to see things (such as pedestrians) on the roadway at night that have *not* been engineered to be visible and conspicuous. On numerous occasions, students have responded (sometimes weeks later) with comments such as "Now I'm scared to drive at night!" and "Since that lecture I've been using my high beams more than ever!" and "Now I'm much more careful when I walk around at night." Although these comments are pleasant enough for a professor to hear (because they suggest that the students actually understood and remembered the material), the comments are, of course, more a tribute to the message than to the messenger. Still, the students' comments seem a bit ironic. After all, a fundamental assertion of the selective degradation theory is that we are not aware of the degree to which nighttime illumination levels degrade our visual abilities. Is it possible that hearing a lecture about these impairments could lead to an appreciation of the impairments while directly experiencing them on a nightly basis does not? If so, might the effect be lasting? And what might be the safety implications? We decided to explore these questions empirically.

To measure the effects of exposure to the selective degradation theory requires, of course, comparing the responses of people who have been exposed to the theory with the responses of those who have not. This seemingly simple idea proved somewhat challenging to implement. We rejected the possibility of measuring the estimated visibility levels of a single group of participants before and after they were exposed to the theory. Because the purpose of such a study would become obvious to its participants, this within-subjects approach would be likely to result in significant "demand characteristics" (e.g., Orne, 1962). As such, the participants' responses might be influenced by their desire to be "good" participants (i.e., to give the responses they believe the researchers want to see). Instead, we decided to compare the estimated visibility levels of multiple groups of participants. The challenge then became how to expose some of the participants to the theory without revealing the purpose of the study. We decided to take advantage of the opportunity afforded by the university classroom setting (where students frequently sit through lectures without questioning the motives of the lecturer). Thus, a group of undergraduate students from different sections of an introduction to psychology course participated in the study in exchange for extra credit. Half of these participants were recruited from sections of the course that had heard the guest lecture described in the next section. The other half were recruited from sections of the course in which the guest lecture had not been given. Because we also wanted to compare the effects of exposure to the selective degradation theory with the effects of having recently been shown a demonstration of pedestrians walking at night under a variety of controlled conditions, half of the participants were shown such a demonstration immediately before data collection.

Thus, the 48 undergraduate students were divided equally into four groups. The lecture group had heard the lecture but had not seen the demonstration. The demo group had seen the demonstration but had not heard the lecture. The combo group had been exposed to both the lecture and the demonstration. The control group had been exposed to neither.

The Lecture

The first author gave a 75-min guest lecture to two sections of an introduction to psychology course (roughly 100 students per section). The lecture was given at the point in the semester when the topic of perception was covered. Later that semester, the second author recruited 24 students from these sections to participate in this research (in the lecture and combo groups). The theme of the lecture, titled "From Hamsters to Highways," was that basic research can help in the understanding of applied problems. The lecture began with a summary of the neurophysiological studies by Gerald Schneider (1969) in which two visual pathways in the golden hamster were first described. The lecture outlined the extension of these results to humans and then emphasized the relevance of these concepts to the problem of night driving as described in the selective degradation theory advanced by Leibowitz and his colleagues (Leibowitz & Owens, 1977; Leibowitz et al., 1982; Owens & Tyrrell, 1999). It is important to note that the theme of the lecture was *not* pedestrian safety. In fact, the pedestrian problem was not raised until the end of the lecture, when the severity of the problem was described and the selective degradation theory was applied to it. Briefly mentioned were the facts that pedestrians typically overestimate their own visibility and that highly reflective clothing, retroreflective materials, and high-beam illumination can all increase the visibility of pedestrians. Although no demonstrations, photographs, or other graphics depicted the specific problem of pedestrian visibility, one nighttime photograph of an underride collision (in which a car had collided with the side of a large tractor trailer) was shown to help make the point that contrast is of fundamental importance in determining visibility.

At no point in the lecture was our research project mentioned, and the person who delivered the lecture was not present during recruiting or data collection. Similarly, the person who recruited the participants and collected the data (the second author) was not present during the guest lectures. Thus the participants were not likely to realize that a connection existed between the guest lecture they had heard and the research project in which they later participated.

The Demonstration

Immediately before data collection, participants in the demo and combo groups watched a demonstration of the visibility of pedestrians at night. This demonstration was done at the test site, with the participant sitting in the front passenger seat of the test vehicle. The participant was told only to observe a pedestrian as he or she walked toward and away from the car under several different conditions; the purpose of the demonstration was not described. An experimenter then walked from the pedestrian's starting point (see further on) toward the car and back again six times in a random order of the same clothing and beam conditions that were later tested (3 clothing conditions × 2 beam conditions). A second experimenter sat in the driver's seat to control the vehicle's headlights and ensure that the participant paid attention to the demonstration. Immediately after this demonstration, the participant walked with the first experimenter to the starting point and began the data collection phase. Participants in the lecture and control groups skipped the demonstration entirely.

Test Site and Test Vehicle

The test site was a private one-lane stretch of asphalt that was approximately 275 m long. The road had not been resurfaced recently and had a reflectance of approximately 15%. The road was adjacent to a golf course and was sufficiently removed from all light sources.

The test vehicle, a 1994 Oldsmobile 98, was parked at one end of the road. The headlights were aligned prior to the study and were cleaned prior to each session. The car idled during data collection to ensure constant headlight power.

Clothing and Illumination Manipulations

Each participant estimated his or her own visibility under each of six combinations of three clothing conditions (black, white, retroreflective) and two illumination settings (low beam, high beam). In the black conditions, participants wore a large black overcoat with a reflectance of 3%. In the white conditions, participants wore a white lab jacket with a reflectance of 79%. When in the retroreflective conditions, the participant wore the same white lab coat but in addition had 2.5-cm-wide silver retroreflective strips attached around the ankles, wrist, elbows, and shoulders. It is important to realize that only the participants who saw the demonstration were given the opportunity to see the retroreflective material "in action" (i.e., from the perspective of a driver sitting above actively burning headlights). The other participants saw the material only from their own perspective (as they donned the material and whenever they looked down at it). From this perspective, of course, retroreflective material does not necessarily appear to be a particularly impressive safety device.

Procedure

Only one participant was tested at a time. Data were collected only on nights that were free from precipitation, and data collection began at least 60 min after sunset. After providing his or her informed consent, the participant was driven to the test site. After the car was parked, the demonstration was presented if the participant was in either the demo or the combo group. The participant then walked with an experimenter to the pedestrian starting point. The six clothing-beam combinations were tested in a random order. After the participant donned the appropriate clothing, he or she was told, "Walk towards the car until you are confident that the driver of the car can recognize you as a pedestrian." The headlights of the car were then turned on in the appropriate setting for the trial, and the trial began. The participant was allowed to walk forward and backward until he or she was satisfied with the estimate. When the participant stopped walking and indicated satisfaction with the estimate, the headlights were turned off, and the participant and the experimenter walked together back to the starting point. During the return walk, the experimenter used a measuring wheel to measure the distance from the participant's estimation point back to the starting point (estimated visibility distance was later calculated by subtracting the distance between the starting point and the participant's estimation point from the distance between the car and the starting point). This procedure was then repeated for the remaining trials. To reduce the usefulness of landmarks, between trials the second experimenter moved the vehicle to a different position in a quasi-random order (235 m, 242 m, or 250 m from the pedestrian starting point). To reduce the salience of the beam manipulation, the headlight beam setting was always switched between trials when the headlights were turned off.

Results and Discussion

To further describe the testing conditions, illuminance was measured on a representative night. Illumination was measured (Minolta Illuminance Meter model T-1, Minolta, Ramsey, NJ) across a range of distances at the height of a pedestrian's head, waist, and ankle under both high- and low-beam conditions. The results are presented in Figure 13.1. The covariation between illuminance and distance can be thought of as one cue to the pedestrians about their own visibility.

The estimated visibility data were analyzed in two steps. In the first step, data from the control group were analyzed separately from that of the other groups. This analysis explored the effects of the clothing and beam manipulations on pedestrians' estimated visibility apart from the educational manipulations used in the other groups. In the second step, the separate and combined effects of the lecture and the demonstration were explored by analyzing the data from the remaining three groups relative to the control group. An alpha level of .05 was used for all statistical tests.

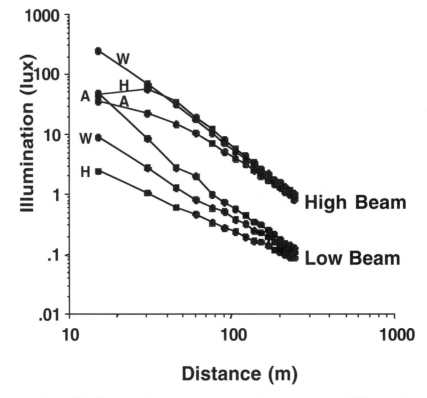

Figure 13.1. Illumination levels measured at the test site at different distances under both low-beam and high-beam settings. Illumination was measured at the height of a pedestrian's ankle (A), waist (W), and head (H).

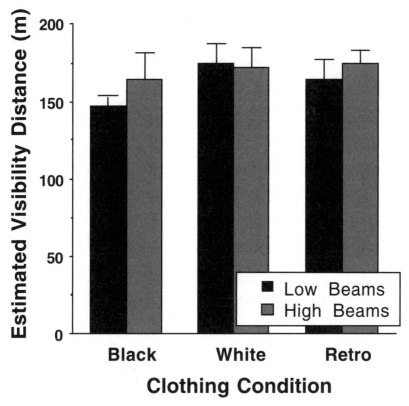

Figure 13.2.   Mean estimated visibility distances (+1 standard error of the mean) of the participants in the control group, who had experienced neither of the educational manipulations.

Effects of Clothing and Beam

Mean estimated visibility distances for the control group are presented in Figure 13.2. A 2 × 3 repeated-measures analysis of variance (ANOVA) revealed a significant main effect of clothing, $F(2, 22) = 15.1$, $p = .0001$. A Newman-Keuls multiple comparison procedure revealed that when averaged across the two beam conditions, visibility estimates from the black clothing condition ($M = 155.9$ m, or 511.5 ft) were significantly less than estimates from both the white condition ($M = 174.1$ m, or 571.2 ft; $p < .01$) and the retroreflective condition ($M = 170.2$ m, or 558.4 ft; $p < .01$) and that estimates from the white condition were not significantly different from the estimates from the retroreflective condition ($p > .05$). The ANOVA also revealed a significant main effect of beam, $F(1, 11) = 15.4$, $p = .002$, indicating that visibility estimates (when averaged across the three clothing conditions) were greater under high-beam illumination ($M = 171.3$ m, or 562.0 ft) than under low-beam illumination ($M = 162.1$ m, or 531.8 ft). The interaction between the clothing and beam variables was marginally significant: $F(2, 22) = 2.8$, $p = .081$. Simple effects tests explored this interaction and revealed that the effect of beam setting was significant for both the black clothing condition—$F(1, 11) = 12.4$,

$p = .005$—and the retroreflective clothing condition—$F(1, 11) = 8.7$, $p = .013$—but not for the White clothing condition, $F(1, 11) = 0.05$, $p = .82$.

Thus, in the control group the influences of the clothing and headlight beam setting manipulations were generally statistically significant and in the expected direction (with greater visibility estimates being associated with higher reflectance clothing and with high beam illumination). At a practical level, however, it is important to evaluate these effects not only by their level of statistical significance but also by their magnitude. The overall effect of beam, for example, was statistically significant ($p = .002$) but surprisingly small: The increase in visibility estimates from low beam to high beam averaged only 5.7%. This effect is dramatically smaller than the effect of high-beam illumination on actual visibility distances. Under no-glare conditions, pedestrian visibility distances under high-beam illumination are between 50% and 100% greater than under low-beam illumination (e.g., Mortimer & Olson, 1974). Thus, although the data indicate that pedestrians' estimates of their own nighttime visibility are influenced by an approaching vehicle's beam setting, the data also suggest that pedestrians appear not to appreciate the magnitude of the effect.

Similarly, pedestrians appear not to appreciate the importance of clothing reflectance. Mean estimated visibility distances from the control group increased by only 11.7% from the black condition to the white condition and by only 9.1% from the black condition to the retroreflective condition. Empirical measurements of the actual benefits of increasing clothing reflectivity vary considerably but range from a minimum of slightly more than a 100% increase (Shinar, 1984; Shinar, 1985) to a maximum of roughly a 600% increase (Hazlett & Allen, 1968; Luoma et al., 1996). Thus it seems clear that pedestrians do not appreciate the importance of the reflectance of their own clothing in determining their visibility to oncoming drivers at night. This is particularly true when retroreflective materials are involved: Despite the fact that in the retroreflective condition participants wore retroreflective material on top of the same white lab coat that was worn in the white condition, estimated visibility distances were actually slightly less in the retroreflective condition than in the white condition.

Previous researchers' findings that pedestrians generally overestimate their visibility suggested that pedestrians may be insufficiently motivated to avoid entering the roadway environment at night whenever possible and less likely to take responsibility for getting out of the way of oncoming vehicles when entering the roadway is unavoidable (Allen et al., 1968; Shinar, 1984). The results from our study's control group underscore this problem but also suggest two others. First, because pedestrians fail to appreciate the benefits of reflective clothing, one might presume that they would also be less likely to seek out, obtain, and wear reflective clothing and retroreflective materials. Indeed, measurements of the reflectance of typical pedestrian garments confirm that pedestrians generally do not dress in a way that enhances their visibility. Bhise et al. (1977) measured the reflectance of clothing worn by 80 individuals at different times of the year and found that more than 60% of the garments had a reflectance of 10% or less. Garments with such low reflectance levels are unlikely to result in substantial contrast when viewed against typical roadways. Second, it seems plausible that one reason many drivers underuse their high beams is that drivers, like pedestrians, fail to appreciate the benefits offered by high beams (Leibowitz et al., 1998). Although most drivers seem acutely aware of the difficulties that high beams can cause for approaching drivers, it seems unlikely given the present data that many fully appreciate the benefits of high beams. Similarly, most driver's manuals seem to emphasize when *not* to use high beams.

Effects of the Lecture and the Demonstration

A mean of 52.8 days (range = 21–88 days) elapsed between when participants in the lecture group heard the lecture and when they participated in the experiment. A mean delay of 49.3 days (range = 21–88 days) elapsed for the combo group, a mean not significantly different from that of the lecture group, $t(22) = .426$, $p = .675$. A regression analysis on the combined data from these two groups revealed no significant relationship between the duration of the delay and the estimated visibility distances ($R^2 = .013$).

Preplanned contrast analyses (Rosenthal & Rosnow, 1985) compared the overall mean from each of the three experimental groups with the overall mean of the control group. This analysis revealed that the mean visibility estimate from the lecture group (151.5 m, or 497.0 ft) was significantly less than the mean of the control group, 166.7 m, or 546.9 ft; $F(1, 44) = 4.06$; $p = .05$. Neither the demo group (174.7 m, or 573.1 ft) nor the combo group (158.1 m, or 518.7 ft) produced overall means that were significantly different from that of the control group ($p > .10$).

To evaluate the separate and combined effects of the lecture and the demonstration more completely, however, the data from the lecture, demo, and combo groups were analyzed relative to the control group by first sub-tracting each of the three groups' observations from the corresponding mean from the control group, then by subjecting the difference scores to an ANOVA. Following this approach, a significant main effect of group—$F(2, 33) = 3.78$; $p = .03$—confirmed that the educational manipulations produced nonequivalent results. When averaged across the six clothing-by-beam combinations, the lecture group estimated their visibility distance to be 15 m (50 ft) less than did the control group. The demo group, however, estimated their visibility distance to be 8 m (26 ft) *greater* than did the control group. This difference between the lecture and demo groups was significant (Newman-Keuls). The estimated visibility distances from the combo group averaged 9 m (28 ft) less than the control group, a mean that was not significantly different from that of either the lecture group or the combo group. Thus, although seeing the demonstration resulted in visibility estimates that were on average farther than those of the control group, hearing the lecture resulted in a reduction in visibility estimates. That said, however, there was a significant interaction between the group and clothing variables, $F(4, 66) = 3.37$; $p = .01$. As can be seen in Figure 13.3, the most striking aspect of this interaction is that the effect of clothing was greatest in the combo group. The combined influence of hearing the lecture and seeing the demonstration was particularly effective at

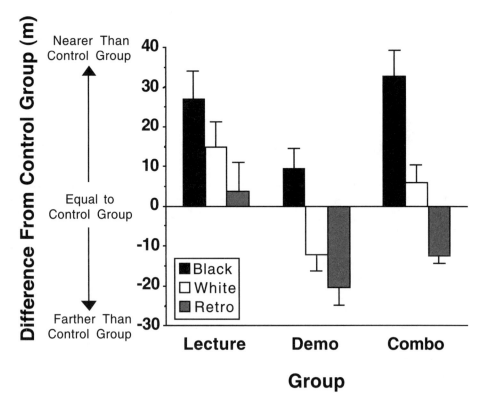

Figure 13.3.   The mean difference (±1 standard error of the mean) in estimated visibility distance for each of the three experimental groups from the control group. These difference scores reflect the influence of the educational manipulations.

reducing participants' estimated visibility while wearing black clothing ($M =$ 32.5 m, or 106.6 ft closer than the control group's average for the two black conditions). Neither the interaction between the group and beam manipulations—$F(2, 33) = 2.6$; $p > .05$—nor the three-way interaction between group, beam, and clothing—$F(4, 66) = 0.6$; $p > .05$—was significant.

Thus these results indicate that visibility estimates can indeed be influenced by relatively simple educational manipulations. On average, the group that heard a Leibowitz-inspired lecture estimated their visibility to be nearly 10% less than the control group did (a 15-m, or 50-ft difference). The effect was even larger (17.4%) when the participants wore black clothing, with estimates from the lecture group 27 m (89 ft) less than those from the control group. In interpreting these effects, it is important to understand that the lecture manipulation was fairly conservative. The lecture was given to a large group of students, more than 7 weeks separated the lecture from the data collection, and every effort was made to minimize the demand characteristics associated with the lecture (the students hearing the lecture were not aware that they would later be asked to participate in the research, and there was no apparent connection between the two events). In addition, the lecture had not been designed specifically to influence the students' visibility estimates.

Although it would, of course, be worthwhile to know whether other lectures would be even more effective, the fact that this particular lecture did have an effect is encouraging. These data suggest that a carefully designed public education campaign has the potential to increase pedestrian safety.

The demo group (participants who watched an experimenter walk in front of the test vehicle under varied clothing and beam conditions immediately before data collection) gave visibility estimates that were on average 8 m greater than those of the control group. Indeed, the demo group had greater visibility estimates in all conditions except when the participants wore black clothing. Thus, although the demonstration appears to have at least partially shown the benefits of wearing reflective clothing (which could potentially result in an increase in the probability of reflective clothing or retroreflective materials being worn at night), it did not serve to decrease visibility estimates overall. When the demonstration was combined with the lecture, however (i.e., in the combo group), visibility estimates were somewhat shorter than those of the control group overall. And as can be seen in Figure 13.3, combining the demonstration and the lecture resulted in a dramatic increase in the effect of clothing: Relative to the control group, visibility estimates of the combo group decreased 21% for the black condition but increased 7% for the retroreflective condition. These results are particularly encouraging, as they indicate both an overall decrease in estimated visibility and an increase in the appreciation for the beneficial effects of reflective clothing.

The finding that participants in the lecture group gave shorter visibility estimates than participants in the control group is similar to the results of a social psychological study on helping behavior. Using a simulated emergency situation, Beaman, Barnes, Klentz, and McQuirk (1978) found that college students who had earlier heard a social psychology lecture on helping behavior in emergencies more frequently helped a simulated victim than students who had not heard such a lecture. Our results and those of Beaman et al. are encouraging, as they indicate that exposure to a lecture might actually result in an increase in the probability of a desired behavior. In the present context, it is hoped that pedestrians who have previously been informed of the limited ability of drivers to see pedestrians at night will be less likely to assume they are visible to approaching drivers and will in turn be more likely to avoid entering the roadway at night, more likely to get out of the way of oncoming vehicles, and perhaps more likely to make use of reflective clothing.

It therefore appears worthwhile to explore even more effective ways to educate pedestrians about the dangers associated with interacting with traffic at night; the selective degradation theory forwarded by Leibowitz and his students seems like a valuable starting point. This theory has effectively described the functional changes in vision that occur with nightfall, and it has received considerable empirical support. Our study further reveals that Leibowitz's theory not only is understandable to nonscientists but also, once presented, can result in lasting and beneficial behavioral changes. Documenting such a blend of teaching, research, and service is perhaps the highest possible tribute that the authors can pay to a psychologist who has spent a long and exceptional career asserting with both words and deeds that psychology really can be useful.

References

Allen, M. J., Hazlett, R. D., Tacker, H. L., & Graham, B. V. (1968, October). Actual pedestrian visibility and the pedestrian's estimate of his own visibility. *Proceedings of the Thirteenth Annual Conference of the American Association for Automotive Medicine*, 293–299.

Ampofo-Boateng, K. A., & Thomson, J. A. (1989). Child pedestrian accidents: A case for preventive medicine. *Health Education Research, 5*, 265–274.

Beaman, A. L., Barnes, P. J., Klentz, B., & McQuirk, B. (1978). Increasing helping rates through information dissemination: Teaching pays. *Personality and Social Psychology Bulletin, 4*, 406–411.

Bhise, V. D., Farber, E. I., Saunby, C. S., Troell, G. M., Walunas, J. B., & Bernstein, A. (1977). *Modeling vision with headlights in a systems context* (SAE Technical Paper Series, No. 770238). Warrendale, PA: Society of Automotive Engineers.

Blomberg, R. D., Hale, A., & Preusser, D. F. (1986). Experimental evaluation of alternative conspicuity-enhancement techniques for pedestrians and bicyclists. *Journal of Safety Research, 17*, 1–12.

Evans, L. (1991). *Traffic safety and the driver.* New York: Van Nostrand Reinhold.

Gregersen, H. P., & Nolen, S. (1994). Children's road safety and the strategy of voluntary traffic safety clubs. *Accident Analysis and Prevention, 26*, 463–470.

Hazlett, R. D., & Allen, M. J. (1968). The ability to see a pedestrian at night: The effects of clothing, reflectorization and driver intoxication. *American Journal of Optometry and Archives of the American Academy of Optometry, 45*, 246–258.

Johansson, G. J., & Rumar, K. (1968). Visible distances and safe approach speeds for night driving. *Ergonomics, 11*, 275–282.

Leibowitz, H. W. (1990, July 30). Studying "human factor" can lead to safer military. *Army Times*, 21.

Leibowitz, H. W. (1996). The symbiosis between basic and applied research. *American Psychologist, 51*(4), 366–370.

Leibowitz, H. W., & Owens, D. A. (1977). Nighttime driving accidents and selective degradation. *Science, 197*, 422–423.

Leibowitz, H. W., & Owens, D. A. (1984, January). We drive by night. *Psychology Today*, 55–58.

Leibowitz, H. W., Owens, D. A., & Post, R. B. (1982). *Nighttime driving and visual degradation* (SAE Technical Paper Series, No. 820414). Warrendale, PA: Society of Automotive Engineers.

Leibowitz, H. W., Owens, D. A., & Tyrrell, R. A. (1998). The Assured Clear Distance Ahead Rule: Implications for traffic safety and the law. *Accident Analysis and Prevention, 30*, 93–99.

Luoma, J., Schumann, J., & Traube, E. C. (1996). Effects of retroreflector positioning on nighttime recognition of pedestrians. *Accident Analysis and Prevention, 28*, 377–383.

Mortimer, R. G., & Olson, P. L. (1974). *Development and use of driving tests to evaluate headlamp beam* (Report UM-HSRI-77-55). Ann Arbor, MI: The Highway Safety Research Institute.

National Highway Traffic Safety Administration. (2002). *Traffic safety facts 2000: Pedestrians.* Washington, DC: U.S. Department of Transportation. Retrieved August 22, 2002, from http://www-nrd.nhtsa.dot.gov/pdf/nrd-30/NCSA/TSF2000/2000pedfacts.pdf

National Research Council's Committee on Trauma Research. (1985). *Injury in America: A continuing public health problem.* Washington, DC: National Academy Press.

Olson, P. L., & Sivak, M. (1983). Comparison of headlamp visibility distance and stopping distance. *Perceptual and Motor Skills, 57*, 1177–1178.

Orne, M. T. (1962). On the social psychology of the psychological experiment: With particular reference to demand characteristics and their implications. *American Psychologist, 17*, 776–783.

Owens, D. A., Antonoff, R., & Francis, E. L. (1994). Biological motion and nighttime pedestrian conspicuity. *Human Factors, 36*, 718–732.

Owens, D. A., & Sivak, M. (1993). *The Role of reduced visibility in nighttime road fatalities* (Report UMTRI-93-33). Ann Arbor, MI: The University of Michigan Transportation Research Institute.

Owens, D. A., & Sivak, M. (1996). Differentiation of visibility and alcohol as contributors to twilight road fatalities. *Human Factors, 38*, 680–689.

Owens, D. A., & Tyrrell, R. A. (1999). Effects of luminance, blur, and age on nighttime visual guidance: A test of the selective degradation hypothesis. *Journal of Experimental Psychology: Applied, 5*, 1–14.

Rosenthal, R., & Rosnow, R. L. (1985). *Contrast analysis: Focused comparisons in the analysis of variance.* Cambridge, England: Cambridge University Press.

Sandels, S. (1975). *Children in traffic*. London: Macmillan.

Schneider, G. E. (1969). Two visual systems: Brain mechanisms for localization and discrimination are dissociated by tectal and cortical lesions. *Science, 163*, 895–902.

Shinar, D. (1984). Actual versus estimated nighttime pedestrian visibility. *Ergonomics, 27*, 863–871.

Shinar, D. (1985). The effects of expectancy, clothing reflectance, and detection criterion on nighttime pedestrian visibility. *Human Factors, 27*, 327–333.

White, M. J. (1987). Big bangs in perception: The most often cited authors and publications. *Bulletin of the Psychonomic Society, 25*(6), 458–461.

Yeaton, W. H., & Bailey, J. S. (1978). Teaching pedestrian safety skills to young children: An analysis and one year follow-up. *Journal of Applied Behavior Analysis, 11*, 315–329.

Part VII

Perceptual Applications to Other Disciplines

14

Basic and Applied Nausea Research Using an Optokinetic Drum

Robert M. Stern

Nausea is a difficult-to-describe sick or queasy sensation usually attributed to the abdominal area. Nausea is similar to pain and fatigue in that it is an unpleasant sensation, but it may be crucial for survival. Very little is known, however, about the complex pathophysiology or biopsychosocial mechanisms of nausea (Koch, 1993). Nausea is often assumed to be the conscious awareness of unusual activity in the chemoreceptor trigger zone, the so-called "vomiting center" in the medulla of the brain stem, but despite numerous references to a vomiting center in the literature, the existence of such an anatomically well localized structure remains controversial (Miller, 1993), as does its relationship, if any, to nausea.

During the past decade, several books with "nausea and vomiting" in their titles have been published by medical investigators (Blum, Heinrichs, & Herxheimer, 2000; Davis, Lake-Bakaar, & Grahame-Smith, 1986; Kucharczyk, Stewart, & Miller, 1991; Sleisenger, 1993), but most of the material deals with vomiting. Psychologists have published a limited number of articles dealing with nausea, including papers on taste aversion (e.g., Smith, Friedman, & Andrews, 2001), motion sickness (e.g., Stern & Koch, 1994, 1996), and studies of nausea and vomiting associated with chemotherapy treatment for cancer (e.g., Morrow, 1989, 1993). The subjective nature of nausea, as opposed to vomiting with its easily observable and quantifiable characteristics, may partly account for the paucity of research and knowledge about nausea.

In addition to being a sensation, nausea is also a complex control mechanism with multiple detectors that inhibits food intake in situations such as the following:

1. When the available food is perceived as disgusting
2. When the available food has been previously associated with nausea—conditioned taste aversion
3. When one's stomach and the related control mechanisms are not functioning normally because of factors such as the ingestion of a toxin, some form of pathology, and stress or anxiety or both

Nausea is frequently followed by vomiting, and sometimes the symptoms of nausea abate following vomiting. This sequence of events has led some to

I would like to acknowledge H. W. Leibowitz, Kenneth L. Koch, Gary Morrow, and several excellent graduate students with whom I have been fortunate to work at Penn State University for their contributions to various aspects of my thinking about nausea and my empirical research.

assume that nausea and vomiting are on a continuum. However, there are situations in which nausea is present in varying degrees but the individual does not vomit (e.g., as occurs in some individuals receiving chemotherapy for cancer) and other situations in which individuals vomit without any sensations of nausea (e.g., as occurs with astronauts in space). Further, drugs such as ondansetron act as antiemetics, effectively reducing vomiting following chemotherapy, but do little to relieve nausea (Levitt et al., 1993; Roscoe, Morrow, Hickok, & Stern, 2000). The relationship of nausea to emesis is obviously not simple or clear.

In the remainder of this chapter I will discuss the possible evolutionary basis for nausea and my view of the "tools" needed to study nausea, including my use of a rotating optokinetic drum. H. W. Leibowitz not only provided me with the optokinetic drum that made possible much of the research described in this chapter but also encouraged me to follow his very productive research approach of simultaneously conducting basic and applied research. As a psychophysiologist, I did basic research to develop techniques that yielded quantifiable subjective and physiological measures of nausea. At the same time, during the past 15 years, I have conducted numerous applied studies that have been aimed at testing my hypothesis that both inherent and situational factors interact to affect one's dynamic nausea threshold. These studies will be briefly described in the latter part of this chapter.

The Role of Nausea in the Survival of the Organism

It is generally thought that when a toxin has been ingested, the biological basis for emesis is to remove the toxin, whereas the role of nausea is to create conditioned aversion to that substance so that it will be avoided in the future (Money & Cheung, 1983). Such life-saving aversion might not develop in the absence of nausea, because uncomplicated vomiting may not be particularly noxious; for example, a person might drink 10 beers, vomit, and drink 10 more beers.

Davis, Harding, Leslie, and Andrews (1986) discussed the role of nausea in each of three levels of toxin defense: (a) nausea and avoidance evoked by smell and taste (b) detection of ingested toxins by gastric receptors followed by a central reflex that evokes nausea and vomiting and (c) detection of circulating toxins by chemoreceptors in the area postrema followed by a central reflex that evokes nausea and vomiting. Treisman (1977) had previously suggested a fourth level of toxin defense, an early warning system that is extremely sensitive to disturbances in normal sensory input or motor control.

As indicated previously, nausea is a control mechanism and as such inhibits ingestion either when there may be something wrong with food being approached or eaten or when there may be something wrong with one's stomach (i.e., it is not functioning normally because of abnormal local activity or because of unusual signals from the central nervous system). The survival value of avoiding foods that have made one nauseated in the past, conditioned taste avoidance, is obvious. Several authors (Bernstein, Vitiello, & Sigmundi, 1980; Garcia, Hankins, & Rusiniak, 1974; Pelchat & Rozin, 1982; Money, 1990) have pointed out that the most potent internal event for producing taste aversion is nausea. In addition, Coil, Hankins, Jenden, and Garcia (1978) have shown that conditioned taste aversion is attenuated by antiemetic agents. And Coil and Norgren (1981) have demonstrated that taste aversion conditioned with intravenous copper sulfate is attenuated by ablation of the area postrema.

Tools Needed to Study Nausea

To study nausea under controlled conditions, the following tools or procedures are needed:

1. A technique for making healthy people nauseous
2. A technique for obtaining subjective reports
3. A technique for obtaining noninvasive quantifiable physiological responses

The Use of a Rotating Optokinetic Drum to Provoke Nausea and Other Symptoms of Motion Sickness

It is difficult to get people to participate in experiments when they are nauseated. For example, women suffering with pregnancy sickness were willing to come to our laboratory on days when they felt well but often canceled their appointments when they were nauseated. Approximately 15 years ago, my colleague H. W. Leibowitz told me that while studying circular vection, the illusion of self-movement, he had noticed that if he left some participants in his rotating optokinetic drum too long, they complained of nausea. Using his drum, I quickly discovered that it was possible to provoke motion sickness symptoms, including nausea, in healthy participants in 5–10 min, and observe their return to their prior healthy state in about 30 min. We are still using Leibowitz's optokinetic drum, which rotates at 10 revolutions per minute around the stationary participant, as shown in Figure 14.1 (for technical specifications of the drum see Stern and Koch, 1994). Within seconds all participants experience vection, the illusion that they are rotating and the drum is still. But feedback from their vestibular system indicates, rightly, that they are sitting still. This visual-vestibular sensory conflict or mismatch provokes the symptoms of motion sickness in approximately 50% of healthy European Americans and African Americans, and in 90% of Asian American participants (Stern, Hu, Uijtdehaage, Muth, Xu, & Koch, 1996). This individual difference will be discussed in a later section of this chapter.

The Subjective Experience of Nausea

Nausea is a subjective experience and, as such, its occurrence and characteristics are best described by the individuals experiencing the feeling. Health care professionals and care givers tend to underestimate significantly the frequency, duration, and severity of nausea experienced by patients. A variety of self-report questionnaires have been developed to describe the experience of

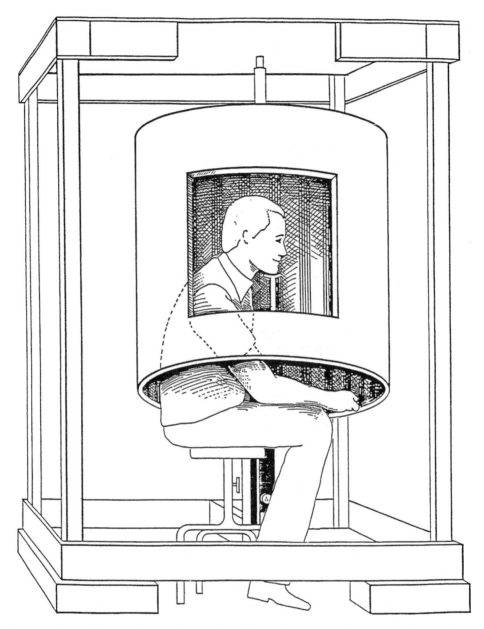

Figure 14.1. The optokinetic drum. The illustration shows the alternating vertical black and white stripes that cover the interior surface of the drum. The actual drum does not have a portion cut out. From "Using the Electrogastrogram to Study Motion Sickness," by R. M. Stern and K. L. Koch in *Electrogastrography*, edited by J. Z. Chen and R. W. McCallum, p. 201. Copyright 1994 by Lippincott Williams & Wilkins. Reprinted with permission.

nausea. Visual analog scales have been used to describe its occurrence and severity. Morrow developed a questionnaire to assess the nausea and vomiting of cancer patients receiving chemotherapy based on the frequency, severity, and duration of nausea and vomiting (Morrow, 1992). In our laboratory studies of motion sickness (Stern & Koch, 1994), we asked participants to report symptoms every 2–3 min. A Subjective Symptoms of Motion Sickness score was determined according to widely used criteria developed by Graybiel, Wood, Miller, and Cramer (1968). Briefly, the motion sickness score depended on the occurrence and severity of symptoms of nausea, sweating, dizziness, headache, increased salivation, stomach awareness, and warmth.

In a recent study designed to explore the possibility that the experience of nausea may be very different in different situations and for different individuals, we obtained descriptors for the sensation of nausea from a large group of participants voluntarily undergoing vection-induced motion sickness; we factor analyzed a set of the most commonly used descriptors and then developed a nausea profile. The results indicated that three dimensions of nausea can be compared across participants or patients in a variety of situations (Muth, Stern, Thayer, & Koch, 1996). From this new questionnaire, a total nausea score is calculated, and a nausea profile is determined for each participant or patient. The profile comprises a score on each of three dimensions: bodily distress, gastrointestinal distress, and emotional distress.

Physiological Changes That Accompany the Development of Nausea

Participants who experience nausea in our optokinetic drum show an increase in sympathetic nervous system activity and a decrease in parasympathetic nervous system activity, followed by a change in gastric myoelectric activity from a regular 3 cycles per minute (cpm), the normal gastric frequency of humans, to dysrhythmic 4–9 cpm activity, or gastric tachyarrhythmia (Hu, Grant, Stern, & Koch, 1991). Using noninvasive electrogastrography (EGG), we record the frequency of gastric myoelectric activity (Stern & Koch, 1994). The left panel (A) of Figure 14.2 shows the normal 3 cpm EGG of a participant prior to drum rotation. The right panel (B) of Figure 14.2 shows gastric tachyarrhythmia, which began at minute 4 of drum rotation. The participant reported nausea at minute 6. The disruption in normal gastric myoelectric activity is usually followed by reports of nausea and an increase in vasopressin levels in the blood (Koch et al., 1990). Similar changes in EGG activity have been found in patients reporting nausea following chemotherapy, suggesting a similar role for the autonomic nervous system in the expression of nausea in that context (Morrow, 1985).

Several studies (e.g., Koch & Stern, 1994) have demonstrated that nausea is accompanied by abnormal dysrhythmic electrical activity in the stomach and little or no normal muscular activity. In short, the stomach is functionally shut down and unable to empty. If one were to eat while one's stomach was in this state, the food would remain in the stomach longer than usual, possibly leading to a feeling of fullness, epigastric discomfort, and more severe nausea.

Vasopressin, an antidiuretic hormone, is released by the posterior pituitary and increases in the blood of individuals who report nausea after injection of apomorphine (Feldman, Samson, & O'Dorisio, 1988), after administration of cancer chemotherapy agents (Edwards, Carmichael, Baylis, & Harris, 1989), and after the stimulation of sitting in a rotating chair (Eversmann et al., 1978). It is not clear in these situations whether the level of plasma vasopressin increases immediately before or immediately after the

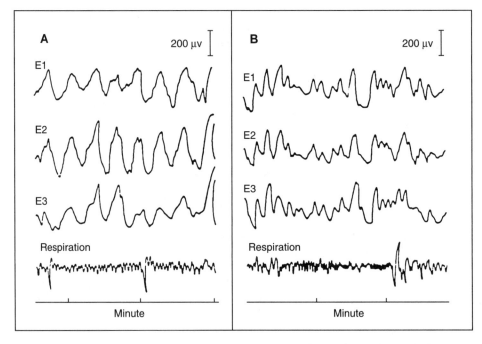

Figure 14.2. Electrogastrography activity recorded from three electrode locations (E1–E3) on the abdomen. Left panel (A) shows normal 3 cpm activity prior to drum rotation. Right panel (B) shows gastric tachyarrhythmia recorded from the same participant during rotation and shortly before he asked that the rotation be stopped. From "Tachygastria and Motion Sickness," by R. M. Stern, K. L. Koch, H. W. Leibowitz, I. Lindblad, C. Shupert, and W. R. Stewart, 1985, *Aviation, Space, and Environmental Medicine, 56,* p. 1075. Copyright 1985 by Aerospace Medical Association. Reprinted with permission.

experience of nausea, although several authors (e.g., Robertson, 1977) have stated that nausea causes an increase in vasopressin release. However, in those few experiments in which several vasopressin measurements were made over time rather than just one prestimulus and one poststimulus measurement (Koch et al., 1990; Xu et al., 1993), reports of nausea do not usually precede increases in vasopressin levels, but rather the two phenomena covary.

In studies in our laboratory, gastric dysrhythmias preceded the onset of nausea and vasopressin release for most participants (Xu et al., 1993). We suggest that the shift to gastric dysrhythmias alters ongoing gastric vagal afferent activity, which then modulates neuronal activity in the tractus solitarius and hypothalamus and ultimately results in vasopressin secretion. Vasopressin levels in the blood of our symptomatic participants increased along with reports of nausea and decreased as nausea subsided. In contrast, levels of stress hormones such as epinephrine increased with reports of nausea but did not decrease until long after nausea subsided. Asymptomatic participants developed neither gastric dysrhythmias nor increased vasopressin release during drum rotation.

To summarize, as is shown in Figure 14.3, the physiological measures that correlate highly with the development of nausea and other symptoms of

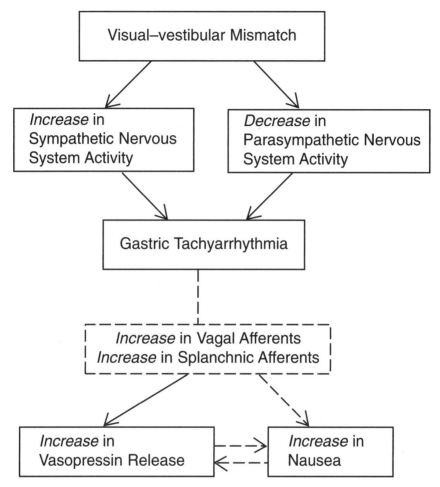

Figure 14.3. Summary of the physiological changes that occur in susceptible participants between exposure to a rotating drum and the sensation of nausea. Solid lines indicate documented relationships; dotted lines indicate hypothesized relationships. From "Using the Electrogastrogram to Study Motion Sickness," by R. M. Stern and K. L. Koch in *Electrogastrography*, edited by J. Z. Chen and R. W. McCallum, p. 209. Copyright 1994 by Lippincott Williams & Wilkins. Reprinted with permission.

motion sickness are increased sympathetic nervous system activity, decreased parasympathetic nervous system activity, increased gastric tachyarrhythmia, and increased plasma vasopressin levels.

Applied Studies of Nausea

The applied studies of nausea that have been done in my laboratory with the use of Leibowitz's rotating optokinetic drum have all been performed within the conceptual framework of a dynamic nausea threshold model. That is, I propose that inherent and situational factors determine one's nausea threshold at any point in time, and these interacting factors set and reset this complex control mechanism. The contributions of some of the factors involved are discussed in the following sections.

Inherent Factors

Age. We found that several infants who sat on the lap of one of their parents in the rotating drum did not seem to develop any symptoms of motion sickness. We have also observed that older participants reported fewer symptoms of motion sickness than those between the ages of 16 and 60. These findings are similar to those of anecdotal reports from other laboratories (Reason & Brand, 1975). Chemotherapy researchers (McMillan, 1989; Morrow, 1984, 1989) have also indicated that older patients report less nausea than young patients.

Gender. Anecdotal reports in the motion sickness literature indicate that women report more symptoms than men (Lentz & Collins, 1977). We (Jokerst et al., 1999) recently completed a study using the optokinetic drum and collecting both subjective reports and EGG activity from the stomach and concluded that, indeed, women reported more symptoms than men, but they did not show greater disturbances in gastric activity. The chemotherapy literature also indicates that women report more nausea than men receiving the same drugs (antiemetic and cytotoxic).

Race. A serendipitous finding in our lab about 10 years ago was that the Chinese friends of one of my graduate students, Senqi Hu, who served as participants so that Senqi could learn how to use the rotating drum, all became extremely motion sick. In the first of three studies, we (Stern, Hu, LeBlanc, & Koch, 1993) reported that 15 Chinese participants experienced significantly more symptoms of vection-induced motion sickness than 15 European American or 15 African American participants (see Figure 14.4A). Further, as can be seen in Figure 14.4B the Chinese participants showed significantly greater gastric tachyarrhythmia during drum rotation than the other two groups. Because the Chinese participants in this study had recently come to the United States, it was possible that non biological factors such as child-rearing practices or diet could account for the difference in susceptibility. To rule out this possibility, in a second study we (Muth, Stern, Uijtdehaage, & Koch, 1994) tested Asian Americans, U.S.-born children of Asian parents, and obtained similar results. A third study (Xu et al., 1993) of the motion sickness susceptibility of Asian participants was conducted at the Hershey Medical Center in the laboratory of my colleague Kenneth L. Koch, a gastroenterologist, and similar results were obtained. In this study, the Asian participants, as compared with European American participants, reported more nausea, showed greater gastric disturbance, and had greater increase in vasopressin levels.

Situational Factors

Anxiety. Reports of nausea are common in patients with various anxiety disorders such as generalized anxiety disorder (Marten, Brown, Barlow, Borkovec, Shear, & Lydiard, 1993). Research has shown that anxious individ-

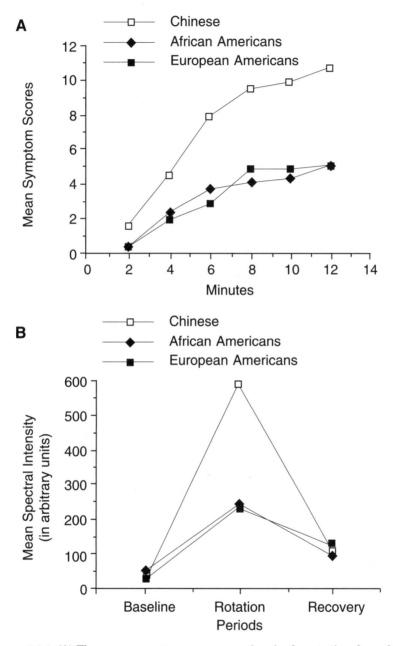

Figure 14.4. (A) The mean symptom scores over time in the rotating drum for Chinese, African American, and European American participants. (B) The amount of gastric tachyarrhythmia for the same participants. Chinese subjects reported significantly more symptoms than the other two groups and showed significantly greater tach-yarrhythmia. From "Chinese Hyper-susceptibility to Vection-induced Motion Sickness," by R. M. Stern, S. Hu, R. LeBlanc, and K. L. Koch, 1993, *Aviation, Space, and Environmental Medicine, 64,* p. 829. Copyright 1993 by Aerospace Medical Association. Reprinted with permission.

uals are hyperalert for any type of threat to their well-being (Mathews, 1990). Therefore, extreme anxiety may lower an individual's threshold for the detection of toxins, resulting in loss of appetite or nausea. It has been found that high anxiety contributes to greater side effects, including more nausea and vomiting, from chemotherapy (Jacobsen et al., 1988) and from the anticipation of chemotherapy (Andrykowski, 1990). Physiologically, many anxious individuals show an increase in sympathetic nervous system activity and vagal withdrawal, the autonomic nervous system profile that often leads to gastric dysrhythmias and reports of nausea. Anxiety often increases plasma vasopressin levels, also related to reports of nausea. We have been surprised that we have not found a relationship between anxiety, measured with various questionnaires, and symptom reports in the rotating drum.

Pregnancy. We know of no studies of the effects of pregnancy on susceptibility to motion sickness, but there is a large literature on the nausea of pregnancy (see Blum et al., 2000; Whitehead, Holden, & Andrews, 1992). Profet (1992) has suggested that the nausea of "morning sickness" is caused by a recalibration of the chemoreceptor trigger zone in the area postrema and a decrease in the mother's threshold for taste and smell as a protective mechanism for screening out toxins from the embryo. As a result of this threshold shift, previously desired foods with strong taste or odors, like coffee, and strong-smelling cheese, are nauseating and are thus avoided. Profet calls attention to the adaptive value of morning or pregnancy sickness and points out that data from several studies have shown that women who experience severe pregnancy sickness have significantly lower rates of spontaneous abortion than do women who experience no or only mild 1st-trimester nausea or vomiting. The results of these studies are summarized by Weigel and Weigel (1989). However, other investigators (e.g., Brown, Kahn, & Hartman, 1997) have questioned the validity of Profet's theory.

Fasting. Preliminary results from our laboratory indicated that after an overnight fast, the electrical activity of the stomach is unstable, showing gastric tachyarrhythmia, the same abnormal pattern of activity seen in motion sickness, and mixed sensations of hunger and nausea are often reported. Individuals who are breaking a fast of several days commonly report nausea and anorexia (Duncan, Jenson, Cristofori, & Schless, 1963). It is interesting that people who are very hungry, who might be expected to approach food with gusto, sometimes avoid it or become highly selective in terms of what they will eat. One possible explanation is that under conditions of prolonged food deprivation, we might be inclined to ingest almost anything, including toxins, and so as a protective mechanism during a prolonged fast, our threshold of acceptable foods shifts, becomes more selective, and favors bland, familiar foods. In fact, Jacobs and Sharma (1969) reported that food-deprived rats and dogs discriminated more with regard to available food than freely fed animals.

Adaptation. My first attempts to adapt participants in the drum by bringing them back for a second session 1 week later were a complete failure. However, comments from two astronauts concerning their pre-space flight training in the "Vomit Comet" were most helpful. The astronauts indicated that almost all trainees get nauseous or vomit, or both, the first time they ride in the roller coaster-like training plane that gives them their first experience of weightlessness, and if they don't get to ride in it again for several days, it is like starting all over and they get sick again. With new insight, I redesigned my adaptation study in the rotating drum and instead of a 7-day intersession interval, I substituted 48 hrs. With the shorter intersession interval, most participants showed a significant reduction in gastric tachyarrhythmia and reports of symptoms of motion sickness, and by the third session they were practically asymptomatic (Stern, Hu, Vasey, & Koch, 1989). In a follow-up study (Hu, et al., 1991) we got similar results and examined a variety of autonomic nervous system measures in an effort to learn more about what adapts. What we observed was that when participants returned for their second and third sessions, they showed less increase in sympathetic nervous system activity and less vagal withdrawal. Such responses would provoke less gastric tachyarrhythmia and thereby less nausea. Perhaps cancer patients who receive a series of chemotherapy treatments do not adapt, in the sense that they often continue to experience nausea following each treatment, because the intertreatment intervals are usually too long.

Expectations. Several studies (e.g., Haut, Beckwith, Laurie, & Klatt, 1991) have found that expectations about nausea prior to one's first chemotherapy treatment can lower that individual's nausea threshold. Is this just a case of self-fulfilling prophecy? In a study recently published (Gianaros, Stern, Morrow, & Hickok, 2001), we reported that the greater the amount of gastric tachyarrhythmia prior to chemotherapy, the greater the chance that the patient will experience nausea during or following the chemotherapy. It may be the case that the expectation of nausea leads to anxiety, which leads to gastric dysrhythmias, which lead to nausea. The issue becomes more complicated when we consider the basis for the individual's expectation, but that is research in progress. In Greece, health care providers are not required to tell patients that they have cancer or what side effects they may experience from chemotherapy. Anecdotal reports from the Oncology Department at the Athens Naval Hospital indicate a much lower incidence of nausea following the same chemotherapy treatment commonly used in the United States.

Conclusion

Nausea is a private sensation and as such is difficult to study. It is hoped that more progress will be made in understanding the causes and prevention of nausea now that better questionnaires are available to quantify the experience of nausea and a quantifiable physiological marker of nausea, gastric tachyarrhythmia, has been identified.

Nausea signals us not to eat. We probably would not be here today if our ancestors did not experience nausea from time to time. The difficult problem facing psychologists and other health care providers at present is how to reduce selectively or turn off this very effective control mechanism when it is unwanted, such as following chemotherapy and surgery, during pregnancy, and during provocative motion. This will be accomplished only after we gain a greater understanding of the interaction of the many factors, inherent and situational, that affect nausea.

References

Andrykowski, M. A. (1990). The role of anxiety in the development of anticipatory nausea in cancer chemotherapy: A review and synthesis. *Psychosomatic Medicine, 52,* 458–475.

Bernstein, I. L., Vitiello, M. V., & Sigmundi, R. A. (1980). Effects of tumor growth on taste aversion learning produced by antitumor drugs in the rat. *Physiological Psychology, 8,* 51–55.

Blum, R. H., Heinrichs, W. L., & Herxheimer, A. (2000). *Nausea and vomiting.* London: Whurr.

Brown, J. E., Kahn, E. S., & Hartman, T. J. (1997). Profet, profits, and proof: Do nausea and vomiting of early pregnancy protect women from harmful vegetables? *American Journal of Obstetrics and Gynecology, 176,* 179–181.

Coil, J. D., Hankins, W. G., Jenden, D. J., & Garcia, J. (1978). The attenuation of a specific cue-to-consequence association by antiemetic agents. *Psychopharmacology, 45,* 21–25.

Coil, J. D., & Norgren, R. (1981). Taste aversions conditioned with intravenous copper sulphate: Attenuation by ablation of the area postrema. *Brain Research, 212,* 425–433.

Davis, C. J., Harding, R. R., Leslie, R. A., & Andrews, P. L. R. (1986). The organization of vomiting as a protective reflex. In C. J. Davis, G. V. Lake-Bakaar, & D. G. Grahame-Smith (Eds.), *Nausea and vomiting: Mechanisms and treatment* (pp. 65–77). Berlin: Springer-Verlag.

Davis, C. J., Lake-Bakaar, G. V., & Grahame-Smith, D. G. (Eds.). (1986). *Nausea and vomiting: Mechanisms and treatment.* New York: Springer-Verlag.

Duncan, G. G., Jenson, W. K., Cristofori, F. C., & Schless, G. L. (1963). Intermittent fasts in the correction and control of intractable obesity. *American Journal of Medical Science, 245,* 515–520.

Edwards, C., Carmichael, J., Baylis, P., & Harris, A. (1989). Arginine vasopressin—A mediator of chemotherapy induced emesis? *British Journal of Cancer, 59,* 467.

Eversmann, T., Gottsmann, M., Uhlich, E., Ulbrecht, G., von Werder, K., & Scriba, P. C. (1978). Increased secretion of growth hormone, prolactin, antidiuretic hormone, and cortisol induced by the stress of motion sickness. *Aviation, Space, and Environmental Medicine, 49,* 53–57.

Feldman, M., Samson, W. K., & O'Dorisio, T. M. (1988). Apomorphine-induced nausea in humans: Release of vasopressin and pancreatic polypeptide. *Gastroenterology, 95,* 721–726.

Garcia, J., Hankins, W. G., & Rusiniak, K. W. (1974). Behavioral regulation of the milieu interne in man and rat. *Science, 185,* 824–831.

Gianaros, P. J., Stern, R. M., Morrow, G. R., & Hickok, J. T. (2001). Relationship of gastric myoelectrical and cardiac parasympathetic activity to chemotherapy-induced nausea. *Journal of Psychosomatic Research, 50,* 263–266.

Graybiel, A., Wood, C. D., Miller, E. F., & Cramer, D. B. (1968). Diagnostic criteria for grading the severity of acute motion sickness. *Aerospace Medicine, 39,* 453–455.

Haut, M. W., Beckwith, B., Laurie, J. A., & Klatt, N. (1991). Postchemotherapy nausea and vomiting in cancer patients receiving outpatient chemotherapy. *Journal of Psychosocial Oncology, 9,* 117–130.

Hu, S., Grant, W., Stern, R. M., & Koch, K. L. (1991). Motion sickness severity and physiological correlates of repeated exposure to a rotating optokinetic drum. *Aviation, Space, and Environmental Medicine, 62,* 308–314.

Jacobs, H. L., & Sharma, K. N. (1969). Taste versus calories: Sensory and metabolic signals in the control of food intake. *Annals of the New York Academy of Science, 157,* 1084–1125.

Jacobsen, P. B., Andrykowski, M. A., Redd, W. H., Die-Trill, M., Hakes, T. B., Kaufman, R. J., et al. (1988). Nonpharmacologic factors in the development of posttreatment nausea with adjuvant chemotherapy for breast cancer. *Cancer, 61,* 379–385.

Jokerst, M. D., Gatto, M., Fazio, R., Gianaros, P. J., Stern, R. M., & Koch, K. L. (1999). Effects of gender of subjects and experimenter on susceptibility to motion. *Aviation, Space, and Environmental Medicine, 70,* 962–965.

Koch, K. L. (1993). Motion sickness. In M. H. Sleisenger (Ed.), *Handbook of nausea and vomiting* (pp. 43–60). New York: Parthenon.

Koch, K. L., & Stern, R. M. (1994). Electrogastrographic data acquisition and analysis: The Penn State experience. In J. Z. Chen & R. W. McCallum (Eds.), *Electrogastrography: Principles and applications* (pp. 31–44). New York: Raven Press.

Koch, K. L., Stern, R. M., Vasey, M. W., Seaton, J. F., Demers, L. M., & Harrison, T. S. (1990). Neuroendocrine and gastric myoelectric responses to illusory self-motion in men. *American Journal of Physiology, 258,* E304–E310.

Kucharczyk, J., Stewart, D. J., & Miller, A. D. (Eds). (1991). *Nausea and vomiting: Recent research and clinical advances.* Boca Raton, FL: CRC Press.

Lentz, J. M., & Collins, W. E. (1977). Motion sickness susceptibility and related behavioral characteristics in men and women. *Aviation, Space, and Environmental Medicine, 48*(4), 316–322.

Levitt, M., Warr, D., Yelle, L., Rayner, H. L., Lofters, W., & Perrault, D. J. (1993). Ondansetron compared with dexamethasone and metoclopramide as antiemetics in the chemotherapy of breast cancer with cyclophosphamide, methotrexate, and fluorouracil. *New England Journal of Medicine, 328,* 1081–1084.

Marten, P. A., Brown, T. A., Barlow, D. H., Borkovec, T. D., Shear, K. M., & Lydiard, R. B. (1993). Evaluation of the ratings comprising the associated symptom criterion of DSM-III-R Generalized Anxiety Disorder. *Journal of Nervous and Mental Disorders, 181,* 676–682.

Mathews, A. (1990). The cognitive function of anxiety. *Behavioral Research and Therapy, 28,* 455–468.

McMillan, S. L. (1989). The relationship between age and intensity of cancer-related symptoms. *Oncology Nurses Forum, 16,* 237–241.

Miller, A. D. (1993). Neuroanatomy and physiology. In M. H. Sleisenger (Ed.), *Handbook of nausea and vomiting* (pp. 1–9). New York: Parthenon.

Money, K. E. (1990). Motion sickness and evolution. In G. H. Crampton (Ed.), *Motion and space sickness.* Boca Raton, FL: CRC Press.

Money, K. E., & Cheung, B. S. (1983). Another function of the inner ear: Facilitation of the emetic response to poisons. *Aviation, Space, and Environmental Medicine, 54,* 208–211.

Morrow, G. R. (1984). Susceptibility to motion sickness and the development of anticipatory nausea and vomiting in cancer patients undergoing chemotherapy. *Cancer Treatment Reports, 68,* 1177–1178.

Morrow, G. R. (1985). The effect of a susceptibility to motion sickness on the side effects of cancer chemotherapy. *Cancer, 55,* 2766–2770.

Morrow, G. R. (1989). Chemotherapy-related nausea and vomiting: Etiology and management. *Cancer, 39,* 89–104.

Morrow, G. R. (1992). A patient report measure for the quantification of chemotherapy-induced nausea and emesis: Psychometric properties of the Morrow Assessment of Nausea and Emesis (MANE). *British Journal of Cancer, 66,* S72–S74.

Morrow, G. R. (1993). Psychological aspects of nausea and vomiting: Anticipation of chemotherapy. In M. H. Sleisenger (Ed.), *Handbook of nausea and vomiting* (pp. 11–25). New York: Parthenon.

Muth, E. R., Stern, R. M., Thayer, J. F., & Koch, K. L. (1996). Assessment of the multiple dimensions of nausea: The nausea profile (NP). *Journal of Psychosomatic Research, 40,* 511–520.

Muth, E. R., Stern, R. M., Uijtdehaage, S. H. J., & Koch, K. L. (1994). Effects of Asian ancestry on susceptibility to vection-induced motion sickness. In J. Z. Chen & R. W. McCallum (Eds.), *Electrogastrography: Principles and applications* (pp. 227–234). New York: Raven.

Pelchat, M. L., & Rozin, P. (1982). The special role of nausea in the acquisition of food dislikes by humans. *Appetite, 3,* 341–351.

Profet, M. (1992). Pregnancy sickness as adaptation: A deterrent to maternal ingestion of teratogens. In J. Barkow, L. Cosmides, & J. Tooby (Eds.), *The Adapted mind* (pp. 327–365). New York: Oxford University Press.

Reason, J. T., & Brand, J. J. (1975). *Motion sickness.* London: Academic Press.

Robertson, G. L. (1977). The regulation of vasopressin function in health and disease. *Recent Progress in Hormonal Research, 33,* 333–385.

Roscoe, J. A., Morrow, G. R., Hickok, J. T., & Stern, R. M. (2000). Nausea and vomiting remain a significant clinical problem: Trends over time in controlling chemotherapy-induced nausea and vomiting in 1413 patients treated in community clinical practices. *Journal of Pain and Symptom Management, 20,* 113–121.

Sleisenger, M. H. (Ed.). (1993). *Handbook of nausea and vomiting*. New York: Parthenon.

Smith, J. E., Friedman, M. I., & Andrews, P. L. (2001). Conditioned food aversion in *Suncus murinus* (house musk shrew)—A new model for the study of nausea in a species with an emetic reflex. *Physiology and Behavior, 73,* 593–598.

Stern, R. M., Hu, S., LeBlanc, R., & Koch, K. L. (1993). Chinese hyper-susceptibility to vection-induced motion sickness. *Aviation, Space, and Environmental Medicine, 64,* 827–830.

Stern, R. M., Hu, S., Uijtdehaage, S. H. J., Muth, E. R., Xu, L. H., & Koch, K. L. (1996). Asian hypersusceptibility to motion sickness. *Human Heredity, 46,* 7–14.

Stern, R. M., Hu, S., Vasey, M. W., & Koch, K. L. (1989). Adaptation to vection-induced symptoms of motion sickness. *Aviation, Space, and Environmental Medicine, 60,* 566–571.

Stern, R. M., & Koch, K. L. (1994). Using the electrogastrogram to study motion sickness. In J. Z. Chen and R. W. McCallum (Eds.), *Electrogastrography: Principles and applications* (pp. 199–218). New York: Raven Press.

Stern, R. M., & Koch, K. L. (1996). Motion sickness and differential susceptibility. *Current Directions in Psychological Science, 5,* 115–120.

Stern, R. M., Koch, K. L., Leibowitz, H. W, Lindblad, I., Shupert, C., & Stewart, W. R. (1985). Tachygastria and motion sickness. *Aviation, Space, and Environmental Medicine, 56,* 1074–1077.

Treisman, M. (1977). Motion sickness: An evolutionary hypothesis. *Science, 197,* 493–495.

Weigel, R. M., & Weigel, M. M. (1989). Nausea and vomiting of early pregnancy and pregnancy outcome. A meta-analytical review. *British Journal of Obstetrics and Gynecology, 96,* 1312–1318.

Whitehead, S. A., Holden, W. A., & Andrews, P. L. R. (1992). Pregnancy sickness. In A. L. Bianchi, L. Grelot, A. D. Miller, & G. L. King (Eds.), *Mechanisms and control of emesis* (pp. 297–306). Montrouge, France: John Libbey Eurotext.

Xu, L. H., Koch, K. I., Summy-Long, J., Stern, R. M., Seaton, J. F., Harrison, T. S., et al. (1993). Hypothalamic and gastric myoelectric responses during vection-induced nausea in healthy Chinese subjects. *American Journal of Physiology, 265,* E578–E584.

15

What Is the Role of Vision During Stair Descent?

Peter R. Cavanagh and Jill S. Higginson

Introduction

More than 1,000 fatalities occur each year as a direct result of falls on stairs (National Safety Council, 1994). The vast majority of falls occur on the top three or bottom three steps (Templer, 1992), but the features that make these regions of the staircase particularly dangerous remain unclear. Our interest in the role of vision during stair descent was stimulated by a visit to our laboratory by Hersh Leibowitz and Johannes Dichgans. Among the issues that we discussed during a lively hour was the question, "Is vision needed for safe stair descent?" Discussion soon turned to demonstration as we took turns negotiating the main stairway of the building with vision absent during various phases of our descent. We rapidly came to the same conclusion as Templer (1992), who has suggested that vision is essential at the upper and lower transitions but relatively unimportant during midstair descent. These speculations by biased observers have been formed into hypotheses for quantitative testing in a simple experiment.

The role of vision during locomotion has been actively addressed in biomechanics and psychology literature for more than 40 years (Gibson, 1958). Patla (1998) has recently summarized the conclusions drawn from theory and empirical research about visually guided locomotion: Visual information from the environment and about the position of our body segments is sampled intermittently and used to actively control locomotion. These generalizations have been demonstrated empirically during level walking, obstacle clearance, and walking to a target but have not been applied to more complex locomotor tasks like stair negotiation.

A characteristic of visual scanning during locomotion is the ability to acquire information about environmental features at a distance. Successful locomotion requires accurate perception and periodic monitoring of the surroundings in an active feedback loop that controls and modifies body action.

We are grateful for the inspiration that Hersh Leibowitz has provided to direct our attention toward visual factors in the control of locomotion. Mary Becker took leadership in recruitment and data collection, and Fred Owens and Steve Arnold provided valuable input on experimental design and statistics. Nori Okita and Kate Christina were generous in giving time for data analysis and Katie McClelland reviewed videotapes. We thank Mrs. Esther Boone and Mrs. Diane Plummer for their dedicated editorial contributions, and Rick Tyrrell and Fred Owens for their comments on the manuscript. This work was supported in part by the National Institute on Aging through grants AG14073 and AG09345.

This requirement is particularly important when obstacles are encountered or the terrain and surroundings are irregular. Presumably, stair negotiation is a combination of target seeking (tread placement) and obstacle avoidance (edge clearance).

Templer (1992) has suggested that prior to stair negotiation, visual inspection must occur and typically includes the detection of hazards, selection of route, and accurate perception of desired step location (i.e., where the first step is located). The majority of visual information concerning the location for impending foot placement may be gained while the foot to be placed is still on the previous step (Hollands, Marple-Horvat, Henkes, & Rowan, 1995). Interruption of these processes via distraction, abrupt changes in motion, or lack of awareness puts the stair user at increased risk of falling. Templer has also proposed that stair descent behavior is different in each of the following five phases: the upper landing, the early stairs, the midstair, the lower stairs, and the lower landing.

The intrasubject joint motion of healthy adults on stairs is most variable at the transitions to and from the staircase (Yu, Kienbacher, Growney, Johnson, & An, 1997). The variations in performance can perhaps be best attributed to reduced constraints on foot placement in these regions (i.e., on the upper landing foot placement may vary freely in relation to the stair edge, whereas on the lower landing the stair tread no longer serves as a target for the stance foot). These variations also suggest that locomotor strategies can be easily modified, deliberately or otherwise. However, the lack of habitual strategies at the transitions to the staircase may instigate instability and falls and may provide some explanation for the increased incident rates of falls at the transition regions.

Research in our laboratory has shown that foot clearance over the stair edge during swing and placement on the tread during stance are particularly useful in revealing characteristics about stair negotiation. Simoneau, Cavanagh, Ulbrecht, Leibowitz, and Tyrrell (1991) observed that the foot trajectory was characterized by lower clearance and decreased surface area between the foot and the tread in the midstair region than on stairs in the transition regions. From these results, we presume that caution is taken at the beginning and end of the staircase but that there is an apparent trend toward more confident behavior in the midstair region, where the staircase features are assumed and internalized based on previous experience. We have also found evidence to suggest that young adults sometimes use foot clearance smaller than 5 mm (Startzell, 1998), which is comparable to the smallest foot clearance observed for older adults by Simoneau et al. (1991). With such a small margin for error and great risk for injury, the safety of the stair user is heavily dependent on accurate perception and synthesis of critical stair and environmental features.

When vision is degraded or absent due to pathologic or environmental conditions, modifications are made to locomotor strategies to enhance safety. Automatic spatial updating during locomotion without vision is known to occur (i.e., we still know where we are even though our eyes are closed). The goal of two studies by Farrell and Thomson (1998) was to discriminate between the persistence of visual information and the role of proprioception during locomotion without vision. Participants were asked to walk blindfolded to a target and then point to a secondary target relative either to the initial position (ignoring condition) or to the new position (updating condition). The first task (ignoring condition) was significantly more difficult for the participants because it involved suppression of somatosensory processing (the current body configuration was consciously ignored). These results suggest that assumptions about spatial configuration are made based on previous experience with the coordination of movement and are supportive of the automatic role of the somatosensory system during locomotion.

Ambient vision, which helps to control posture and body orientation, is relatively unaffected by reduced illuminance (Leibowitz & Owens, 1977). Conversely, focal vision is seriously degraded by reduced illuminance, resulting in reduced resolution acuity, contrast sensitivity, and stereoscopic depth perception, which are all important for identifying critical features in the environment. Consequently, when illuminance is less than optimal (e.g., in the range of civil twilight, or 3 lux), we experience "selective degradation" of focal vision while ambient vision remains intact. Beyond the context of locomotion, others (Leibowitz & Owens, 1977; Owens & Tyrrell, 1992) have shown that those visual limitations are undetected by drivers, and consequently the appropriate precautions are not made.

Studies in our own laboratory have shown that degraded visual acuity resulted in modification to stair descent strategy in older women (Simoneau et al., 1991). Healthy women aged 55 to 70 exhibited significantly greater foot clearance when vision was blurred that in the high visual contrast condition.

To examine further the role of vision in stair descent, we devised a simple experiment using only three body-mounted markers tracked by video analysis. We postulated the following:

1. More precautions would be taken at the beginning and end of the staircase than in the midstair region.
2. Vision would be critical in the transitions to and from the stairs but less important in the midstair region.
3. At the top and bottom of the staircase, all available sensory information would be integrated to enhance secure foot placement on the first few steps and to internalize the dimensions of the staircase.
4. When vision was occluded or degraded, significant changes would be made to the stair negotiation strategy to promote safety on the stairs.

Methods

An instrumented staircase (Figure 15.1) was used to test our hypotheses. This adjustable modular staircase with seven steps, set to a tread depth of 29.9 cm (11 in.) and riser height of 17.8 cm (7 in.), was custom designed for our laboratory and has been described previously (Startzell, 1998). Two portable force plates (Kistler Instrument Corporation, Amherst, NY) were incorporated into the staircase on the second and fourth steps. A third force plate was installed in the floor at the lower landing of the staircase. (Force measurements are not

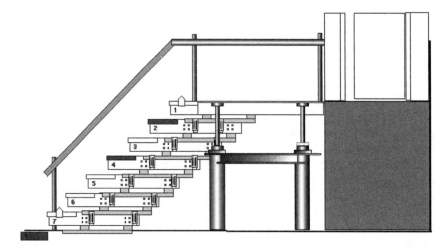

Figure 15.1. A schematic diagram of the experimental staircase. In this experiment, rise and run were set at 17.8 cm (7 in.) and 29.9 cm (11 in.), respectively. The shaded areas on Steps 2, 4, and 8 are force platforms, which were not used in this study.
From "How Do the Elderly Negotiate Stairs?" by P. R. Cavanagh, L. M. Mulfinger, and D. A. Owens, 1997, *Muscle and Nerve, 20,* (Suppl. 5), p. S52–S55. Copyright 1997 by John Wiley and Sons. Adapted with permission.

reported here.) A steel handrail paralleled the slope of the staircase. A global coordinate reference frame was established according to International Society of Biomechanics (ISB) conventions (Wu & Cavanagh, 1995) with positive x in the direction of travel and positive y upward. Reasonably uniform illumination was achieved with a mean value over the entire staircase of approximately 550 lux.

Ten young healthy participants—six men, four women, mean age of 23.3 years (standard deviation, *SD,* 2.11), height of 175.4 cm (*SD* 10.05), and weight of 73.33 kg (*SD* 11.84)—performed 18 trials starting on the upper landing at one of three randomized distances (0.5, 1, 1.5 m) from the stair edge. The experimental design also included three levels of vision (full vision, limited vision, no vision). Two replicate blocks of nine trials were designed to examine the effects of learning. Within each block, the experimental conditions were randomly presented.

Instructions to participants were as follows: "Please hold your left arm at your waist at all times. When told to go, please descend to the bottom landing at a pace that is comfortable for you. Use the handrail with your right hand as required."

Limited vision was achieved with the use of 1% transmission glasses, resulting in illuminance of approximately 5.5 lux, which is just outside the range of civil twilight (3 lux). In the "no vision" condition, dark goggles were worn to eliminate the transmission of light. Before each trial in altered visual conditions, the participants stood at the top of the stairway for 1 min to acclimate to the new condition. They wore a harness and were secured by an overhead gantry to prevent injury in case of a fall.

The dependent variables included the velocity profile of a single marker on the left lateral pelvis, which was intended to approximate hip or center-of-mass motion and variables derived from the motion of single markers placed on the dorsum of both feet (Figure 15.2). All stairs and the upper and lower landings were studied, and divisions were adapted from Templer's stair model (1992). Mean speed was detected by photocells placed at the edge of stairs 1 and 7.

A Vicon 370 motion analysis system (Vicon Motion Systems, Lake Forest, CA) was used to collect the three-dimensional position of the body-mounted markers with respect to the global reference frame throughout the stair descent at 60 Hz (2-mm accuracy). The stair geometry with respect to the global reference frame was determined prior to the experiment by acquisition of stair landmarks with use of a calibration wand. Although measurement of actual foot clearance over the stair and placement on the stair requires a three-dimensional approach to the calculation of shoe orientation (Startzell & Cavanagh, 1999), the single shoe markers allowed estimates of these quantities to be obtained as shown in Figure 15.2. While the shoe was placed flat on the stair during the placement phase, the position of the shoe marker in relation to the tread allowed a correction distance (a in Figure 15.2A) to be measured. An estimate of placement was also obtained at this time (p in Figure 15.2A). During the swing phase of the limb, the distance of the marker from the stair tread or edge (m in Figure 15.2B) was measured continuously. When the correction distance, a, was subtracted from this measured distance, m, an estimate of clearance of the shoe over the stair (c in Figure 15.2B) was obtained. Note that this estimate did not represent the minimum clearance of any part of the shoe over the stair, because it would have been quite possible for the heel of the shoe to touch the stair while the distance, c, for the trial indicated that the clearance was greater than zero. Nevertheless, this simple approach to the estimation of clearance provided comparative values among the various experimental conditions. Note also that the placement was

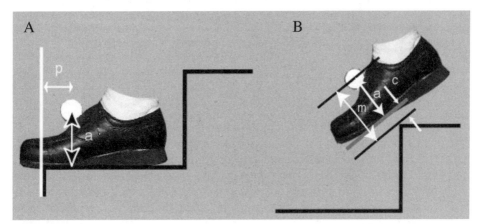

Figure 15.2. The approach used to obtain estimates of relative placement (A) and shoe clearance (B) during the placement and swing phases, respectively. The foot markers used in the experiment are shown. A similar marker was also placed over the left greater trochanter at the hip. Measurements are as follows: a is the height of the shoe marker from the stair tread during placement; p is the placement of the shoe relative to the stair edge (negative if the marker is behind the stair edge, as it is in the figure); m is the smallest distance between the marker and the stair edge at any time during the trial; and c is the estimate of clearance between the shoe sole and the stair (calculated from $m - a$).

relative to the marker on the shoe and this varied between subjects. However, it did not vary among conditions for the same participant, and therefore it provided a good measure of differences in placement among conditions.

Displacement data were filtered at 6 Hz before finite difference differentiation with respect to time. Hip velocity was plotted against the x-coordinate to allow the profile in each phase of descent to be examined. Maximal forward velocity and peak and minimum vertical velocity were determined. The individual stairs corresponding to these velocity measures were also identified. Mean speed was compared with the calculated measures of velocity. In addition, an elementary frequency analysis was performed on the velocity profiles to determine the number and magnitude of oscillations during each trial for comparison among conditions. The vertical component of velocity of the shoe markers was taken as a measure of foot velocity during clearance.

Adverse events were identified subjectively from a wide-angle video of the entire stairway. Among the events included in this analysis were falls, slips, and trips, contact with the stair during swing, the clear expectation of another stair after the last stair (indicated by inappropriate knee flexion at foot strike); and a loss of orientation that resulted in walking dangerously close to the stair edge.

Statistical analyses were conducted using Minitab 12 (Minitab Inc, State College, PA).

Results

Order Effects

An analysis of variance (ANOVA) was conducted using average speed determined from the photocells as the dependent variable. Out of a total of 180 trials, 13 trials had missing data, because of photocell malfunction. The model used was as follows:

$$\text{Speed} = \text{Participant} + \text{Visual Condition} + \text{Starting Position} + \text{Block} +$$
$$(\text{Vis} \times \text{Pos}) + (\text{Vis} \times \text{Block})$$

Visual condition, starting position, block, and vis × block were all statistically significant ($p < .05$). Learning or habituation clearly occurred between the first and second block of trials when vision was degraded (both limited vision and no vision) as participants increased their speed as the experiment progressed. The interaction plot of visual conditions over the two blocks of trials shown in Figure 15.3 indicates that decrements in vision resulted in greater speed reductions during the first block of nine trials than during the second, but the speed with full vision did not change. When participants started at the farthest distance from the stairs (1.5 m), there was a nonsignificant trend ($p = .062$) for speed to be slower than when they started at the two other positions (0.5 m and 1.0 m).

Because of learning effects, we chose to present the results for the first block of trials in this chapter. The first trials best represent the situation that would occur when a stair user made his or her initial traversing of the stairway, before becoming fully habituated to the geometry of the stairway.

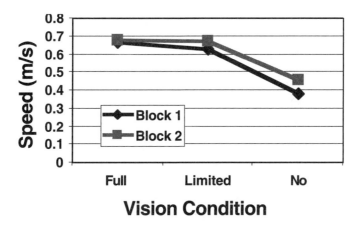

Figure 15.3. The interaction between vision condition and trial blocks in the average speed of stair descent. Note that greater familiarity during block 2 resulted in greater speeds under reduced vision conditions.

Accidents and Incidents

Thirteen adverse events in six participants were noted during 9 trials (from a total of 81 trials available for video viewing of the entire descent). The majority of incidents (85%) occurred during no vision trials, with the remainder occurring during the limited vision trials. The incident rates for the no vision and limited vision trials were 40.7% and 7.4%, respectively. More than 50% of the adverse events occurred at the bottom of the stairway (Table 15.1).

For the remaining analysis of clearance, placement, and foot and hip velocity, the trials in which an adverse event occurred were excluded. The rationale for this exclusion was that we wished to describe successful strategies for adaptation to altered visual conditions.

Placement

Placement of the foot on the stair (estimated as shown in Figure 15.2A) varied from −269.0 mm (a placement well behind the edge of stair 1) to a value of +94 mm (an overhanging placement in which only the rear part of the shoe was in contact with the stair). It should be recalled that the measure of placement used

Table 15.1. Summary of Adverse Events in the Experiment.

Description of event	Number of events
Error on bottom landing (expected another stair/slip)	6
Loss of orientation in no vision condition	3
Missed stair 1	2
Missed stair 7	1
Fell from stair 1 to stair 2	1

Note. Eighty-five percent of adverse events were in the no vision condition. All others were in the limited vision condition.

in this study is dependent on both marker placement and shoe size; thus the main utility of this measure is in comparing results between vision conditions.

A three-factor ANOVA similar to that conducted for speed (discussed previously) showed no interactions between starting position, stair number, and vision conditions, but a significant main effect for vision ($p < .001$) and a trend for stair ($p = .071$). The placement under the no vision condition was significantly less than that under the other two conditions ($p < .05$). The mean values for placement were -210 (± 24.4 mm), -208 (± 28.5), and -164 (± 52.65) mm for full, limited, and no vision conditions, respectively. This finding means that the foot was farther forward on the stair in the no vision condition. In the full vision condition, the placement on stair 1 (the upper landing) was significantly less (farther back on the stair) than on all other stairs ($p < .05$). Placement on stair 8 (the lower landing) was not analyzed because this foot placement was outside the field of view on many trials.

Clearance

Clearance of the shoe over the stair (estimated as shown in Figure 15.2B) varied from 0 to 122.6 mm. The smooth marker trajectories over the stair edge shown in Figure 15.4A were typical of those seen during descent with full vision, whereas the more uneven trajectories shown in Figure 15.4B were typical of those seen during descent with no vision.

A three-way ANOVA for clearance, similar to that described earlier for speed, showed a highly significant interaction between visual condition and stair as well as significant main effects of starting position, stair, and vision condition ($p < .05$). The interaction plot for stair and vision condition (Figure 15.5) suggests that the absence of vision caused a decrease in clearance on stair 1, no changes in clearance on stairs 2 and 7, and increases in clearance on the intermediate stairs 3 through 6. Post hoc analyses using a Tukey test indicated that clearance over stair 1 with no vision was significantly less than clearance in both of the other visual conditions ($p < .05$). At stairs 4, 5, and 6, clearance with no vision was significantly higher than in either of the other two visual conditions (all comparisons, $p < .05$). The increment in clearance over the middle stairs in the no vision condition was approximately 15–20 mm. With regard to clearance of any stair, there were no significant differences between the full vision and limited vision conditions. The average clearance when participants started 1.5 m from the stair edge was significantly greater (by approximately 3.4 mm) than when they started from the two positions closer to the stair edge ($p < .05$).

A comparison of clearance over different stairs was made within each vision condition. In the full vision condition, a number of significant differences were found: stair 1 < stairs 2, 3, 4, and 7; stair 2 > stairs 4, 5, and 6; stair 3 < stair 7; stairs 4, 5, and 6 < stair 7 (all comparisons $p < .05$). However, in the no vision condition, only stair 1 clearance was significantly ($p < .05$) and substantially less (21.8 mm vs. > 60 mm) than clearance on all other stairs. The low values for stair 1 clearance were due to a lower overall trajectory of the clearance foot (see Figure 15.4B for a typical pattern) and to those participants who deliberately tapped the foot on the stair (zero clearance) in

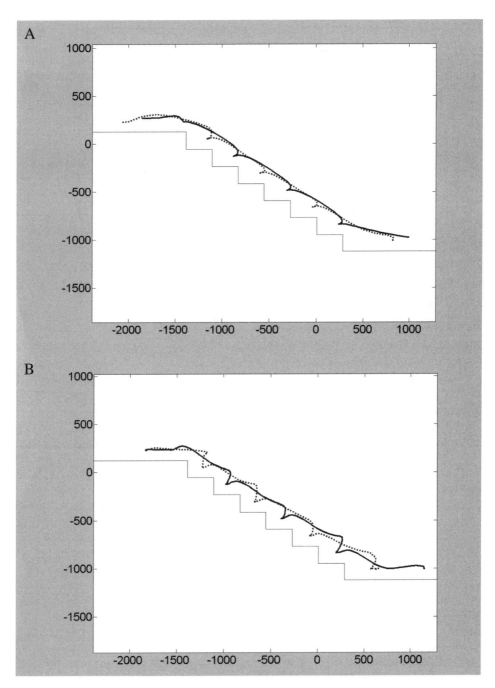

Figure 15.4. Exemplary shoe marker trajectories (in millimeters) for both feet during stair descent. The point of minimum clearance over each stair is shown during the clearance phase by the line extending from the stair edge. (A) Smooth clearance trajectories during descent in full vision. (B) Uneven clearance trajectories during a no vision trial.

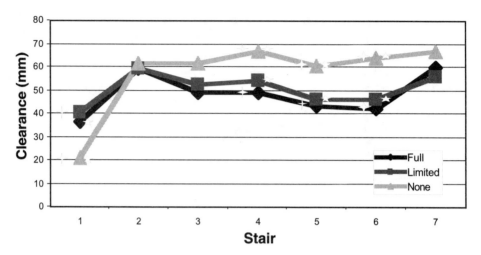

Figure 15.5. The interaction of vision condition and stair number in the clearance of the foot over the stair. Clearance values that share the same symbol on a stair were significantly different ($p < .05$).

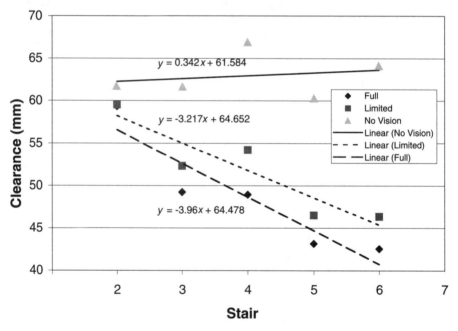

Figure 15.6. Linear regression of clearance vs. stair number over a range of stair 2 to stair 6 during descent with full vision (solid line), limited vision (dotted line), and no vision (dashed line). Note that clearance decreases progressively as descent progresses with full vision and limited vision but does not change with no vision.

order to locate the stair edge in the no vision condition (see Search Strategies section further on).

Regression plots of clearance vs. stair position for stairs 2 through 6 in all visual conditions are shown in Figure 15.6. This stair range was chosen because the upper and lower stairs appear to be special cases that are less constrained by stair geometry. During descent with full vision and limited vision, the clearance decreased on each successive stair by 4 mm and 3.2 mm, respectively, whereas with no vision, clearance was almost unchanged as the descent progressed (change in clearance was +0.3 mm per stair).

Foot Velocity

The maximum downward component of velocity (numerically, this is the minimum y component because a downward velocity is negative) represents the greatest downward speed of the foot as it reaches toward placement on the next step. ANOVA indicated that there was a significant main effect for starting position, vision, and stair number ($p < .05$) but no significant interactions. Follow-up analysis of the stair main effect with use of Tukey's test indicated that the velocity on stair 1 was significantly less than that on every other stair. Additional differences were stair 2 < stairs 3 and 4, and stairs 3 and 4 > stairs 6 and 7 (all comparisons $p < .05$). This finding suggests a more cautious approach to stair 1, increasing confidence up to stair 4, followed by a more tentative approach to the final stairs. This pattern is exemplified by the complete velocity-time profiles for a single participant shown in Figure 15.7. Maximum downward velocity was significantly less when participants started 1.5 m from the stair edge than when they started at 1 m.

Hip Kinematics

Hip velocity decreased in general as vision was progressively degraded ($p < .001$), but starting position had no significant effect and showed no apparent trends. However, there was a significant interaction effect ($p < .05$) of vision condition and starting position on maximum forward velocity (Figure 15.8).

For most participants, peak forward and upward velocity occurred on the bottom landing, with maximal downward velocity occurring in the middle of the staircase (stairs 3, 4, and 5) regardless of vision condition. There was a slight effect of starting position on the location of maximal forward velocity ($p < .05$) such that peaks occurred higher on the staircase when participants started the trial farther from the edge of the first stair.

To isolate the effects of the dependent variables on the descent portion of the trial, further analyses were confined to the segment of data between stairs 1 and 7. In "full vision," velocity gradually increased during descent, and the peak occurred on stair 7. In the limited vision and no vision condition, peak forward velocity occurred on stairs 6 and 4, respectively, indicating a decline in forward velocity as the transition to level walking was sought. As is apparent from the representative hip profiles shown in Figure 15.9 (see p. 226), the peak velocity was generally not much greater than the overall mean velocity for the trial.

We initially planned to analyze the effect of visual conditions on variations in velocity of the hip marker within individual cycles of stair descent (e.g., from placement on stair 1 to placement on stair 2). As shown in Figure 15.9, this would be straightforward in the full vision and limited vision conditions (Figures 15.9A and B). On each stair between stairs 1 and 6, a single

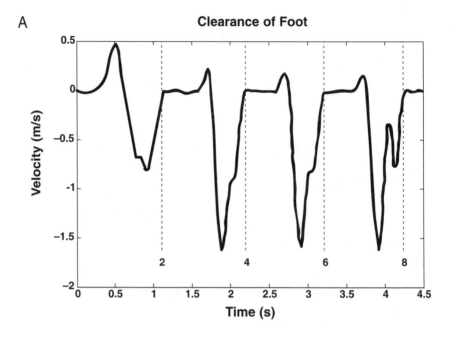

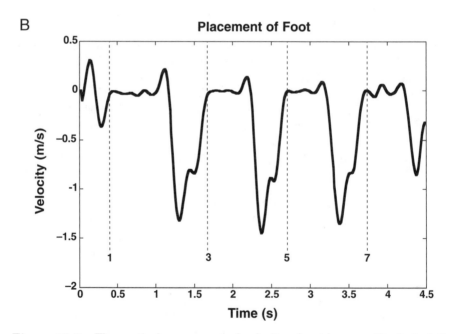

Figure 15.7. The vertical component of velocity of markers on the foot plotted as functions of time. The numbers associated with the dashed vertical lines identify the times at which foot placement occurred on the indicated step. (A) The foot that clears the top stair and is placed on stair 2. (B) The foot that clears stair 2 and is placed on stair 3.

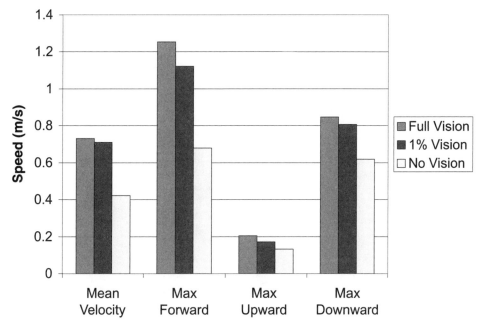

Figure 15.8. Hip velocity measures by vision condition.

major peak and a single major valley typically occurred in the velocity curve. However, as shown in Figure 15.9C, the profile of velocity versus the x-coordinate was radically different during the no vision condition. In addition to an overall lower average velocity mentioned previously, there were many more fluctuations in velocity and no clear peaks coincident with the stair edge.

The overall maximum and minimum forward and vertical velocities were extracted from the data. A threshold for peak and valley detection of 0.03 m · s^{-1} was established, and the number of reversals per stair was taken as the dependent variable. The number of reversals per stair above threshold was remarkably similar for full vision and limited vision conditions (mean values of 1.3 and 1.4, respectively) but increased dramatically, as shown in Figure 15.9C for the no vision condition (mean value of 2.3, $p < .001$). Starting position had no significant effect.

Search Strategies

An examination of the strategies used by participants to locate the first step in the no vision condition provided insight into how locating a stair might be performed under conditions of poor or absent illumination in a real setting. Information on the strategies used was available from two sources: First, a subjective analysis of video was used to evaluate clues to the method used in detecting the top stair; second, the trajectories of the foot markers in the region of the top stair were studied.

In the absence of vision, participants often approached the first stair cautiously, sometimes shuffling with small steps on the upper landing. Some individuals used tactile information from the handrail to locate the region where

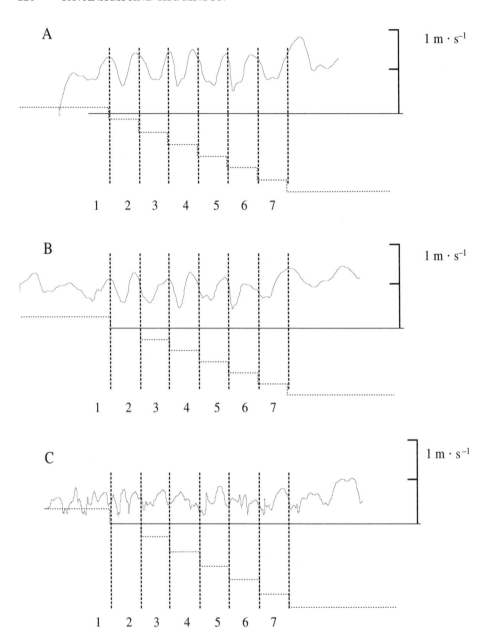

Figure 15.9. Typical hip velocity versus x-coordinate profiles for a single subject. The dashed vertical lines correspond to the edge of each stair. A scale for velocity is also shown. (A) Full vision (number of reversals/stair = 1.6). (B) Limited vision (number of reversals/stair = 1.6). (C) No vision (number of reversals/stair = 4.8).

the first stair edge could be located. This was possible because the slope of the stair rail changed at the first stair edge. Many participants used the foot as a sensory organ to search for the edge of the first stair, tapping it with the sole of the foot before advancing the limb in an exaggerated arc to the second stair.

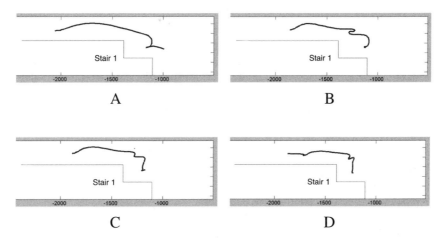

Figure 15.10. A selection of spatial trajectories in the plane of progression of the placement foot on stair 2 from walking in the full vision condition (A) and in the no vision condition (B–D). Axis labels are millimeters, x- and y-scales are the same.

Some participants also used the back of the heel to gauge the starting point of the tread on which the next foot placement would occur. Both of these strategies presumably use the perception of touch and pressure on the skin of the foot as well as muscle and tendon receptors in the leg as the joint angle profiles are interrupted by contact with the stair.

A selection of foot marker trajectories on the upper stair from participants walking with full vision (Figure 15.10A) can be compared with trajectories from participants in no-vision trials (Figure 15.10 B–D). In a sagittal (ISB x–y) plane, the forward and backward movement of the foot that is searching for stair 2 is clearly seen. The first backward movement appears to be related to locating the edge of stair 1 with the heel so that placement on stair 2 is not too far forward.

Discussion

Our young participants proved highly successful and safe during stair descent with full vision and reasonably successful with "limited vision" when 99% of the illuminance was eliminated. Of the "limited vision" trials, 92% were completed without an adverse event. In other words, performance on stairs was not severely degraded in reduced-illuminance conditions, emphasizing the dominant role of ambient vision in stair descent. This latter finding supports the observations of steering accuracy retained by young drivers in blurry or poorly lit environments (Owens & Tyrrell, 1999). In the same experimental situation, older drivers exhibited reductions in steering performance with degraded visual conditions. It remains to be seen whether elderly participants would be equally successful as our participants were in low-light conditions on stairs.

The incident rate during no vision trials was high, with an adverse event occurring in 1 of every 5.5 trials and many more unusual events occurring (such as a forward placement on the stair). Depending on footwear and stair conditions, these events could lead to a slip off the stair tread. In the absence of vision, participants implemented a multifaceted conservative strategy. They reduced average speed, decreased the downward velocity of the foot, and used the foot to search for the first stair edge and, sometimes, the hand to locate the change in handrail inclination. Once participants were on the stairs, the smooth cyclic pattern reflected by the motion of the hip marker was abandoned in favor of an irregular, uncertain descent. In the midstair region, foot clearance in the no-vision trials was increased by approximately 20 mm, but placement was consistently increased throughout by a mean of approximately 40 mm, so that less of the foot was placed on the stair tread. Thus, the challenge of removing vision resulted in a safer strategy as far as clearance was concerned but a less safe strategy for placement of the foot. The latter is probably the result of the higher clearance and a desire to make sure that the previous stair edge was cleared before placement.

The search behaviors just discussed did not extend to other stairs. Once the top stair edge had been located and the foot was placed safely on the second stair, participants appeared to have sufficient information to allow the remainder of the stairs to be negotiated successfully. An exception to this statement was the location of the bottom landing. Half of the adverse events occurred on the bottom landing, where several participants expected another step down. There appeared to be no consistent search strategy used for locating the last stair or the bottom landing. These results corroborate the observation by Yu et al. (1997) that kinematic variability is heightened at the transitions to and from the staircase. These findings are also in agreement with reports showing that most stairway incidents occur on the top three or bottom three steps (Templer, 1992).

The clearance values found in our study are considerably greater than those reported previously (Simoneau et al., 1991; Startzell & Cavanagh, 1998). This finding is probably a result of the different approaches used to characterize clearance of the foot over the stair in the different studies. As emphasized previously, the method used in our study estimated the clearance only as the midregion of the shoe crossed the stair.

Several aspects of our results showed adaptation of movement patterns as the participants became accustomed to the stairs. In the no vision condition, participants descended faster with repeated trials. Within a full vision trial, there was progressively smaller clearance between stairs 2 and 6 as the participant became accustomed to the stair geometry. It is of considerable interest that such adaptation did not occur in the no vision trials, in which clearance over the same stairs was unchanged from stair 2 through stair 7. The same proprioceptive information on stair geometry was available in both conditions, but vision was clearly needed by these participants to allow them to integrate the proprioceptive input they were receiving. The participants knew that all the stairs were the same size, and yet when vision was occluded, they used the same conservative strategy of increased clearance throughout the midstair region.

We found some evidence to support the idea of different behavior in different regions of the stairway that has been proposed by Templer (1992), although our seven-stair experimental arrangement does not allow the kind of regional differences seen on a larger stairway. In particular, the downward velocity of the foot appeared to be maximized in midstair and reduced at either end of the stairway. However, the most important differences that we have found are between the first and second stairs and the remainder of the stairway, particularly in the no-vision condition. It is clear that locating the edge of the first stair and appropriate placement on the second stair are the key events that determine safety during descent of stairs. The likely consequences of a fall are also most serious at these times. This finding implies that in conditions in which lighting or vision may be compromised, measures should be taken to allow the stair user to locate the stair edge by using proprioceptive means. This may include a change of surface hardness or cues on the handrail.

These findings also emphasize the need to study large stairways (longer than three steps), as done in other studies, because the staircase has clearly defined regions that are identified by distinct kinematic and potentially kinetic characteristics. In addition, it would be of great interest to study stairs of differing dimensions to see how individuals respond to unexpected features in the environment (as might be encountered in some public settings where applicable building codes are not met). Several variables also showed a dependence on the starting position of the participant on the landing, and this deserves further exploration.

In addition to providing insight into strategies used in stair negotiation, our results confirm the dangers involved in stair descent in conditions in which vision is seriously compromised. Although the National Bureau of Standards has suggested that greater than 200 lux is required for safe illuminance of stairways (Archea, Collins, & Stahl, 1979), this recommendation is not commonly heeded. In fact, substandard lighting levels were apparent in 95% of stairways surveyed by Carson et al. (Carson, Archea, Margulis, & Carson 1978). These authors also reported that in sites where accidents had occurred, the stairway was three times as likely to be poorly lit. This finding has particular implications for older people, who experience major age-related declines in visual performance in moderate and low illumination, due in part to a reduction in maximum pupillary dilation (*senile miosis;* see Pitts, 1982). If older individuals need to negotiate stairs at night, efforts should be made to provide permanent illumination of the stairway, particularly the upper and lower boundaries.

Conclusion

We conclude that vision is critical for the safe descent of stairs. Locating the upper two stairs appeared to be crucial in ensuring safe descent. Once participants were on the stairs, they adopted conservative strategies that appeared generally successful in allowing safe stair negotiation. During locomotion with vision, we found evidence of progressive adaptation in the midstair region. However, the inability to use vision to determine the location of the bottom landing instigated adverse events. These experiments have validated Templer's (1992) contention that vision is important to safe stair negotiation, especially at the upper and lower transitions to the staircase. Young individuals were easily able to modify their gait parameters, but it remains to be seen whether older adults would cope as well with challenges that accompany stair negotiation, particularly in poorly illuminated public places.

References

Archea, J., Collins, B. L., & Stahl, F. I. (1979). *Guidelines for stair safety.* Washington, DC: U.S. Department of Commerce, National Technical Information Service.

Carson, D. H., Archea, J. C., Margulis, S. T., & Carson, F. E. (1978). *Safety on stairs.* Washington, DC: U.S. Department of Commerce, National Technical Information Service.

Cavanagh, P. R., Mulfinger, L. M., & Owens, D. A. (1997). How do the elderly negotiate stairs? *Muscle and Nerve, 20* (Suppl. 5), S52–S55.

Farrell, M. J., & Thomson, J. A. (1998). Automatic spatial updating during locomotion without vision. *The Quarterly Journal of Experimental Psychology, 51A*(3), 637–654.

Gibson, J. J. (1958). Visually controlled locomotion and visual orientation in animals. *British Journal of Surgery, 49,* 182–194.

Hollands, M. A., Marple-Horvat, D. E., Henkes, S., & Rowan, A. K. (1995). Human eye movements during visually guided stepping. *Journal of Motor Behavior, 27*(2), 155–163.

Leibowitz, H. W., & Owens, D. A. (1977). Nighttime driving accidents and selective visual degradation. *Science, 197,* 422–423.

National Safety Council. (1994). *Accident facts 1994 edition.* Itasca, IL: Author.

Owens, D. A., & Tyrrell, R. (1992). Visual guidance of young and older drivers in challenging conditions. *Investigative Ophthalmology and Visual Science, 34*(4), 1418.

Owens, D., & Tyrrell, R. (1999). Effects of luminance, blur, and age on nighttime visual guidance: A test of the selective degradation hypothesis. *Journal of Experimental Psychology: Applied, 5*(2), 115–128.

Patla, A. E. (1998). How is human gait controlled by vision? *Ecological Psychology, 10*(3–4), 287–302.

Pitts, D. G. (1982). The effects of aging on selected visual functions: Dark adaptation, visual acuity, stereopsis, and brightness contrast. In R. Sekuler, D. Kline, & K. Dismukes (Eds.), *Aging and human visual function* (pp. 131–159). New York: Alan R. Liss.

Simoneau, G. G., Cavanagh, P. R., Ulbrecht, J. S., Leibowitz, H. W., & Tyrrell, R. A. (1991). The influence of visual factors on fall-related kinematic variables during stair descent by older women. *Journal of Gerontology, 46*(6), M188–M195.

Startzell, J. K. (1998). *Foot clearance and placement during stair descent: The effect of speed and illumination.* Unpublished master's thesis, The Pennsylvania State University.

Startzell, J. K., & Cavanagh, P. R. (1999). A three-dimensional approach to the calculation of foot clearance during locomotion. *Human Movement Science, 18,* 603–611.

Templer, J. (1992). *The staircase. Studies of hazards, falls, and safer design.* Cambridge, MA: Massachusetts Institute of Technology Press.

Wu, G., & Cavanagh, P. R. (1995). ISB recommendations for standardization in the reporting of kinematic data. *Journal of Biomechanics, 28*(10), 1257–1261.

Yu, B., Kienbacher, T., Growney, E. S., Johnson, M. E., & An, K. N. (1997). Reproducibility of the kinematics and kinetics of the lower extremity during normal stair-climbing. *Journal of Orthopaedic Research, 15,* 348–352.

Appendix: Selected Publications by Herschel W. Leibowitz

Abernethy, C. N., III, & Leibowitz, H. W. (1971). The effect of feedback on luminance thresholds for peripherally presented stimuli. *Perception and Psychophysics, 10*(3), 172–174.

Andre, J. T., Muth, E. R., Stern, R. M., & Leibowitz, H. W. (1996). The effect of tilted stripes in an optokinetic drum on gastric myoelectric activity and subjective reports of motion sickness. *Aviation, Space, and Environmental Medicine, 67,* 30–33.

Andre, J. T., Tyrrell, R. A., Leibowitz, H. W., Nicholson, M. E., & Wang, M. (1994). Measuring and predicting the effects of alcohol consumption on contrast sensitivity for stationary and moving gratings. *Perception and Psychophysics, 56,* 261–267.

Andre, J. T., Tyrrell, R., Nicholson, M., MinQi, W., & Leibowitz, H. (1992). Measuring and predicting the effects of alcohol on contrast sensitivity for static and dynamic gratings. *Investigative Ophthalmology and Visual Science, 33*(4), 1416.

Berman, P. W., & Leibowitz, H. W. (1965). Some effects of contour on simultaneous brightness contrast. *Journal of Experimental Psychology, 9,* 251–256.

Braida, L. D., Cornsweet, T. N., Durlach, N. I., Green, D. M., Leibowitz, H. W., Liberman, A., et al. (1982). Research in psychophysics. In R. McAdams, N. J. Smelzer, & D. J. Thomas (Eds.), *Behavioral and social sciences: A national resource* (pp. 373–405). Washington, DC: National Academy Press.

Brislin, R. W., & Leibowitz, H. W. (1970). The effect of separation between test and comparison objects on size constancy at various age-levels. *American Journal of Psychology, 83,* 372–376.

Brown, J. L., Graham, C. H., Leibowitz, H., & Ranken, H. B. (1953). Luminance thresholds for the resolution of visual detail during dark adaptation. *Journal of the Optical Society of America, 43,* 197–202.

De Soto, C., & Leibowitz, H. (1956). Perceptual organization and intelligence: A further study. *Journal of Abnormal and Social Psychology, 53,* 334–337.

Dunn, B., & Leibowitz, H. (1961). The effect of separation between test and inducing fields on brightness constancy. *Journal of Experimental Psychology, 61,* 505–507.

Farquhar, M., & Leibowitz, H. W. (1971). The magnitude of the Ponzo illusion as a function of age for large and for small stimulus configurations. *Psychonomic Science, 25*(2), 97–99.

Farr, J., & Leibowitz, H. W. (1976, September). An experimental study of the efficacy of perceptual-motor training. *American Journal of Optometry and Physiological Optics, 53*(9), 451–455.

Francis, E. L., Jiang, B. C., Owens, D. A., Tyrrell, R. A., & Leibowitz, H. W. (1989). "Effort to see" affects accommodation and vergence but not their interactions. *Investigative Ophthalmology and Visual Science, 30,* 135.

Furst, D. M., Leibowitz, H. W., Landers, D. M., & Rodemer, C. S. (1980). The effect of the size of the visual field on foveal reaction time. In G. C. Roberts, & D. M. Landers (Eds.), *Psychology of motor behavior and sport–1980.* Champaign, IL: Human Kinetics.

Gish, K. W., Sheehy, J. B., & Leibowitz, H. W. (1988). Decreased visual performance resulting from temporal uncertainty, target movement and background movement. *Perception and Psychophysics, 44*(2), 142–150.

Gish, K., Shulman, G. L., Sheehy, J. B., & Leibowitz, H. W. (1986). Reaction times to different spatial frequencies as a function of detectability. *Vision Research, 26,* 745–747.

Graham, C., & Leibowitz, H. W. (1972). The effect of suggestion on visual acuity. *The International Journal of Clinical and Experimental Hypnosis, 20*(3), 169–186.

Graham, C., Olsen, R. A., Parrish, M., & Leibowitz, H. (1968). The effect of hypnotically induced fatigue on reaction time. *Psychonomic Science, 10,* 223–224.

Guzy, L. T., Leibowitz, H. W., & Scialfa, C. T. (1991). Can vehicle speed be estimated accurately? *Journal of Applied Social Psychology, 21*(2), 172–174.

Harpster, J. L., Freivalds, A., Shulman, G., & Leibowitz, H. W. (1989). Visual performance on VDT screens and hard copy displays. *Human Factors, 31*(3), 24–257.

Harvey, L. O., Jr., & Leibowitz, H. W. (1967). Effects of exposure duration, cue reduction, and temporary monocularity on size matching at short distances. *Journal of the Optical Society of America, 57,* 249–253.

Harvey, L. O., Jr.,& Leibowitz, H. W. (1976). [Review of the book *The Telltale Eye*]. *Contemporary Psychology, 21,* 640–641.

Held, R., & Leibowitz, H. (1994). The significance of vection: Thoughts provoked by Gunnar Johansson's studies on visual perception of locomotion. In G. Jannsen, S. S. Bergstrom, & W. Epstein (Eds.), *Perceiving events and objects* (pp. 449–454). Hillsdale, NJ: Erlbaum.

Held, R., Leibowitz, H. W., & Teuber, H. L. (Eds.) (1978). *Perception. Handbook of sensory physiology: Vol. 8.* Berlin, Germany: Springer-Verlag.

Hennessy, R. T., Iida, T., Shiina, K., & Leibowitz, H. W. (1976). The effect of pupil size on accommodation. *Vision Research, 16,* 587–589.

Hennessy, R. T., & Leibowitz, H. W. (1970). Subjective measurement of accommodation with laser light. *Journal of the Optical Society of America, 60,* 1700–1701.

Hennessy, R. T., & Leibowitz, H. W. (1971). The effect of a peripheral stimulus on accommodation. *Perception and Psychophysics, 10*(3), 129–132.

Hennessy, R. T., & Leibowitz, H. W. (1972). Laser optometer incorporating the Badal principle. *Behavioral Research Methods and Instrumentation, 4*(5), 237–239.

Hennessy, R. T., & Leibowitz, H. W. (1972). Perceived vs. retinal relationships in the Ponzo illusion. *Psychonomic Science, 28*(2), 111–112.

Hicks, L. H., Ross, S., Leibowitz, H. W., & Paller, M. (1970). A 1970 overview of sources of support for psychological research. *American Psychologist, 25,* 1013–1025.

Jiang, B. C., Gish, K., & Leibowitz, H. W. (1991). The effect of luminance on the relation between accommodation and convergence. *Optometry and Vision Science, 68,* 220–225.

Jiang, B. C., Scialfa, C. T., Tyrrell, R. A., Garvey, P. M., & Leibowitz, H. W. (1990). Bandwidth of the contrast sensitivity function as an index of spatial vision with application to refraction. *Optometry and Vision Science, 67,* 260–267.

Johnson, C. A., & Leibowitz, H. W. (1974). Practice, refractive error and feedback as factors influencing peripheral motion thresholds. *Perception and Psychophysics, 15,* 276–280.

Johnson, C. A., & Leibowitz, H. W. (1976). Velocity-time reciprocity in the perception of motion: Foveal and peripheral determinations. *Vision Research, 16,* 177–180.

Johnson, C. A., & Leibowitz, H. W. (1979). Practice effects for visual resolution in the periphery. *Perception and Psychophysics, 25*(5), 439–442.

Johnson, C. A., Leibowitz, H. W., Millodot, M., & Lamont, A. (1976). Peripheral visual acuity and refractive error: Evidence for two visual systems? *Perception and Psychophysics, 20*(6), 460–462.

Kilbride, P. L., & Leibowitz, H. W. (1975). Factors affecting the magnitude of the Ponzo perspective illusion among the Baganda. *Perception and Psychophysics, 17*(6), 543–548.

Kilbride, P. L., & Leibowitz, H. W. (1977). The Ponzo illusion among the Baganda of Uganda. In L. L. Adler (Ed.), *Issues in cross cultural research, Annals of the New York Academy of Sciences, 285*, 408–417.

Kilbride, P. L. & Leibowitz, H. W. (1984). The Ponzo illusion among the Baganda of Uganda: Implications for ecological and perceptual theory. In L. L. Adler (Ed.), *Issues in cross cultural research* (pp. 31–44). New York: Academic Press.

Leibowitz, H. (1952). The effect of pupil size on visual acuity for photometrically equated test fields at various levels of luminance (Doctoral dissertation, Columbia University, 1951). *Journal of the Optical Society of America, 42*(6), 416–422.

Leibowitz, H. (1952). Photometric scales and the duplicity theory of vision. *American Journal of Psychology, 65*, 632–634.

Leibowitz, H. (1953). Some observations and theory on the variation of visual acuity with the orientation of the test-object. *Journal of the Optical Society of America, 43*, 902–905.

Leibowitz, H. (1954). The use and calibration of the "Maxwellian View" in visual instrumentation. *American Journal of Psychology, 67*(3), 530–532.

Leibowitz, H. (1955). Some factors influencing the variability of vernier adjustments. *American Journal of Psychology, 68*, 266–273.

Leibowitz, H. (1955). Effect of reference lines on the discrimination of movement. *Journal of the Optical Society of America, 45*, 829–830.

Leibowitz, H. (1956). Relation between Brunswick and Thouless ratios and functional relations in experimental investigations of perceived shape, size, and brightness. *Perceptual and Motor Skills, 6*, 65–68.

Leibowitz, H. (1958). Über die verschiedenen Mechanismen der Sehgrössenkonstanz [On the different mechanisms of size constancy]. *Naturwissenschaften, 45*(24), 621–622.

Leibowitz, H. (1961). Apparent visual size as a function of distance for mentally deficient subjects. *American Journal of Psychology, 74*, 98–100.

Leibowitz, H. (1963). Some trends in perceptual theory. In M. H. Marx (Ed.), *Theories in contemporary psychology* (2nd ed). New York: Macmillan.

Leibowitz, H. (1967). *The human visual system and image interpretation*. Arlington, VA: Institute for Defense Analysis.

Leibowitz, H. (1971). Sensory, learned and cognitive mechanisms of size perception. In H. E. Adler (Ed.), Orientation: Sensory basis. *Annals of the New York Academy of Sciences, 188*, 47–62.

Leibowitz, H. (1973). Detection of peripheral stimuli under psychological and physiological stress. In National Research Council Committee on Vision (Eds.), *Visual Search*. Washington DC: National Academy of Sciences–National Research Council.

Leibowitz, H. (1975). Visual perception and hypnosis. In M. H. Siegel, & H. P. Zeigler (Eds.), *Psychological research: The inside story* (pp. 272–290). New York: Harper & Row.

Leibowitz, H. (1979). The two visual systems concept and some applications. *Journal of the Association of Engineers and Architects in Israel, 39*, 45–48.

Leibowitz, H. (1979). Stress and visual perception. *Journal of the Association of Engineers and Architects in Israel, 39*, 49–52.

Leibowitz, H. (Chair, Working Group 39, Committee on Vision, Assembly of Behavioral and Social Sciences, National Research Council). (1980). Recommended standard procedures for the clinical measurement and specification of visual acuity. *Advances in Ophthalmology, 41*, 103–148.

Leibowitz, H. (1983, January/February). The need to know. *The Penn Stater, 20*, 34.

Leibowitz, H. (1984, June). *Traffic safety: Nighttime and alcohol related accidents*. Paper presented at the Science and Public Policy Seminar of the Federation of Behavioral, Psychological, and Cognitive Sciences, Washington, DC.

Leibowitz, H. (1994). A note on the synergy between basic and applied research. In G. Jannsen, S. S. Bergstrom, & W. Epstein (Eds.), *Perceiving events and objects* (pp. 329–331). Hillsdale, NJ: Erlbaum.

Leibowitz, H., Brislin, R., Perlmutter, L., & Hennessy, R. (1969). Ponzo perspective illusion as a manifestation of space perception. *Science, 166,* 1174–1176.

Leibowitz, H., Bussey, T., & McGuire, P. (1957). Shape and size constancy in photographic reproductions. *Journal of the Optical Society of America, 47,* 658–661.

Leibowitz, H., & Chinetti, P. (1957). Effect of reduced exposure duration on brightness constancy. *Journal of Experimental Psychology, 54,* 49–53.

Leibowitz, H., Chinetti, P., & Sidowski, J. (1956). Exposure duration as a variable in perceptual constancy. *Science, 123,* 668–669.

Leibowitz, H., & Dichgans, J. (1977, June). Zwei verschiedene Seh-Systeme [A review of the two-visual-systems concept in science and technology]. *Umschau in Wissenschaft und Technik, 77*(11), 353–354.

Leibowitz, H., & Hartman, T. (1959). Magnitude of the moon illusion as a function of the age of the observer. *Science, 130,* 569–570.

Leibowitz, H., & Harvey, L. O., Jr. (1973). Perception. *Annual Review of Psychology, 24,* 207–229.

Leibowitz, H., & Heisel, M. A. (1958). L'evolution de l'illusion de Ponzo en fonction de l'age [The development of the Ponzo illusion as a function of age]. *Archives de Psychologie, 36,* 328–331.

Leibowitz, H., Johnson, C. A., & Guez, J. R. (1977). Differences in the processing of peripheral stimuli. *Documenta Ophthalmologica Proceedings Series, Second International Visual Field Symposium, 14,* 299–302.

Leibowitz, H., & Kaestner, N. (1954). *The effect of exposure time, individual variability and practice on the precision of vernier adjustments* (Technical Report, WADC TR 54–77). Wright-Patterson Air Force Base, OH: Wright Air Development Center.

Leibowitz, H., Kraft, C. L., & Johnson, C. A. (1976). *Evaluation of visual function* (pp. 7–23), Kalamazoo Workshop on Low Vision Mobility. Washington, DC: Veterans Administration, Department of Medicine and Surgery.

Leibowitz, H., Leon, G. R., & Bourne, L. E. (1969). Some observations on the stability of matched shape. *Perception and Motor Skills, 28,* 329–330.

Leibowitz, H., Lundy, R. M., & Guez, J. R. (1980). The effect of testing distance on suggestion-induced visual field narrowing. *International Journal of Clinical and Experimental Hypnosis, 28,* 409–420.

Leibowitz, H., Mitchell, E., & Angrist, N. (1954). Exposure duration in the perception of shape. *Science, 120,* 400.

Leibowitz, H., & Moore, D. (1966). Role of changes in accommodation and convergence in the perception of size. *Journal of the Optical Society of America, 56,* 1120–1123.

Leibowitz, H., Mote, F. A., & Thurlow, W. R. (1953). Simultaneous contrast as a function of separation between test and inducing fields. *Journal of Experimental Psychology, 46*(6), 453–456.

Leibowitz, H., Myers, N. A., & Chinetti, P. (1955). The role of simultaneous contrast in brightness constancy. *Journal of Experimental Psychology, 50,* 15–18.

Leibowitz, H., Osaka, R., & Oyama, T. (Eds.) (1979). *Perception of space and motion: An international symposium.* Kyoto, Japan: Psychologia Society.

Leibowitz, H., & Owens, D. A. (1993). Visibility and the basic visual functions. In *Second International Symposium on Visibility and Luminance in Roadway Lighting* (pp. 121–132). New York: Lighting Research Institute.

Leibowitz, H., Owens, D. A., & Helmreich, R. L. (1995). Transportation. In R. S. Nickerson (Ed.), *Emerging needs and opportunities for human factors research* (pp. 241–261). Washington, DC: National Academy Press.

Leibowitz, H., Post, R., and Ginsburg, A. (1980). The role of fine detail in visually controlled behavior. *Investigative Ophthalmology and Visual Science, 19,* 846–848.

Leibowitz, H., & Toffey, S. (1966). The effect of rotation and tilt on the magnitude of the Poggendorff illusion. *Vision Research, 6,* 101–103.

Leibowitz, H., & Walker, L. (1956). Effect of field size and luminance on the binocular summation of suprathreshold stimuli. *Journal of the Optical Society of America, 46,* 171–172.

Leibowitz, H., Waskow, I., Loeffler, N., & Glaser, F. (1959, May). Intelligence level as a variable in the perception of shape. *Quarterly Journal of Experimental Psychology, 11,* 108–112.

Leibowitz, H. W. (1955). The relation between the rate threshold for the perception of movement and luminance for various durations of exposure. *Journal of Experimental Psychology, 49,* 209–214.

Leibowitz, H. W. (1961). Some visual illusions and the mechanisms of size perception. Proceedings of the 16th International Congress of Psychology, Bonn, Germany. *Acta Psychologica, 19,* 844–845.

Leibowitz, H. W. (1965). *Visual perception.* New York: Macmillan.

Leibowitz, H. W. (1968). [Review of the book *The Nature of Psychology*]. *Contemporary Psychology, 13,* 3.

Leibowitz, H. W. (1974). Multiple mechanisms of size perception and size constancy. *Hiroshima Forum for Psychology, 1,* 47–53.

Leibowitz, H. W. (Chair, Working Group 39 on Visual Field and Acuity Standards). (1976). *First interprofessional standard for visual field testing.* Washington, DC: National Academy of Sciences—National Research Council Vision Committee.

Leibowitz, H. W. (1976). Cross-cultural and personality factors influencing the Ponzo perspective illusion. In K. F. Riegel & J. A. Mescham (Eds.), *The developing individual in a changing world: Vol. 1, Historical and Cultural Issues.* The Hague: Mouton.

Leibowitz, H. W. (1976). Visual perception and stress. In G. Borg, (Ed.), *Wenner-Gren International Symposium Series*: Vol. 28. *Physical work and effort* (pp. 25–37). Oxford, England: Pergamon Press.

Leibowitz, H. W. (1978). The two visual systems concept and some applications. In *Proceedings of the Fifth Annual IRA Symposium on Human Engineering and Quality of Work Life* (pp. 56–65). Ramat Efal, Israel: The IRA Memorial Foundation.

Leibowitz, H. W. (1983). A behavioral and perceptual analysis of grade crossing accidents. In *Proceedings of the 1982 Operation Lifesaver National Symposium* (pp. 12–15). Chicago, IL: National Safety Council.

Leibowitz, H. W. (1984). Preface. In W. D. Froelich, G. J. Smith, J. G. Draguns, & U. Hentschel (Eds.), *Psychological processes in cognition and personality.* Washington, DC: Hemisphere.

Leibowitz, H. W. (1985). Grade crossing accidents and human factors engineering. *American Scientist, 73*(6), 558–562.

Leibowitz, H. W. (1985). Sensation and perception. In A. Kuper & J. Kuper (Eds.), *The social science encyclopedia* (pp. 744–746). London: Routledge and Kegan Paul.

Leibowitz, H. W. (1986). Recent advances in our understanding of peripheral vision and some implications. In *Proceedings of the 1986 Human Factors Society Meeting.* Santa Monica, CA: Human Factors Society.

Leibowitz, H. W. (1987). Ambient illuminance during twilight and from the moon. In *Proceedings of the 1985 Conference on Night Vision* (pp. 19–22). Washington, DC: National Research Council.

Leibowitz, H. W. (1987). *Some basic mechanisms in spatial orientation.* Paper presented at Air Force Conference on Spatial Disorientation, Bolling Air Force Base, Washington, DC.

Leibowitz, H. W. (1987). *The two modes of processing visual information and implications for spatial orientation.* Paper presented at Aircraft Altitude Awareness

Workshop, Flight Dynamics Laboratory, Wright-Patterson Air Force Base, OH, 1-9-1 to 1-9-5.

Leibowitz, H. W. (1988). The human senses in flight. In E. L. Wiener & D. C. Nagel (Eds.), *Human factors in aviation* (pp. 83–110). San Diego, CA: Academic Press.

Leibowitz, H. W. (1989). [Review of the book *Blindsight: A case study and implications*] *Contemporary Psychology, 34*(11), 1035–1036.

Leibowitz, H. W. (1991, July). The importance of behavioral research to national defense. *Bulletin of the Human Factors Society, 34,* 4–5.

Leibowitz, H. W. (1991). Perceptually induced misperception of risk: A common factor in transportation accidents. In L. P. Lipsitt & L. P. Mitnick (Eds.), *Self-regulatory behavior and risk taking: Causes and consequences* (pp. 219–229). Norwood, NJ: Ablex.

Leibowitz, H. W. (1992). Functional psychology and its societal contributions. In D. A. Owens & M. Wagner (Eds.), *Progress in contemporary psychology: The legacy of American functionalism* (pp. 17–29). Westport, CT: Praeger.

Leibowitz, H. W. (1992). Perception in flight: Shape and motion perception, space perception, spatial orientation and visual-vestibular interaction. In *Visual problems in night operations, AGARD (North Atlantic Treaty Organization) lecture series,* LS-187, 3–1 to 3–9.

Leibowitz, H. W. (1993) Some basic mechanisms in spatial orientation. In *Vision topics for aviation: A new look at traditional concerns* (pp. 1–15). Orlando, FL: University of Central Florida.

Leibowitz, H. W. (1993). Vision and driving: Past limitations and future possibilities. *Alcohol, Drugs and Driving, 9,* 211–218.

Leibowitz, H. W. (1996), The symbiosis between basic and applied research. *American Psychologist, 51,* 366–370.

Leibowitz, H. W., Abernethy, C. N., III, Buskirk, E. R., Bar-Or, O., & Hennessy, R. T. (1972). The effect of heat stress on reaction time to centrally and peripherally presented stimuli. *Human Factors, 14*(2), 155–160.

Leibowitz, H. W., Andre, J., Tyrrell, R., Hewitt, F. G., Cavanagh, P., & Simoneau, G. G. (1992). Contrast sensitivity during locomotion: The effect of alcohol. *Investigative Ophthalmology and Visual Science, 33*(4), 14–15.

Leibowitz, H. W., & Appelle, S. (1969). The effect of a central task on luminance thresholds for peripherally presented stimuli. *Human Factors, 11*(4), 387–392.

Leibowitz, H. W., & Bourne, L. E., Jr., (1956). Time and intensity as determiners of perceived shape. *Journal of Experimental Psychology, 51,* 277–281.

Leibowitz, H. W., & Crassini, B. U. (1986). [Review of the book *The Athletic Eye*] *Journal of Sport Psychology, 8,* 139–141.

Leibowitz, H. W., & Dato, R. A. (1966). Visual size constancy as a function of distance for temporarily and permanently monocular observers. *American Journal of Psychology, 79*(2), 279–284.

Leibowitz, H. W., & Dichgans, J. (1980). The ambient visual system and spatial orientation. *Proceedings of the AGARD Conference on spatial Disorientation in Flight: Current Problems, 287,* B4–1 to B4–4 .

Leibowitz, H. W., Farrell, R. J., Anderson, C.D., Kraft, C. L., & Boucek, G.P., Jr. (1971, July). The effect of the accommodation-convergence relationship on stereopsis. *Proceedings of the Symposium Sehleistung beim Gebrauch optischer Instrumente.* [Visual performance while using optical instruments]. Munich, Germany: University of Munich, International Commission for Optics, Institute of Medical Optics.

Leibowitz, H. W., Gish, K. W., & Sheehy, J. B. (1988). Role of vergence accommodation in correcting for night myopia. *American Journal of Optometry and Physiological*

Optics, 65, 383–386.

Leibowitz, H. W., Graham, C., & Parrish, M. (1972). The effect of hypnotic age regression on size constancy. *American Journal of Psychology, 85,* 271–276.

Leibowitz, H. W., Guzy, L. T., Peterson, E., & Blake, P. T. (1993). Quantitative perceptual estimates: Verbal versus nonverbal retrieval techniques. *Perception, 22,* 1051–1060.

Leibowitz, H. W., & Gwozdecki, J. (1967). The magnitude of the Poggendorff illusion as a function of age. *Child Development, 38,* 573–580.

Leibowitz, H. W., & Harvey, L. O., Jr. (1967). Size matching as a function of instructions in a naturalistic environment. *Journal of Experimental Psychology, 74,* 378–382.

Leibowitz, H. W., & Harvey, L. O., Jr. (1968–69). Comparaison de l'approche expérimentale et non-expérimentale de la perception de la taille [Comparison of experimental and nonexperimental approaches to the perception of size]. *Bulletin de Psychologie, (Paris), 22*(9–13), 716–724.

Leibowitz, H. W., & Harvey, L. O., Jr. (1969). Effect of instructions, environment, and type of test object on matched size. *Journal of Experimental Psychology, 81,* 36–43.

Leibowitz, H. W., & Hennessy, R. T. (1975). The laser optometer and some implications for behavioral research. *American Psychologist, 30*(3), 349–352.

Leibowitz, H. W., Hennessy, R. T., & Owens, D. A. (1975). The intermediate resting position of accommodation and some implications for space perception. *Psychologia, 18,* 162–170.

Leibowitz, H. W., Hennessy, R. T., & Owens, D. A. (1980). The intermediate resting position of accommodation and some implications for space perception. In H. Leibowitz, R. Osaka, & T. Oyama (Eds.), *Perception of space and motion: An international symposium* (pp. 14–22). Kyoto, Japan: Psychologia Society.

Leibowitz, H. W., & Johnson, C. A. (1972). Dioptrics of the periphery of the eye. *Science, 182,* 87.

Leibowitz, H. W., Johnson, C. A., & Isabelle, E. (1972). Peripheral motion detection and refractive error. *Science, 177,* 1207–1208.

Leibowitz, H. W., & Judisch, J. M. (1967). The relation between age and the magnitude of the Ponzo illusion. *American Journal of Psychology, 80,* 105–109.

Leibowitz, H. W., & Judisch, J. M. (1967). Size constancy in older persons: A function of distance. *American Journal of Psychology, 80,* 294–296.

Leibowitz, H. W., & Meneghini, K. A. (1966). Shape perception for round and elliptically shaped test-objects. *Journal of Experimental Psychology, 72,* 244–249.

Leibowitz, H. W., Myers, N. A., & Grant, D. A. (1955). Frequency of seeing and radial localization of single and multiple visual stimuli. *Journal of Experimental Psychology, 50,* 369–373.

Leibowitz, H. W., Myers, N. A., & Grant, D. A. (1955). Radial localization of a single stimulus as a function of luminance and duration of exposure. *Journal of the Optical Society of America, 45,* 76–78.

Leibowitz, H. W., & Owens, D. A. (1975). Anomalous myopias and the intermediate dark focus of accommodation. *Science, 189,* 646–648.

Leibowitz, H. W., & Owens, D. A. (1975, October). Night myopia and the intermediate dark-focus of accommodation. *Journal of the Optical Society of America, 65,* 1121–1128.

Leibowitz, H. W., & Owens, D. A. (1977). Nighttime driving accidents and selective visual degradation. *Science, 197,* 422–423.

Leibowitz, H. W., & Owens, D. A. (1977). Oculomotor adjustments and space perception. In G. Oléron (Ed.), *Psychologie Expérimentale et Comparée, Homage à Paul Fraisse* (pp. 99–112). Paris: Presses Universitaire de France.

Leibowitz, H. W., & Owens, D. A. (1978). New evidence for the intermediate position of relaxed accommodation. *Documenta Ophthalmologica, 46,* 133–147.

Leibowitz, H. W., & Owens, D. A. (1981, February). The intermediate dark focus of accommodation and some implications. *Southern Journal of Optometry, 23*(2), 8–12.

Leibowitz, H. W., & Owens, D. A. (1986, January). We drive by night. *Psychology Today, 20*(1), 55–58. Sudden Death at Night, *Reader's Digest,* September 1986, 77–80.

Leibowitz, H. W., & Owens, D. A. (1989). Multiple mechanisms of the moon illusion and size perception. In M. Hershenson (Ed.), *The moon illusion* (pp. 281–286). Hillsdale, NJ: Erlbaum.

Leibowitz, H. W., & Owens, D. A. (1990). Behavioral implications of civil twilight. In *Light and color in the open air* (Technical Digest Series, Vol. 12, pp. 105–108). Washington, DC: Optical Society of America.

Leibowitz, H. W., & Owens, D. A. (1990). The moon illusion and relevant perceptual mechanisms. In *Light and color in the open air* (Technical Digest Series, Vol. 12, pp. 98–101). Washington, DC: Optical Society of America.

Leibowitz, H. W., & Owens, D. A. (1991). Can normal activities be carried out during civil twilight? *Applied Optics, 30,* 3501–3503.

Leibowitz H. W., Owens, D. A., & Post, R. B. (1982, September). Nighttime driving and visual degradation. (Society of Automotive Engineers Technical Paper Series, No. 820414). *Transactions of the Society of Automotive Engineers.*

Leibowitz, H. W., Owens, D. A., & Tyrrell, R. A. (1998). The assured clear distance ahead rule: Implications for nighttime traffic safety and the law. *Accident Analysis and Prevention, 38,* 93–99.

Leibowitz, H. W., & Pick, H. A., Jr. (1972). Cross-cultural and educational aspects of the Ponzo perspective illusion. *Perception and Psychophysics, 12*(5), 430–432.

Leibowitz, H. W., & Pishkin, V. (1961). Perceptual size constancy in chronic schizophrenia. *Journal of Consulting Psychology, 25,* 196–199.

Leibowitz, H. W., Pollard, S. W., & Dickson, D. (1967). Monocular and binocular size-matching as a function of distance at various age-levels. *American Journal of Psychology, 80,* 263–268.

Leibowitz, H. W., & Post, R. B. (1982). Capabilities and limitations of the human being as a sensor. In J. T. Kuznicki, R. A. Johnson, & A. F. Rutkiewic (Eds.), *Selected sensory methods: problems and approaches to measuring hedonics* (ASTM STP 773, pp. 3–10). Philadelphia: American Society for Testing and Materials.

Leibowitz, H. W., & Post, R. B. (1982). Some implications of gaze stability mechanisms for vision in aviation. In *Conference proceedings: Vision as a factor in military aviation.* Brooks Air Force Base, TX: School of Aviation Medicine.

Leibowitz, H. W., & Post, R. B. (1982). The two modes of processing concept and some implications. In J. Beck (Ed.), *Organization and representation in perception* (pp. 343–363). Hillsdale, NJ: Erlbaum.

Leibowitz, H. W., Post, R. B., Brandt, T., & Dichgans, J. (1982). Implications of recent developments in dynamic spatial orientation and visual resolution for vehicle guidance. In A. H. Wertheim, W. A. Wagenaar, & H. W. Leibowitz (Eds.), *Tutorials on motion perception* (pp. 231–260). New York: Plenum.

Leibowitz, H. W., Post, R. B., & Sheehy, J. B. (1986). Efference, perceived movement, and illusory displacement. *Acta Psychologica, 63,* 23–34.

Leibowitz, H. W., Post, R. B., Shupert-Rodemer, C., Wadlington, W. L., & Lundy, R. M. (1980). Roll vection analysis of suggestion-induced visual field narrowing. *Perception and Psychophysics, 28*(2), 173–176.

Leibowitz, H. W., Rodemer, C. S., & Dichgans, J. (1979). The independence of dynamic spatial orientation from luminance and refractive error. *Perception and Psychophysics, 25,* 75–79.

Leibowitz, H. W., & Sacca, E. J. (1971). Comparison of matching and drawing in the perception of shape at various intelligence levels. *Perception and Psychophysics, 9*(5), 407–409.

Leibowitz, H. W., Sheehy, J. B., & Gish, K. W. (1987). Correction of night myopia: The role of vergence accommodation. In *Proceedings of the 1985 Conference on Night Vision* (pp. 116–123). Washington, DC: National Research Council.

Leibowitz, H. W., Shiina, K., & Hennessy, R. T. (1972). Oculomotor adjustments and size constancy. *Perception and Psychophysics, 12*(6), 497–500.

Leibowitz, H. W., & Shupert, C. L. (1984). *Low luminance and spatial orientation.* [Naval Aerospace Medical Research Laboratory Monograph, Vol. 33.]. Washington, DC: Naval Aerospace Medical Research Laboratory.

Leibowitz, H. W., & Shupert, C. L. (1985). Spatial orientation mechanisms and their implications for falls. *Clinics in Geriatric Medicine, 1,* 571–580.

Leibowitz, H. W., & Shupert, C. L. (1985). Spatial orientation mechanisms and their implications for falls. In T. S. Radebaugh, E. Hadley, & R. Suzman (Eds.), *Falls in the elderly: Biologic and behavioral aspects.* Philadelphia: W. B. Saunders.

Leibowitz, H. W., Shupert, C. L., & Post, R. B. (1983, March). Peripheral vision horizon display (PVHD). In *Proceedings of Conference, NASA Ames Research Center, Dryden Flight Facility* (pp. 41–44). Edwards, CA: NASA Ames Research Center.

Leibowitz, H. W., Shupert, C. L., & Post, R. B. (1983). *The two modes of visual processing: Implication for spatial orientation.* (NASA Conference Publication, No. 2306). Washington, DC: NASA.

Leibowitz, H. W., Shupert, C. L., Post, R. B., & Dichgans, J. (1983). Autokinetic drifts and gaze deviation. *Perception and Psychophysics, 33*(5), 455–459.

Leibowitz, H. W., Shupert, C. L., Post, R. B., & Dichgans, J. (1983). Expectation and autokinesis. *Perception and Psychophysics, 34*(2), 131–134.

Leibowitz, H. W., & Sulzer, R. L. (1965). *An evaluation of three-dimensional displays* (pp. 1–27). Washington, DC: Armed Forces–National Research Council, Committee on Vision.

Leibowitz, H. W., Toffey, S. E., & Searle, J. L. (1966). Intensity-time relationship and perceived shape. *Journal of Experimental Psychology, 72,* 7–10.

Leibowitz, H. W., Tyrrell, R. A., Andre, J. T., Eggers, B. G., & Nicholson, M. E. (1993, June). *Dynamic visual contrast sensitivity.* Washington, DC: AAA Foundation for Traffic Safety.

Leibowitz, H. W., Vinger, P. F., & Landers, D. M. (1988). Can visual training improve athletic performance? *Proceedings of the United States Olympic Academy, 22,* 177–185. United States Olympic Committee.

Leibowitz, H. W., Wilcox, S. B., & Post, R. B. (1978). The effect of refractive error on size constancy and shape constancy. *Perception, 7,* 557–562.

MacDuffee, E. J., Shupert, C. L., & Leibowitz, H. W. (1988). The influence of peripheral stimuli on the amount and direction of autokinesis. *Perception and Psychophysics, 43,* 395–400.

Mattas, R. B., Townsend, J. C. & Leibowitz, H., (1978). Some effects of chromostereopsis on stereoscopic performance: Implications for microscopes. *Human Factors, 20*(4), 401–408.

Meneghini, K. A. & Leibowitz, H. W. (1967). Effect of stimulus distance and age on shape constancy. *Journal of Experimental Psychology, 74,* 241–248.

Miller, R. J., Hennessy, R. T., & Leibowitz, H. W. (1973). The effect of hypnotic ablation of the background on the magnitude of the Ponzo perspective illusion. *International Journal of Clinical and Experimental Hypnosis, 21,* 180–191.

Miller, R. J., & Leibowitz, H. W. (1976). A signal detection analysis of hypnotically induced narrowing of the peripheral visual field. *Journal of Abnormal Psychology, 85,* 446–454.

Millodot, M., Johnson, C. A., Lamont, A., & Leibowitz, H. W. (1975). Effect of dioptrics on peripheral visual acuity. *Vision Research, 15,* 1357–1362.

Nicholson, M. E., Andre, J. T., Tyrrell, R. A., Wang, M., & Leibowitz, H. W. (1995). Effects of moderate dose alcohol on visual contrast sensitivity for stationary and moving targets. *Journal of Studies on Alcohol, 56,* 261–266.

Owens, D. A., Francis, E. L., & Leibowitz, H. W. (1989). *Visibility distance with headlights: A functional approach* (Society of Automotive Engineers Paper No. 890684). Warrendale, PA: Society of Automotive Engineers.

Owens, D. A., & Leibowitz, H. W. (1975, March). Chromostereopsis with small pupils. *Journal of the Optical Society of America, 65,* 358–359.

Owens, D. A., & Leibowitz, H. W. (1975). The fixation point as a stimulus for accommodation. *Vision Research, 15*(10), 1161–1163.

Owens, D. A., & Leibowitz, H. W. (1975). The intermediate resting position of accommodation and its implications for night driving. In Proceedings of 1st International Conference on Vision and Road Safety, *Editions La Prevention Routiere Internationale* (pp. 147–152). Paris: Linas-Monttheiry.

Owens, D. A., & Leibowitz, H. W. (1976, November). Night myopia: Cause and a possible basis for amelioration. *American Journal of Optometry and Physiological Optics, 53*(11), 709–717.

Owens, D. A. & Leibowitz, H. W. (1976). Oculomotor adjustments in darkness and the specific distance tendency. *Perception and Psychophysics, 20*(1), 2–9.

Owens, D. A., & Leibowitz, H. W. (1980). Accommodation, convergence, and distance perception in low illumination. *American Journal of Optometry and Physiological Optics, 57,* 540–550.

Owens, D. A., & Leibowitz, H. W. (1983). Perceptual and motor consequences of tonic vergence. In C. M. Schor & K. J. Ciuffreda (Eds.), *Vergence eye movements: Basic and clinical aspects* (pp. 25–74). Boston: Butterworth.

Owens, D. A., Leibowitz, H. W., & Norman, J. (1976, December). Pedestrian night accidents and night myopia. *Proceedings of International Conference on Pedestrian Safety* (pp. 4B1–4B5). Technion, Haifa University, Israel: Society for Medicine and Law in Israel.

Parrish, M., Lundy, R. M., & Leibowitz, H. W. (1968). Hypnotic age-regression and magnitudes of the Ponzo and Poggendorff illusions. *Science, 159,* 1375–1376.

Parrish, M., Lundy, R. M., & Leibowitz, H. W. (1969). Effect of hypnotic age regression on the magnitude of the Ponzo and Poggendorff illusions. *Journal of Abnormal Psychology, 74,* 693–698.

Pick, H. L., Jr., Leibowitz, H., Singer, J. E., Stevenson, H. W., & Steinschneider, A. (1978). *Psychology: From research to practice.* New York: Plenum.

Pishkin, V., Smith, T. E., & Leibowitz, H. W. (1962). The influence of symbolic stimulus value on perceived size in chronic schizophrenia. *Journal of Consulting Psychology, 26,* 323–330.

Post, R. B., & Leibowitz, H. W. (1980). Independence of radial localization from refractive error. *Journal of the Optical Society of America, 70,* 1377–1379.

Post, R. B., & Leibowitz, H. W. (1981). The effect of refractive error on central and peripheral motion sensitivity at various exposure durations. *Perception and Psychophysics, 29*(2), 91–94.

Post, R. B., & Leibowitz, H. W. (1982). The effect of convergence on the vestibulo-ocular reflex and implications for perceived movement. *Vision Research, 22,* 461–465.

Post, R. B., & Leibowitz, H. W. (1985). A revised analysis of the role of efference in motion perception. *Perception, 14,* 631–643.

Post, R. B. & Leibowitz, H. W. (1986). The two modes of processing visual information: Implications for assessing visual impairment. *American Journal of Optometry and Physiological Optics, 63,* 94–96.

Post, R. B., Leibowitz, H. W., & Shupert, C. L. (1982). Autokinesis and peripheral stimuli: Implications for fixational stability. *Perception, 11,* 477–482.

Post, R. B., Owens, R. L., Owens, D. A., & Leibowitz, H. W. (1979). Correction of empty-field myopia on the basis of the dark-focus of accommodation. *Journal of the Optical Society of America, 69*(1), 89–92.

Post, R. B., Shupert, C. L., & Leibowitz, H. W. (1984). Implications of OKN suppression by smooth pursuit for induced motion. *Perception and Psychophysics, 36*(5), 493–498.

Raymond, J. E., & Leibowitz, H. W. (1985). Reduction of body sway by stimuli imaged within a cortical scotoma: A case study. *Investigative Ophthalmology and Visual Science, 26,* 1021–1024.

Raymond, J. E. & Leibowitz, H. W. (1985). Viewing distance and the sustained detection of high spatial frequency gratings. *Vision Research, 25,* 1655–1659.

Raymond, J. E., Lindblad, I. M., & Leibowitz, H. W. (1982). Contrast sensitivity of the accommodative system [Abstract]. *Investigative Ophthalmology and Visual Science, 22*(3), (Suppl.), 126.

Raymond, J. E., Lindblad, I. M., & Leibowitz, H. W. (1984). The effect of contrast on sustained detection. *Vision Research, 24,* 183–188.

Scialfa, C. T., Garvey, P. M., Gish, K. W., Deering, L. M., Leibowitz, H. W., & Goebel, C. (1988). Relationships among measures of static and dynamic acuity. *Human Factors, 30,* 677–687.

Scialfa, C. T., Garvey, P. M., Tyrrell, R., & Leibowitz, H. W. (1992). Age differences in dynamic contrast thresholds. *Journal of Gerontology: Psychological Sciences, 47,* 172–175.

Scialfa, C. T., Guzy, L. T., Leibowitz, H. W. Garvey, P.M., & Tyrrell, R. A. (1991). Age differences in estimating vehicle velocity. *Psychology and Aging, 6,* 60–66.

Scialfa, C. T., Leibowitz, H. W., & Gish, K. W. (1989). Age differences in peripheral refractive error. *Psychology and Aging, 4*(3), 372–375.

Shupert, C. L., Lindblad, I. M., & Leibowitz, H. W. (1983). Visual testing for competition diving: A two systems approach. In D. Golden (Ed.), *Proceedings of the 1983 United States Diving Sports Sciences Seminars,* (pp. 99–115).

Shupert, C. L., Post, R. B., Leibowitz, H. W., & Dichgans, J. (1982). Autokinesis and fixational stability. *Investigative Ophthalmology and Visual Science, 22*(3), (Suppl.), 85.

Simoneau, G. G., Cavanagh, P. R., Ulbrecht, J. S., Leibowitz, H. W., & Tyrrell, R. A. (1991). The influence of visual factors on fall-related kinematic variables during stair descent by older women. *Journal of Gerontology: Medical Sciences, 46*(6), M188–M195.

Simoneau, G. G., & Leibowitz, H. W. (1996), Posture, gait, and falls. In J. E. Birren & K. W. Schaie (Eds.), *Handbook of the psychology of aging* (4th ed.). San Diego, CA: Academic Press.

Simoneau, G. G., Leibowitz, H. W., Cavanagh, P. R., Ulbrecht, J. S., & Tyrrell, R. A. (1992). The effects of visual factors and head orientation on postural steadiness in women 55 to 70 years of age. *Journal of Gerontology: Medical Sciences, 47*(5), M151–158.

Starr, B. J., Leibowitz, H. W., & Lundy, R. M. (1968). Size constancy in catatonia. *Perception and Motor Skills, 26,* 747–752.

Stern, R. M., Hu, S., Anderson, R. B., Leibowitz, H. W., & Koch, K. L. (1990). The effects of fixation and restricted visual field on vection-induced motion sickness. *Aviation, Space, and Environmental Medicine, 61,* 712–715.

Stern, R. M., Koch, K. L., Leibowitz, H. W., Shupert, C., Lindblad, I. M., & Stewart, W. R. (1985). Tachygastria and motion sickness. *Aviation, Space, and Environmental Medicine, 56,* 1074–1077.

Tyrrell, R. A., Andre, J. T., Boonie, K. K., Peasley, C. E., & Leibowitz, H. W. (1993). On the visual information that supports blind walking. *Investigative Ophthalmology and Visual Science, 34,* 1418.

Tyrrell, R. A., Daniels, C. M., Andre, J. T., Lundy, D. H., Eggers, B. G., & Leibowitz, H. W. (1991). The effects of time and eye movements on pointing performance. *Investigative Ophthalmology and Visual Science, 32,* 1272.

Tyrrell, R. A., Garvey, P. M., Deering, L. M., & Leibowitz, H. W. (1988). Age differences in Vistech near contrast sensitivity. *American Journal of Optometry and Physiological Optics, 65,* 951–956.

Tyrrell, R. A., & Leibowitz, H. W. (1990). The relation of vergence effort to reports of visual fatigue following prolonged near work. *Human Factors, 32*(3), 341–357.

Tyrrell, R. A., Rudolph, K. K., Eggers, B. G., & Leibowitz, H. W. (1993). Evidence for the persistence of visual guidance information. *Perception and Psychophysics, 54*(4), 431–438.

Tyrrell, R. A., Rudolph, K. K., Eggers, B. G., Li, Y., & Leibowitz, H. W. (1990). Do ambient orientation cues persist in the absence of visual stimulation? *Investigative Ophthalmology and Visual Science, 31* (Suppl.), 327.

Tyrrell, R. A., Thayer, J. F., Friedman, B. H., Leibowitz, H. W., & Francis, E. L. (1995). A behavioral link between the oculomotor and cardiovascular systems. *Integrative Physiological and Behavioral Science, 30,* 46–67.

Wertheim, A. H., Bouma, H., Wagenaar, W. A., & Leibowitz, H. W. (Eds.). (1981). Special issue on Motion Perception. *Acta Psychologica, 48.*

Wertheim, A. H., Wagenaar, W. A., & Leibowitz, H. W. (Eds.) (1982). *Tutorials on motion perception.* New York: Plenum.

White, K., Post, R., & Leibowitz, H. (1980). Saccadic eye movements and body sway. *Science, 208,* 621–623.

Woolsey, C. N., Akert, K., Benjamin, R. M., Leibowitz, H., & Welker, W. I. (1955). The visual cortex of the marmoset. *Federation Proceedings, 14,* 1–3.

Zeigler, H. P., & Leibowitz, H. (1957). Apparent visual size as a function of distance for children and adults. *American Journal of Psychology, 70,* 106–109.

Zeigler, H. P., & Leibowitz, H. (1958). A methodological study of "shape constancy" in the Rhesus monkey. *Journal of Comparative and Physiological Psychology, 51,* 155–160.

Author Index

Numbers in italics refer to listings in the reference sections.

Abrams, R. A., 149, *152*
Adams, C. W., 47, 52, *54,* 75, *78*
Agent, K. R., 163, 171, *178*
Aglioti, S., 146, 147, *152*
Alf, E., Jr., 28, *39*
Allen, M. J., 20, *21,* 182, 183, 184, 190, *194*
Amblard, B., 139, *140*
Ampofo-Boateng, K. A., 184, *194*
An, K. N., 214, 228, *230*
Anand, S., 146, 149, 150, *152*
Anderson, D. R., 50, *55*
Andre, J. T., 71, 75, 76, *78, 79,* 170, *179*
Andrews, C., 61, 62, *66*
Andrews, P. L. R., 199, 200, 208, *210, 212*
Andronicos, M., 59, 63, *66*
Andrykowski, M. A., 208, *210*
Anker, S., 91, *93*
Annis, R. C., 89, *93*
Antonoff, R. J., 20, *21,* 176, *179,* 183, *194*
Antonucci, G., 126, *141*
Arango, S., 54, *56*
Archea, J., 229, *230*
Archea, J. C., 229, *230*
Arnold, P., 91, *94*
Asch, S. E., 126, *141,* 151, *154*
Atkinson, J., 83, 91, *93, 94*
Aulhorn, E., 27, *39*
Avery, G. C., 119, *121*

Baginski, T. A., 47, *56*
Bailey, J. S., 184, *195*
Baird, J. C., 100, *121*
Ballinger, C. J., 151, *153*
Banta, C., 126, *140*
Barlow, D. H., 206, *211*
Barnes, P. J., 193, *194*
Barraud, P. A., 128, 131, 132, 138, *140*
Bauer, J., 83, 89, 90, *94*
Baylis, P., 203, *210*
Beaman, A. L., 193, *194*
Beavers, L. L., 28, *39*
Beckwith, B., 209, *210*
Bernstein, A., 190, *194*
Bernstein, I. L., 200, *210*
Bhise, V. D., 190, *194*
Billingham, B., 91, *94*
Birdsall, T. G., 24, 25, *40*
Blackwell, A. W., 170, *180*
Blomberg, R. D., 183, *194*
Blum, R. H., 199, 208, *210*
Boisson, D., 146, *154*
Boltz, R. L., 81, 90, 92, *94*
Boring, E. G., 118, *121,* 164, *177*

Borkovec, T. D., 206, *211*
Bouquillon, A., 59, *66*
Boussaoud, D., 164, *177*
Braddick, O., 83, 91, *93, 94*
Brand, J. J., 206, *211*
Braun, J., 144, *153,* 163, *178*
Brenner, E., 149, *154*
Bridgeman, B., 144, 145, 146, 148, 149, 150, *152*
Brill, S., 83, 85, 89, *94*
Brooks, J. C., 164, *178*
Brown, D. R., 169, *180*
Brown, J. E., 208, *210*
Brown, T. A., 206, *211*
Bullimore, M. A., 47, 52, *54*
Bultkoff, H. H., 148, *153*

Caleca, A., 62, *66*
Campion, J., 144, *153*
Canon, L., 149, *153*
Carey, D. P., 146, *154*
Carmichael, J., 203, *210*
Carson, D. H., 229, *230*
Carson, F. E., 229, *230*
Cavanagh, P. R., 214, 215, 216, 217, 228, *230*
Cello, K. E., 51, 54, *54*
Chambers, D., 148, *153*
Charman, W. N., 75, *79,* 81, 84, *93*
Chaturvedi, N., 47, *54*
Chauhan, B. C., 47, *55*
Cheung, B. S., 200, *211*
Chieffi, S., 146, 148, *153*
Cioffi, G. A., 47, 54, *55*
Ciuffreda, K. J., 71, 76, *78, 79*
Cobb, S. R., 83, 88, 93, *93*
Cogan, D. G., 74, *78,* 159, *178*
Cohen, M. M., 126, 136, *140, 141,* 150, 151, *153, 154*
Cohn, T. E., 46, *55*
Coil, J. D., 201, *210*
Collins, B. L., 206, *211,* 229, *230*
Collobi, L. R., 62, *66*
Collon, D., 61, *66*
Coppola, D. A., 81, 89, 93, *93*
Coren, S., 120, *121,* 135, *140*
Cornelius, C. S., 74, *78,* 159, *178*
Cornwell, P., 163, *179*
Cramer, D. B., 203, *210*
Creelman, C. D., 26, *40*
Creem, S. H., 146, 148, *153*
Cremieux, J., 139, *140*
Cristobal, G., 89, 93, *94*
Cristofori, F. C., 208, *210*
Crooks, L. E., 177, *178*

Subject Index

About the Editors

Jeffrey Andre, PhD, is assistant professor of psychology at James Madison University. After receiving his BA in psychology from Muhlenberg College, Dr. Andre attended the Pennsylvania State University, where he earned an MS (1993) and a PhD (1995) in experimental psychology under the mentorship of Herschel W. Leibowitz. As Leibowitz's last graduate student, Dr. Andre investigated in his dissertation the individual and combined effects of low luminance, glare, alcohol consumption, stimulus motion, and spatial frequency on human visual contrast sensitivity. Prior to his current position, he was a NIH/NRSA postdoctoral research fellow working with D. Alfred Owens at Franklin & Marshall College (F & M) and held positions at Texas Tech University and Lewis & Clark College. Dr. Andre's current research interests include night driving, verbal and nonverbal estimations of distance, and the role of the oculomotor systems in the development of visual fatigue.

D. Alfred Owens, PhD, is associate dean of the faculty and Charles A. Dana Professor of Psychology at Franklin & Marshall College. Dr. Owens obtained his PhD under the direction of Herschel W. Leibowitz at the Pennsylvania State University in 1976, with a dissertation on factors influencing steady-state accommodation. Following an NIH/NRSA postdoctoral fellowship with Richard Held at the Massachusetts Institute of Technology (MIT), he joined the faculty of his undergraduate alma mater, F & M. There, Dr. Owens has continued active investigation into perception and action, with emphasis on problems of night vision and transportation safety. Dr. Owens's research has been energized not only by his students but also by collaborations with colleagues at MIT, the University of Bielefeld (Germany), the University of Michigan Transportation Research Institute, the Center for Locomotion Studies at Penn State University, and the Queensland University of Technology (Australia).

Lewis O. Harvey, Jr., PhD, is full professor at the University of Colorado, Boulder. He received his PhD from the Pennsylvania State University in 1968, where his dissertation, *Critical Flicker Fusion As a Function of Viewing Distance, Stimulus Size, and Luminance*, was supervised by Herschel W. Leibowitz. Following a postdoctoral year in the Department of Psychology at MIT with Whitman Richards and Hans-Lukas Teuber, Dr. Harvey spent a year in the Netherlands as a scientific coworker at the Institute for Perception RVO-TNO in Soesterberg, working with John Michon on problems of motion perception and nighttime automobile driving. He returned to the United States and held assistant professor and associate professor positions at the Massachusetts College of Optometry in Boston and was research associate in psychology at MIT. In 1974 he accepted a faculty position in the Department of Psychology at the University of Colorado. Dr. Harvey's research interests range from basic psychophysics of spatial frequency mechanisms to the application of signal detection theory to complex human judgments. He has been guest professor at the Institute for Medical Psychology, University of Munich, and in the Department of Neurology, University of Frieburg, Germany.